EDUCATION
TRANSFORMATION

How K-12 online learning is bringing the greatest
change to education in 100 years.

RON PACKARD

Herndon, Virginia

BEYOND WORDS
Hillsboro, Oregon

To the students of K^{12}, who have kept me going the last twelve years and who will encourage me for years to come.

BEYOND WORDS

20827 N.W. Cornell Road, Suite 500
Hillsboro, Oregon 97124-9808
503-531-8700 / 503-531-8773 fax
www.beyondword.com

Copyright © 2013 by Ron Packard

Interior design and composition: Devon Smith

First Beyond Words hardcover edition April 2013
Beyond Words Publishing is an imprint of Simon & Schuster, Inc., and the Beyond Words logo is a registered trademark of Beyond Words Publishing, Inc.

For information about special discounts for bulk purchases, please contact Beyond Words Special Sales at 503-531-8700, or specialsales@beyondword.com.

Manufactured in the United States of America

10 9 8 7 6 5 4 3 2 1

Library of Congress Control Number: 2013930520

ISBN: 978-1-58270-385-5

The corporate mission of Beyond Words Publishing, Inc.: *Inspire to Integrity*

CONTENTS

CONTENTS

INTRODUCTION

Technology Sped Past Our Schools

*O*n a crisp fall morning in 1999, I found myself on a train speeding up the New England Corridor from New York City, bound for New Haven, Connecticut. It was a commuter special, cars filled with business-people, most of them nosed into their *New York Times* or hunched over their briefcases and laptops, lawyers poring over legal briefs, bankers sweating out spreadsheets, and knots of others engaged in quiet but intense conversations that appeared to be strategy sessions for high-stakes meetings that could spell ruin or riches by day's end.

I was headed for such a meeting, one that I knew could change my life—and just maybe the face of American education.

Tucked into my attaché case that morning was a twenty-page plan to create a new type of school, the idea for which had originated with my attempt to find an online math course for my six-year-old daughter a few months earlier. I had discovered hundreds of supplemental math sites, but I could not find any high quality, fully formed, grade-level courses. I wanted an assessment that told me if my child took this course and passed this test that she was on par with the best students in the world's top schools. Believing that other parents might be facing the same predicament, I became determined to create something that would put the full power of technology in the hands of parents, teachers, and students who wanted access to a rigorous, engaging, and interactive curriculum—something that would have been impossible only five years earlier.

At that moment, I realized it was now possible to deliver a world-class education to anyone on the globe. There was no reason why students couldn't go to school online full-time or part-time. Geography would no longer matter. Economic means would no longer matter. As long as people had access to the internet, they could receive a world-class education and become anything they wanted to be. This idealistic, chimerical dream would eventually become reality. Education would finally be individualized with regard to a student's program, learning style, prior knowledge, and pacing. What I didn't realize was that my idea had far-reaching implications for the nature of schooling itself. Even more broadly, it could greatly improve human capital not just in the United States but around the world. In fact, less wealthy nations that could not afford the high costs of a brick-and-mortar education stood to benefit even more than the United States. They would eventually leapfrog brick-and-mortar schools and move straight to online education in the same way many nations have skipped landlines and moved straight to cellular phones. In this vision, children everywhere would have access to the education previously only available in the best schools in developed nations. It would no longer matter whether you lived in a remote village in China or a city in Africa. If you wanted an education, you would be able to get it.

I sketched out an idea for what I called an online school, wrote a business plan, and then contacted Bill Bennett, US Secretary of Education during the Reagan administration and one of the most visible and respected names in education. I wasn't sure how he would react since his new book at the time, *The Educated Child: A Parent's Guide from Preschool through Eighth Grade*, was about to become a national bestseller, and it specifically warned, "When you hear the next pitch about cyber-enriching your child's education, keep one thing in mind: so far, there is no good evidence that most uses of computers significantly improve learning."[1]

I explained that technology was simply a tool to get children to the right content and teach them the necessary skills in a more engaging way. That hit a chord; Bennett perked up. As we talked, he became more enthusiastic about the possibilities of online schooling, but he wanted confirmation from a reputable expert that technology could indeed be used the way that I wanted to use it. He didn't want to hear from just any technologist; he told me to "talk to Gelernter."

Gelernter was David Gelernter, professor of computer science at Yale University and the author of a terrific book, *Machine Beauty: Elegance and the Heart of Technology*, about how aesthetic beauty was important to the rise of personal computers. That was where I was going that fall morning in 1999, to Yale. I had read *Machine Beauty* and had sensed in Gelernter's views of technology a comrade. He knew the frustrations but also the grand possibilities:

> Good technology is terribly important to our modern economy and living standards and comfort levels, the "software crisis" is real, we do get from our fancy computers a tiny fraction of the value they are capable of delivering: we are a nation of Ferrari drivers tooling around with kinked fuel lines at fifteen miles per hour.[2]

INTRODUCTION

Everything Online—Except Our Schools

Today, it's possible to order everything from cars to cornflakes on the internet, download music with wireless iPods, and customize our shirts as easily as our vacations—all of it by using sophisticated computer technology. The internet has made our lives more efficient. It has touched every aspect of American business and American lives. It would be simple to assume that the Ferrari has been unleashed. The idea of online education sounds simple and should be obvious and accepted by everyone.

Yet American schools seem to have been left behind on this high-speed journey. Just about every part of our political, economic, and cultural world has joined the technology revolution except our $550-billion-a-year education system. "Many areas of American life have changed for the better during the past two decades," said Paul Peterson, director of Harvard's Program on Education Policy and Governance (PEPG), "except, it appears, the K-12 education system."[3]

Or consider what Frederick Hess, director of education policy studies at the American Enterprise Institute, has said:

> The emergence of near-universal computing and wireless communications, a large college-educated workforce marked by professional mobility, and information technology and accountability tools that make feasible niche services and multisite operations have radically altered the landscape. Yet schools and school districts have remained largely impervious to these advancements.[4]

In many fundamental ways, American education has not changed much over the past one hundred years, let alone the last twenty. True, many schools now have computer labs or students with laptops. For most of the day, however, computers remain idle, never integrated into the core parts of teaching and learning. They are barely on the periphery of the core educational process, let alone integral to it. It is no wonder technology has failed to have an impact on results. It is there, but on the sidelines.

While technology has blazed a remarkable trail of transformation in the larger culture the last twenty years, our schools have not kept pace. To anyone who has spent time in a business or organization that thrives on technology, this is the American education system's most glaring omission. Schools throughout the country have not adequately incorporated the advances in how technology can deliver information, communicate, respond, and shape learning. The ineffective use of technology has left education behind in the enormous productivity gains the US economy has achieved over the past twenty-five to fifty years. There are nearly twice as many teachers per student in the American education system today as there were in 1960, while the outcomes are practically unchanged.[5] It is tough to think of another sector with a similar decline in productivity. Healthcare has seen an explosion in costs, but the outcomes have certainly improved as the result of innovative drugs and procedures.

Decades of Reform, Little Progress

As I write this book, America—and most of the world—is faced with an economic crisis. We also face an educational crisis. As President Barack Obama said in his first inaugural address, "Our schools fail too many."[6] In fact, our national high school dropout rate is 30 percent. In our fifty largest school districts, the dropout rate is now 50 percent and almost 70 percent in some cities.[7] If this is not a national tragedy, I am not sure what is. What chance do these students have at economic success? To make matters worse, barely 18 percent of American students who enter high school finish college.[8] America cannot afford to have that many children dropping out of high school and not finishing college.

In the highly competitive "flat world" described by Thomas Friedman, education is more important than ever.[9] Yet America's relative position compared to other nations is declining. In 1950, 80 percent of US jobs were unskilled. Today, that number is less than 20 percent.[10] Future generations of Americans will face increasingly intense competition for jobs from workers around the globe. If America's educational system is not up to the competition, our workforce is not up to the competition, and our economy is destined to lag behind nations with better-educated citizens.

Education may be the only way to achieve a more equal and just society—and a more robust and globally competitive economy. The wealth of nations is now determined more by brains than by brawn. Every nation's GDP is determined by their success in deploying their human capital, and that success is heavily influenced by the education process, both formal and informal. Nations that fail to educate their youth will experience an erosion of their economic standing in the world. Failing to educate a subsector of our population means that subsector will be denied the opportunities presented by the dynamic twenty-first-century economy. When large segments of the population have little opportunity to raise their living standards, the risk of political strife becomes much larger (as we have recently seen in the Middle East and North Africa).

At a time when education is more important than ever, more American children than ever seem to be opting out. "Among industrialized nations," reported the education advocacy group Education Trust, "the United States is the only country in which today's young people are less likely than their parents to have earned a high school diploma. Reversing this trend could hardly be more urgent."[11]

The poor performance of so many American schools is even more worrisome when we consider the extraordinary reform efforts and massive infusions of money over the last two decades. Education spending has increased faster than inflation. The nation has tried charter schools, vouchers, open classrooms, uniforms, small class sizes, year-round schools, merit pay for teachers, leadership schools for administrators, and high-stakes testing. The list is long, and the needle has barely moved. The reasons underpinning the lack of progress are complex, but the common denominator is that these reforms all lack one thing: scalability.

The reform efforts have not delivered higher student achievement. Moreover, the large increase in the number of adults per student in the system has led to underpaid educators and an underinvestment in technology, research, and student materials. The pupil–teacher ratio has fallen close to 50 percent since 1960. Thus, productivity in the education sector has fallen close to half over the last fifty years. This is an extraordinary decline in an era when some industries have seen a tenfold increase in productivity. To see how scalable technology can lead to greater outcomes and efficiency, we can look at almost any industry, but the steel industry in particular shows how dramatic the effect can be. Clearly, manufacturing is different from a service industry like education, but imagine if education could achieve even a portion of these gains.

Impact of Technological Advancements on the Productivity of Employees in the Steel Industry

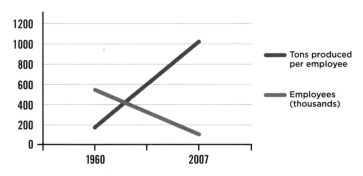

Source: National Center for Education Statistics, Institute of Education Sciences/ US Department of Education, http://nces.ed.gov/programs/digest/d11/tables/dt11_069.asp.

The Evidence So Far:
Technology's Remarkable Classroom Achievements

In 1999, I didn't fully appreciate the complexity of the problems facing public schools—or how fundamentally the system would resist on-line education. I had long believed that technology would transform our lives for the better, but I did not know until I looked for an online math course for my daughter how immune education had been to the benefits of technology and how far-reaching those benefits could be.

My meeting with David Gelernter lasted almost two hours. We discussed the state of public education in the United States relative to other nations. We agreed that public education is the country's most valuable resource and functions as the fuel that drives our economic engine. We agreed that if the United States was going to be globally competitive for the next one hundred years, it needed the best public school system possible.

I explained that my mission was not to compete with the public education system but to support its promise of an excellent education for every child. The company I envisioned would create a high quality curriculum and deliver it electronically. It would be a partner for states, schools, teachers, and parents, and it would help public schools deliver customized, individualized, interactive, and engaging education to students—in any setting.

In fact, technology could—and would—make education more efficient, more effective, and more engaging. It would not matter where a child lived—it could be urban or rural, and it could be in the United States, the United Kingdom, or the United Arab Emirates. We would, through the internet, offer every child a world-class education, and while doing so, we could solve a multitude of education problems. (K^{12}, the company I founded to meet the goal, now has online schools serving children in eighty-five countries.)

The other part of the story is that online education encountered tremendous institutional resistance. We had to overcome an array of legislative obstacles, as well as a number of lawsuits. Fortunately for American students and America as a whole, there were visionary, courageous school boards, legislators, governors, and educators who were willing to lead this new exciting wave in education. In the fall of 2011, K¹² was in more than half of the states, touching over five hundred thousand students in individual courses and full-time programs. The number would be far larger if many of these states didn't limit enrollment in online schools and courses. Online education is now approaching the tipping point, and the question has shifted from "Will we do this?" to "When and how will we do this?"

Online learning is a phenomenon that's playing out across the country. In November 2005, the North American Council on Online Learning listed 157 unique online learning programs in forty-two states, including thirty-two virtual charter schools, three online homeschool programs, and fifty-three public, noncharter virtual schools.¹² That was more than five years ago—a lifetime in computer technology terms. The number has grown significantly since then. The US Department of Education's 2004 National Education Technology Plan predicted that with the "explosive growth in the availability of online instruction and virtual schools…we may well be on our way to a new golden age in American education."¹³ That age is coming quickly both in K-12 and college. The creation of MOOCs (Massive Open Online Courses) by top universities will accelerate this trend. These MOOCs have the potential to both expand access and lower costs.

Indeed, we are building new learning systems with the internet, creating what amounts to entirely new schools. The most dated concept in education is that technology in the classroom only means a computer on a student's desk. The possibilities of the new paradigm are so much more advantageous. Technology is changing how curricula are delivered, how students and teachers interact, how progress is monitored, and how different methods of learning can be accommodated.

Online education is moving from virtual schools to the classroom. In 2003, K[12] was part of an experiment in Philadelphia to create an online school within a steel-and-glass building where teachers taught using an online basal curriculum that the company developed. This was an existing public middle school in a new building in a poor section of the city (see chapter 5). The then superintendent, Paul Vallas (who subsequently took over New Orleans schools), wanted to use online curriculum in a brick-and-mortar setting (even if it was steel-and-glass). All the classrooms had laptops and interactive whiteboards (big interactive computer screens that replaced chalkboards and overhead projectors) and wireless access to the internet.

The teachers at the school voted almost unanimously to participate in this pilot. This didn't surprise me, but it did surprise some district officials who thought teachers would be reluctant to embrace technology and new ways of teaching. In my experience, teachers are very willing to embrace new technology—if properly introduced to it—including the latest interactive software; real-time, computer-based student assessments; and online access to high quality curriculum. The Philadelphia teachers took to it immediately. After just one year, student achievement soared: more than a 20 percent improvement in fifth-grade math and 40 percent in third-grade math. This improvement occurred without changing the faculty or the school day.

Two years later, a different type of school was launched, in Chicago: a hybrid school, part brick-and-mortar school and part online school where students attend classes one to two days per week and do the rest online, providing them with face-to-face instruction in small groups and creating a strong social environment for the students. This school has proven to be a wonderful success, and there is now a long waiting list to enroll. K[12] alone has opened thirty-five of these hybrid facilities where instruction is done both online and in the classroom.

Hybrid schools specifically designed for high school dropouts are demonstrating remarkable results in that they are graduating over 90 percent of the dropouts who enroll, and many of these graduates are going on to postsecondary education. Many types of hybrid schools are emerging: a flex academy—a flip school where much of the instruction takes place out of the classroom, and actual classroom time is reserved for discussions and project-based learning—is an example of this. The first flex academy opened in San Francisco and offers students a completely individualized education in a brick-and-mortar setting that they attend full-time. This allows them to get the extraordinary, individualized education that can be obtained in a virtual school while having the social and custodial benefits offered by brick-and-mortar schools. These schools work for students behind grade level, at grade level, and ahead of grade level. I expect that many more new models will emerge in the coming years.

Technology-based education brings individualized education to classrooms, hybrid settings, and full-time virtual schools, but it's only part of the solution. While full-time virtual schools receive much attention, they will likely serve only a small total percentage of students. The primary reason for this is that the majority of Americans do not have the custodial situation at home to do full-time online education. Additionally, many families prefer the traditional classroom setting. The biggest impact of online education will likely be in the classroom and individualized courses.

Education's Equalizer:
Beyond Computers in the Classroom

These experiments demonstrate how technology, when used in the right way, can trigger a transformation in the way students learn. I believe that technology is now the most powerful, scalable, and hopeful force in education reform—with nothing over the past one hundred years offering the same potential for progress. While we have learned a great deal about how it works best—financially, pedagogically, and cognitively—the most exciting part is that we are just at the beginning.

We know, for instance, that computer equipment will never compensate for poor curriculum content. We know that young children do not retain what they have to scroll down the screen to see; they get confused when wrong answers to questions are accompanied by fancy (and fun) animation. We know that children love interactive whiteboards and that teachers feel almost liberated by their computer assistants and interactive curricula. The new software not only allows instant assessments—it can also instantly adjust to compensate for the comprehension gaps.

The bottom line: we can now customize and individualize education without hiring armies of tutors, and this can be achieved at scale. In other words, school districts, which do not have funds for research and development, can buy sophisticated technology services from private companies in the same way they have been buying textbooks. Technology is the greatest leveling force in education since Brown v. Board of Education, the 1954 Supreme Court case that ruled segregation in public schools to be unconstitutional.[14]

In this book, I try to make an uncomplicated case for technology and show how some of the newest computer and software innovations can solve many of our oldest educational problems. Some of the advantages of the new technology that I address include:

- Establishing crucial links between school and afterschool programs and home
- Enabling truly individualized learning and adaptive learning that will serve children with special needs and challenge gifted students
- Empowering parents and students
- Delivering sophisticated software that can make gaming a content-rich educational experience

- Making online teacher training available 24/7
- Letting students tutor themselves with genuine twenty-four-hour access to school and curricula
- Giving teachers and parents a way to monitor individual student needs and progress
- Customizing curricula to meet not just different state standards but also the needs of the individual student, both gifted and challenged
- Giving all students access to the best resources on any topic, from anywhere in the world
- Diminishing the need for remedial education as well as individual-ized remediation
- Dramatically increasing early learning proficiency by the crucial third-grade year
- Saving the public school system billions of dollars as productivity improves and the need for physical buildings declines
- Significantly improving academic results for all schools
- Educating the incarcerated and reducing recidivism
- Expanding the number of courses and programs available to all students
- Creating a global education system and allowing high quality learn-ing in the developing world
- Allowing women and other people who are oppressed to obtain an education where it might not be permitted

The promise of public education can now be extended as never before—and the worrisome trends of the last thirty years can be reversed. Similarly, the universal education system that once made America the envy of the world can be revived. It is no magic bullet—and it is not sim-ple—but thanks to the new technology, children no longer have to live in the "right" zip code to get a good public school education. They need not have to wait for a bus or travel an hour on three different subway lines to find a class in AP Calculus or Latin that their public school doesn't offer. Students can get a world-class education as easily from their Bronx tenement as from their Nob Hill loft—and for the same price. When the tragic earthquake struck Haiti a few years back, the American school was destroyed. K[12] had all the school's students back in class online within two weeks!

The Haiti experience is an example of learning available anytime, anywhere. Even the most persistently low-performing schools can learn to incorporate technology that will change the way their students absorb new ideas and provide more time on task. As I explain in the pages that follow, the new technology will help solve the teacher-shortage challenge, the summer-regression problem, and the credit-recovery dilemma that is one of the primary causes of our dropout crisis. No longer will students who fail a single course in the fall of a school year have to wait a full year to retake the course, dropping a whole year behind their graduating class in the process. No longer are motivated students in rural districts kept from taking courses in advanced physics or Chinese. No longer do the gifted students need to be held back or the special needs students pushed more quickly than they can comprehend. No longer will mastery of concepts and skills be limited only to those who are easy to teach in the classroom.

Pie in the sky? It was ten years ago, perhaps, as was the idea of carrying the contents of your office around with you. All of this was surely not part of my original plan or vision. As I worked the past decade in education, however, the potential of technology to revolutionize our public school system kept revealing itself. Yes, I am well aware of the promises made by other technologists—in 1926 Thomas Edison predicted that film would "revolutionize" education.[15] Similar predictions were made for television, but they failed because they did not offer what the new technology does: access to a customized, engaging, and interactive world-class education.

We have focused on building an educational network that joins the best of technology with a world-class curriculum because I believe those are the essential elements of a twenty-first-century education. I called my company K¹² because I knew this new approach could work for every child at every stage of education. The business has been exhilarating, as most start-up ventures are, but the most exciting and rewarding part is contributing to a revolution that can benefit society in so many ways.

Indeed, we are still at the earliest stage of creating a new model for American education, centered on technological innovation. The computer and the internet are an order of technological innovation the magnitude of which hasn't been seen since the printing press. In fact, the computer revolution is the joining of Gutenberg and Gates—and everything in between. We don't have a choice about new technologies; we have to be ready to know how to use them when they arrive—as they inevitably will. This book will help in that transformation.

For the first time in history, we can provide education to the public without having to erect thousands of buildings. The quick transition from dial-up to broadband to wireless in less than a decade has sealed the deal, even for our education system, which has been notoriously slow in seizing the opportunities presented by technological progress. It is the technology era; virtual reality is a reality.

A Blueprint for Technology Revolution in Schools

So, how do we best use technology to educate our children? I answer that question in the pages that follow.

I have learned a great deal about education in the past decade, and I have more confidence than ever that school systems can evolve to meet the demands of the twenty-first century. Is it the perfect public school system? No, but to borrow from our Founding Fathers, it is more perfect than what has preceded it.

With economic opportunity increasingly driven by knowledge and critical thinking, never before have the stakes been so high. Never before have stakeholders had such a range of opportunities to obtain a rigorous, first-class education—not just as consumers but as providers. For that reason, this book has been written with these stakeholders in mind:

Parents: Technology will unite school and afterschool with home as never before. With online schools, parents will have a detailed understanding of their child's education and what they are being taught, regardless of whether that school is in their living room or in a building across town. Parental empowerment goes much beyond that, of course, since the internet gives you access to a multitude of educational options. If your children are not getting the education that you believe they need, you will have many full-time and part-time options to choose from.

Educators: Teachers will get a more detailed understanding of online schools and how to use them to maximize educational achievement. You will see that there is no reason to fear technology but that it is a wonderful—and liberating—ally in the task of teaching. Technology-based curriculum can be used in the classroom to produce remarkable results, providing you use it correctly. Differentiated instruction will finally become a reality. In fact, it will be completely individualized. Adaptive assessments will allow more accurate measures of learning gains.

Administrators: School leaders, from superintendents to principals, will receive broad-based exposure to the role of technology in education and emerge with ideas on how you can use it to raise student achievement and do so cost effectively. Technology can greatly help schools do more with less, as is being necessitated by the current fiscal crisis in most states.

Policy makers: Almost every state and school district in the country is currently trying to understand how technology can lower costs, improve education outcomes, and meet the needs of students for flexibility and increased course offerings. This book highlights best practices in technology, virtual education, and online learning, with the idea of helping policy makers understand what works and doesn't work and showing how technology can improve school systems without unleashing strong institutional resistance.

University leaders: Technology is already revolutionizing higher education. This book offers postsecondary leaders insights into developments at the elementary and secondary education level, so you can fashion better relationships between high school and beyond. It also provides a roadmap for a more cost-effective college education. With the creation of MOOCs, college education is rapidly changing and there is no turning back.

As someone who runs a business centered on education, I know that no education experiment can have a lasting effect if it does not raise student achievement. Too often, however, when businesspeople look at education, they only want to measure customer and market satisfaction statistics. For K^{12}, those metrics have been off the charts. What's more meaningful are student test-score growth and achievement, reduced dropout rates, and increased learning—the real bottom line for any education enterprise.

We may not be ready for "Beam me up, Scotty," but we can squeeze an extraordinary amount of data into our portable flash drives, including a world-class education. In order to seize the opportunities presented by this new environment, we do not need new laws—only new understandings about how to most effectively use these amazing new tools to educate our children. This book is a roadmap for how we can do so.

1

WHY WE CAN'T WAIT ANY LONGER

*T*he rallying cry for American education reform traces back to a slim report by the National Commission on Excellence in Education released in 1983. *A Nation at Risk: The Imperative for Educational Reform* warned that "the educational foundations of our society are... being eroded by a rising tide of mediocrity that threatens our very future as a Nation and a people."[1]

One other memorable line still resonates: "If an unfriendly foreign power had attempted to impose on America the mediocre educational performance that exists today, we might well have viewed it as an act of war."[2]

The sixty-five-page report, with its explosive rhetoric and dire conclusions, touched a national nerve and unleashed an unprecedented wave of education reform efforts and actions.

In the intervening years, the United States has poured billions more dollars into schools, hiring new teachers, offering more incentives for professional development and more pay for teachers who stay longer. Average class size in the United States dropped by more than one-third— from twenty-three students per teacher to fourteen—between 1991 and 1999. Between 1971 and 2001, the percentage of teachers holding advanced degrees more than doubled, from 27.5 percent to 56.8 percent. The average teacher in 2001 had fourteen years of experience, compared with eight years of experience in 1971. It was an impressive—and extremely expensive—effort.[3]

A Nation Still at Risk?

Unfortunately, all the spending does not seem to have significantly raised student achievement. This is not a surprise. There are no studies that strongly correlate money spent with improved student performance. Indeed, most studies show little relationship at all.

From 1971 to 2001, overall student achievement stayed more or less the same. It's possible that, in the absence of the increased spending, the results would have declined over that period, but it's also possible that the money did little to improve educational outcomes. What's clear is that progress was not proportional to the money spent.

Scores on the National Assessment of Education Progress (NAEP), which is often referred to as the nation's report card, have been flat since the 1970s. The average seventeen-year-old student's score on the NAEP reading test was 285 in 2004, exactly the same as in 1971. Math results are no different, going from a score of 304 in 1973 to 307 in 2004. "Despite twenty years of agitation and reform, much of it sparked by the Risk report," said Paul Peterson, of Harvard University, "student achievement has at best stagnated, if not declined."[4]

Similarly, scores on the Scholastic Aptitude Test (the infamous SAT), taken by college-bound high school students, have not improved much. SAT scores in reading dropped from 537 in 1970 to 507 in 2003. Math SAT scores have inched up from 512 in 1970 to 519 in 2003.[5] Given the reduction in class sizes (and thus more individualized attention from teachers), these results are unimpressive. While SAT scores are not a comprehensive measurement of a quality education, they are a valuable indicator of how students are performing and also an indicator of college headlines.

There are other concerns besides standardized test scores. Many students enter college unprepared. According to the 2008 NAEP test, a significant percentage of twelfth graders were not proficient in math or in reading.[6] More alarming, said Jay Greene, professor of education reform at the University of Arkansas, is the fact that almost half of the students who do graduate from high school are essentially ineligible for a four-year college because they have not taken the minimal coursework required for admission to virtually any four-year institution. According to the American College Testing (ACT) program, which has been administering a math, science, and English test to high school seniors since 1959, the nation has a "college readiness crisis": only one-fourth of the students who took the test recently met the readiness benchmark.[7] (The remediation is already beginning online, as that forum is less expensive and can be done before the student matriculates.)

Perhaps more troubling is that the United States is falling further behind other countries where school systems are improving. In fact, the *Risk* report exclaimed rather bluntly in 1983 that "what was unimaginable a generation ago has begun to occur—others are matching and surpassing our educational attainments." Unfortunately, this report prediction has come true.

This is an enormous blow because the United States at one time led the world by a large margin in educational attainment and achievement. The International Association for the Evaluation of Education Achievement (IEEA) has administered tests of math and science in countries around the world since the 1960s. And while our scores have remained pretty constant (the same flat line as indicated in the NAEP and SAT), other countries have charged ahead. American students are now scoring below those from Singapore, Korea, Japan, Hong Kong, and the Netherlands on the Trends in International Mathematics and Science Study (TIMSS) and other international exams.[8]

The United States was the first country to offer universal elementary education and the first to make an attempt to offer secondary education to all citizens. As late as 1970, a higher percentage of US teenagers completed secondary education than did their peers in any other nation. Today, the United States falls in the middle of the pack.[9] Even those who do go to college are, increasingly, not finishing. Nationally, fewer than 20 percent of high school freshmen will go on to finish college. No wonder the Education Trust concluded that the United States is alone among industrialized countries whose children will not be better educated than their parents.

America has fallen into a vicious cycle. As the country loses ground to other countries on test scores, we have also lost the ability to keep children in school. High school dropout rates are appalling, approaching 70 percent in some of our inner cities. While the 2012 report showed some improvement, the rates are still too high.[10]

US Dropout Rate in 2005

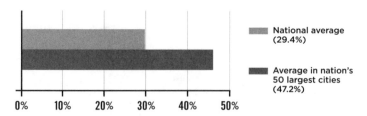

Source: America's Promise Alliance, *Cities in Crisis 2009: Closing the Graduation Gap*, Editorial Projects in Education Research Center (April 2009).

Highest Dropout Rates in US Cities in 2005

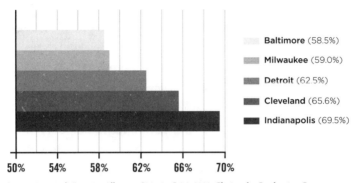

Baltimore (58.5%)

Milwaukee (59.0%)

Detroit (62.5%)

Cleveland (65.6%)

Indianapolis (69.5%)

50% 54% 58% 62% 66% 70%

Source: America's Promise Alliance, *Cities in Crisis 2009: Closing the Graduation Gap,* Editorial Projects in Education Research Center (April 2009).

Even more alarming is that these numbers do not include the students who drop out before high school or are not officially listed as dropouts. *Los Angeles Times* columnist Tim Rutten wrote about the City of Angels' Unified School District in July of 2008.

> We've all become so inured to the unending stream of dreary and dispiriting news that Thursday's horrific report on the high school dropout rate came and went with barely a civic whimper…. In an economy that increasingly rewards participation in knowledge-based industries, failure to graduate from high school is a virtual guarantor of perpetual helotry.[11]

As Rutten pointed out, the social cost of our dropout crisis is monumental: a high school graduate is 20 percent less likely to commit a violent crime than a dropout is, 11 percent less likely to commit a crime against property, and 12 percent less likely to be arrested for breaking the drug laws.[12]

All of these numbers hit African American and Latino students much harder than Caucasian students, which is why so much of educa-

5

tion reform is about civil rights. "Despite concerted efforts by educators," reported the *New York Times* in 2006, "the test-score gaps are so large that, on average, African-American and Hispanic students in high school can read and do arithmetic at only the average level of whites in junior high school."[13] The US Secretary of Education, Arne Duncan, rightly called this gap the modern era's civil rights challenge. The infamous digital divide, which refers to the gap between different racial and economic groups in accessing digital and information technology, is more important than ever.[14]

As grim as these statistics are, there is a larger peril. American schools are not producing the skilled labor and lifelong learners with twenty-first-century skills that are a cornerstone of America's future prosperity. In 1950, when most of American jobs were unskilled, failing to graduate from high school might have been less consequential. Today, with only a small percentage of jobs being unskilled, the consequences could be catastrophic—we are essentially committing millions of children to a lifetime of poverty.

According to a study by the Alliance for Excellent Education, "The nation would save approximately $45 billion if it could cut the number of dropouts in half." The Alliance study showed that "if high school dropouts who currently head households in the United States had earned their diplomas, the US economy would have benefited from an additional $74 billion in wealth accumulated by families."[15]

The Need Is Greater than Ever

It's increasingly difficult to realize the American dream without a quality education, particularly for children from impoverished areas and rural areas, and all of us should find it appalling that a good education is the exception, not the norm. The effect is to leave these kids far behind their counterparts in higher-performing schools. If underperforming schools can improve (and closing the digital divide can spark the improvements), the benefits will be felt in communities throughout the world. Absent these improvements, countless children will be ill prepared to seize the opportunities of the knowledge economy.

There have been many harsh critics who say the US education system is steadily sliding into mediocrity. While I don't believe we are in a state of absolute decline, we are clearly in a state of relative decline. The facts are that we were quantum leaps ahead of the rest of the world; now that education is more important than it ever was, the world has caught up. This is a frightening realization for Americans in an increasingly flat world—a realization compounded by the fact that the United States may no longer be the benefactor of the world's brain drain. More and more students and entrepreneurs stay in China, India, and other fast-growing nations because they believe the opportunities there are perhaps more promising than they are in the United States. Plus, it is difficult to obtain a visa to stay here. Having highly educated foreigners leave the United States is a dramatic change from where we were twenty years ago. If we can no longer import or produce high quality human capital, our economic prosperity is in peril.

In an era of global economic competition, America's schools need—at a minimum—to measure up to those in other nations. There is a need to take a quantum leap akin to the launch of universal free education a century ago, which built one of the most skilled and powerful engines of human capital in history.

If America is going to remain a great nation—that "shining city on a hill" that President Reagan alluded to—a world-class education system is essential, so this dream that many of us have lived will be possible for the next generation of Americans. The next generation of entrepreneurs impacting our world will be created by our current education system, and we need a system that equips them with the knowledge, talents, skills, values, drive, and vision to be entrepreneurs—or anything they want to be. Nations that fail to do this will not remain globally competitive.

2

WHY WE DON'T CHANGE

*I*n the services-driven, information-age economy, the premium attached to a rigorous education is greater than ever. The increasing value placed on skills is the major factor in increasing income disparity, yet the American public school system isn't keeping pace with the dynamism of the US economy. While the United States spends more per student than any other country, SAT and NAEP scores are flat, and other nations are moving forward as the United States remains stagnant. On almost every indicator of student achievement, American students are falling further behind. Almost 30 percent of children don't even finish high school. Productivity in education has fallen almost 50 percent.[1] In a nation that has achieved so much progress over the past fifty years, what is truly remarkable is that education has failed to advance at the same rate. The reasons why are complex and not always clear.

What is clear is that the money and effort pumped into the US public education system over the last twenty years has altered the course of the ship a few degrees, but it has not turned the ship around nor sped it up. Why? This is the crucial question for any education reformer—teacher, parent, and policy maker—to ask.

The first thing to know is how big the ship is. After healthcare, public education is the largest single part of our economy and of government expenditures, accounting for over $500 billion in expenditures, before the recent Obama stimulus.[2] There are so many well-entrenched interests and so many ingrained habits that it is difficult to find the engine room, much less the bridge.

Total Government Spending: $6.3 Trillion for Fiscal Year 2012

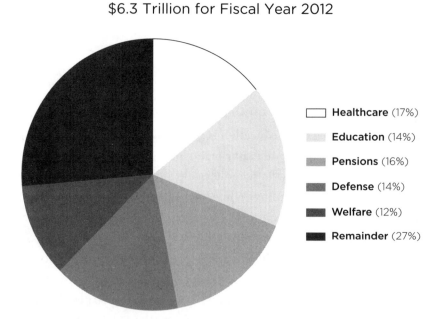

Healthcare (17%)

Education (14%)

Pensions (16%)

Defense (14%)

Welfare (12%)

Remainder (27%)

Source: The Office of Management and Budget and the United States Census Bureau, compiled by http://www.usgovernmentspending.com.

There are now 3.3 million teachers in some ninety-seven thousand elementary and secondary public schools teaching over fifty million students—all of it regulated by fourteen thousand different boards of education, fifty different state legislatures, and the US Congress.[3] Try to find the stop or turnaround button on that ship! This order of magnitude makes education harder to turn around than a company like General Motors, given the decentralized management and board control found in education, as well as the sheer size (five to ten times larger than GM, with even more powerful entrenched interests and unbelievable political power). Reforming the education system requires all of these school boards, legislatures, administrators, unions, and teachers to act in a coordinated fashion. This is almost impossible unless an external force creates the need to do so. In a normal marketplace, this force comes in the form of competition, which drives firms to innovate and continually produce a better product or service in a more cost-efficient way. The education system is mostly insulated from the competitive marketplace and so, like most monopolies, it strives to stifle change and competition.

Change Comes Hard

In public education, change is widespread as long as nothing changes. The title of E. D. Hirsch's bestselling book, *The Schools We Need: And Why We Don't Have Them* implies the obvious: that we should be able to have good schools. So, why can't we have them?

In a perfect education world, students would be put first and we would have comprehensive information and vibrant competition. This is, however, an imperfect—and political—world. Clearly, the politics of policy reform play a major role in the question of education malfunction. There is an enormous number of constituencies and an enormous number of adults in the system. Sometimes their desires align with what's best for student learning, and sometimes they don't.

When *Washington Post* education writer Jay Mathews wrote about attempts to reform Philadelphia's public school system, he concluded that "factors that have little to do with children are often very important." Though the Philadelphia Federation of Teachers' goal is not to oppose good things for students, "its resistance to change," as Matthews pointed out, as well as "the desire to find a political compromise that would give all combatants some sense of victory, "took precedence over student welfare in the working out of these issues."[4]

In other words, there are plenty of ways to fail our children and, apparently, very few ways to successfully encourage them to succeed. As Mathews remarked, "improvement in achievement is not going to be big or fast."[5]

Moreover, educational data is extremely complex, and some might argue they need to be measured over multiple years. For example, advocates of early childhood education rely on social outcomes that occur twenty years later to make their argument. Waiting twenty years to determine whether something works is impractical. By testing on an annual basis and measuring growth as opposed to absolute outcomes, it's possible to arrive at a measurement system that will allow us to continually optimize education much more rapidly. In an online world, it could even be daily.

There are so many powerful engines resisting change that any changes at all are surprising. While not attempting to present a complete list, here are seven factors that play a significant role in preventing the kind of change that could spark fundamental improvement:

- Complexity of the politics and regulations at the local, state, and federal levels
- Large, entrenched groups with very specific agendas
- Lack of competitive forces and large barriers to private-sector involvement

- Short-term nature of leadership and teachers
- Fragmented market with no scalable solutions
- Inadequate investments in research and development
- Lack of valid information and high quality research

These issues are addressed throughout the book, some more directly than others. Let me briefly introduce the key challenges to change in the following pages.

Politics

Anyone involved in the effort to reform education is immediately thrust into a highly charged political climate. Any substantive change in education typically requires modifying legislation and state policies (at a minimum, school board approval is needed). The process of fostering change is often very long and sometimes expensive. When the policy change affects a particular constituency, it becomes extremely expensive and arduous. Consider the structure of American public education, in which power is distributed among local boards of education, state boards of education; mayors; state and federal legislators; and large local, state, and federal education bureaucracies. That alone almost guarantees change will be difficult to implement.

For this reason, it has been historically difficult to start education companies and to receive investment for these companies. Even companies like K^{12}, which eventually became successful, were met with skepticism. Fortunately, in the case of the virtual schools, some states were willing to be trailblazers, as were some very innovative school districts. Once they showed the way, others soon followed. The fact that there are fourteen thousand school boards in fifty states made the K^{12} concept more viable, not less, because the idea could be presented to thousands of different bodies but only needed a few visionaries to say yes in order to launch the concept. Amazingly, this resistance still exists as we see groups (there are still fourteen thousand school boards) continue to fight to stop virtual education in their state or limit the number of students who can enroll. It makes little sense to deny students enrollment in a school that they want to attend and that is willing to take them. Yet it happens all the time, even though the school is significantly more taxpayer efficient.

Complex politics have also led to complex regulations that do not change easily with the times. Often these regulations are so inflexible that they make it hard for principals to run high-performing schools. Freedom from these complexities was a major impetus for charter schools, though many public virtual schools must still operate under the absurd regulations that were written before the internet even existed.

Entrenched Interests

Teachers unions are often blamed for blocking school reform and are sometimes made to be the scapegoats for everything. The reality is that these unions are only doing what they are chartered to do, which is to improve the welfare of teachers. Albert Shanker, the former president of the American Federation of Teachers, is often quoted as saying: When schoolchildren start paying union dues, that's when I'll start representing the interests of school-children. Teachers and their unions clearly want to provide children with the best education possible, and my meetings with union leaders have always been centered on improving education. They may have other issues that matter to them, and these need to be understood before any reform can happen. Innovations that benefit teachers and students *and* have the support of the union are far more likely to be enacted than are reform efforts opposed by the unions. Fortunately, technology has the potential to leverage great teachers, reduce the preparation time needed each day, and make instruction more individualized and more engaging. Thus, I believe technology is something that will eventually be embraced by teachers and their unions, which makes it much more likely to have the impact that it should have.

The behavior of all of these interests is not abnormal or irrational; people are normally resistant to change. However, in the case of education, the size of the education infrastructure and the complexity of the politics exacerbate this problem and slow change to a glacial pace. These groups can pass laws to ban virtual schools or private school management companies, for example. Could one imagine a law to ban iPods or ban private companies from manufacturing them? Of course not! Conduct that encourages a monopoly in a normal market is illegal in the United States. The current ability to enact legislation to protect a monopoly structure in education makes it harder to reform than any commercial market.

Competition

The role of competition and private enterprise in education is a cornerstone of reform efforts. Both have contributed to America's success and unleashed great wealth and prosperity, but if there is an alternative explanation for America's success, it is education. The United States was providing free grade school education to most children by the mid-1800s and free high school to most Americans by the 1930s—a universal education system decades ahead of other nations. Tens of thousands of mostly poor immigrant children disembarked from ships in New York Harbor and attended school *for free*.[6] It wasn't just the universality of opportunity that set America apart. It was the equal access to good schools—and the critical role the marketplace has played in developing successful schools.

Competition can be trusted to deliver better products at better prices. In the history of humankind, economic competition has been an engine of change and progress, almost always providing the consumer with a better product at a better price. Unfortunately, education has been immune from these competitive forces. When AT&T was broken up, innovation in telephony was unleashed. Long-distance calls were once prohibitively expensive, and now they are virtually free. It used to be illegal to put an answering machine on a phone line. Cell phones were once considered commercially unviable. It's remarkable what happens to an industry under competitive forces. This rate of innovation has been remarkable. I hope education soon follows this path.

The American university system is generally considered the best in the world and is the one aspect of the US education system that has seen a significant amount of competition. These universities have competed for professors, students, research grants, and funds for the past fifty years. The GI Bill, which was enacted following World War II, was essentially a voucher system for colleges and universities that allowed potential students to take their voucher to the college of their choice, including public universities and religious universities. This bill not only helped create the world's most educated workforce but also the world's best college system that draws students from throughout the world. Yes, without coincidence our strongest educational system is the one that is subject to competitive forces.

The university system has recently come under stress because of costs that have risen much faster than the rate of inflation for the past forty years. Much of this ineffectiveness emanates from a financial aid structure that, in some ways, discourages efficiency.

For the most selective colleges, price is not a great concern, as there is an insatiable demand to attend these universities, and they subsidize students using the schools' large endowments. We can't argue that something is "too expensive" when there are multiples of qualified applicants for every spot, all willing to pay the price of admission, albeit often through loans and grants. As long as these funding sources are available, price competition will not occur, as the consumer does not bear the cost when the aid is in the form of grants. These universities will be able to continue as is until the cost of their education exceeds the perceived value of their education. My instincts tell me we have a long time before that happens at Harvard, Princeton, Stanford, or the University of Pennsylvania.

Average Undergraduate Tuition, Fees, and Room and Board Rates for Full-Time Students

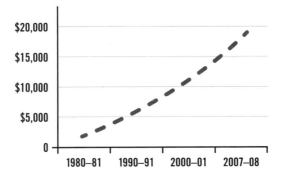

Source: National Center for Education Statistics, Institute of Education Sciences, US Department of Education, *Digest of Education Statistics* (July 2007), table 320.

For the less-selective universities, the model is already beginning to collapse. Many of these colleges are beginning to fail financially. This trend will accelerate, as the market for these colleges cannot support their costs. Does this mean the end of less selective colleges? Hardly! Technology and competition from for-profit colleges will drive the cost of a college education down to a much more affordable price point and will likely improve the quality of the experience from a customer point of view. This can be seen by looking at the rapid growth of the University of Phoenix, which is now the largest university in the United States, with almost four hundred thousand students (up from one hundred thousand just ten years ago).[7] This impressive growth suggests quite clearly they are delivering something that students want and perceive the value of to be greater than the cost. The high price umbrella provided by the nonprofits has allowed this expansion at a relatively high tuition point. With different incentives, the private sector and competition could address the high cost of higher education. In all cases, tuition increasing at multiples of inflation is unsustainable for most colleges, and the best likely solution will be online education and competition. Ideally, government policy will encourage competition, not discourage it. Additionally, MOOCs will have the potential to lower college costs by providing access to great professors at low price points. As their courses become eligible for credit, this will drive down college costs.

Competition needs to be introduced to the public K-12 sector in order to stimulate innovation and efficiency. Philadelphia saw a large rise in test scores when for-profit and nonprofit private operators ran a significant number of its schools. The competition forced the local school district to raise its game, and its improvements were on par with the averages for the private operators. Charter schools have the potential to create this competition, but there are still too few to have a large impact on the overall system.

Leadership, Continuity, and Accountability

The leaders of America's school districts need to be assessed on the basis of concrete results and given the time to enact comprehensive changes. Superintendents are often replaced after a few years for political reasons, or they receive an offer from a bigger district that draws them away. This lack of continuity is a real obstacle to education improvement. Others stay for years without having any meaningful impact because not rocking the boat is often the best recipe for job security in highly political environments.

Leaders of districts need to be given the tools to succeed and be held accountable for their performance. This concept holds true for everyone working in a school system, principals and teachers as well. This is difficult for any organization, and while the private sector is far from perfect on accountability issues, it is generally better than the public and nonprofit sectors.

Teachers also tend to leave the profession or change schools rapidly. The NCES reported that approximately 17 percent of teachers change schools or leave each year.[8] This discontinuity makes it very difficult to improve performance because the workforce at a school needs to be continually trained.

Research and Development

There are many types of education-related research and development (R&D), but relative to other sectors, very little is spent on them. The fragmented nature of the sector combined with the limited involvement of the private sector make doing research difficult. In the defense industry, the private sector does extensive R&D. This does not happen in education, as grants and contracts often exclude for-profit companies. Such a scattershot approach to seeking policies and programs that work has been an enormous drag on improvement, especially in relation to the more focused efforts in other countries. When something does work, it is rarely scalable. I hope this will change with online education and technology-based education. The emergence of large curriculum providers, learning-system companies, and integrated school-management companies may finally create an environment in which large companies can both invest and innovate. While there is some research and development being done in schools of education, it is small relative to the size of education spending.

Knowledge and the Parent Revolution

The strongest catalyst for change in the US education system is likely to be the recognition that American students are not performing as well as students in other nations. Indeed, the fear of falling behind has unleashed changes in the past. In 1959, the country mobilized to increase its emphasis on the sciences in order to thwart the perceived Russian dominance following Russia's launch of a spacecraft. Recall also the *Nation at Risk* report. The report seemed to have mobilized the country to focus on education reform and spend money on the problem. Unfortunately, the results have been limited, which is unsatisfactory in a nation where the vast majority of jobs require skilled labor.

In addition to the *Nation at Risk* report, the TIMSS test and other international benchmarking exams have increased awareness that American students are underperforming relative to students from other developed nations. By the time US students finish high school, they are close to the bottom in math and science.[9]

The intersection of technology and politics can spark change in education, though the most powerful force of all is the consumer. In the case of K-12 education, it comes in the form of parents. They are leading the march to educational equity and excellence by demanding that their children receive a quality education. Parents are increasingly aware of alternatives to simply enrolling their children in the neighborhood school and hoping for the best. This includes charter schools, virtual schools, virtual classes, and anything else that might benefit their children.

In 2009, when the governor of Ohio tried to pass legislation that would have adversely impacted charter schools and virtual schools, legislators were inundated with letters against the bill, and a rally at the state capitol attracted nearly ten thousand parents and students.[10] The rally was just one example of the parent revolution in education, which is only going to intensify as parents use the internet and other media to better understand the full range of schooling options and demand them for their children. Parents want choice, not a one-size-fits-all education. When choice is available in every other part of consumers' lives, it should not be surprising that they want the same opportunities in education.

In countries such as Japan and Korea, where the students generally rank near the top on the international exams, parents are involved at a level that would be almost unimaginable to American parents. Korean students spend as much time in afterschool centers as they do in school itself. This intense effort likely helps these students on the international exams. In fact, these families often spend more money on education than they do on housing, according to the Milken Institute.[11]

What Asian Families Saved for in 2012

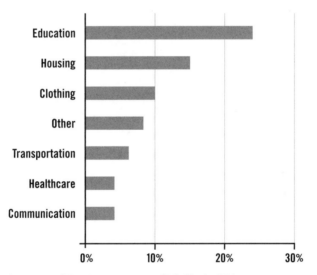

Source: Mr. and Mrs. Asia, 2009 report, published by the CLSA: http://www.bls.gov/cex/2011/standard/multiyr.pdf.

The improvement of the education systems in Korea and Singapore over the past fifty years is remarkable—though not surprising, given the intensity of government actions and parental attitudes. This improvement in education has coincided with significant economic development. We are seeing a similar type of intensity in China. In fact, China (Shanghai) recently topped the list of countries on the Programme for International Student Assessment (PISA) for fifteen-year-olds. Additionally, European and Asian nations and regions within nations outperformed US students in reading, math, and science.[12] Given the economic growth and population in China, I think there is little doubt that China will be a force in the world's economy for a long time to come as educational attainment spreads to the rest of China and this well-educated, English-fluent generation enters the workforce.

2009 PISA Test Scores

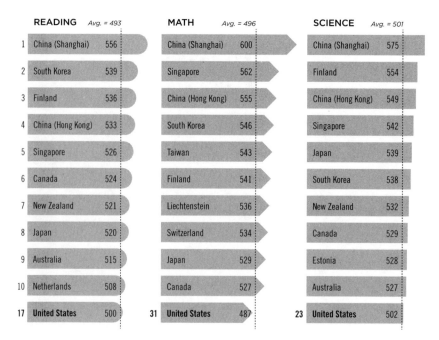

READING *Avg. = 493*		MATH *Avg. = 496*		SCIENCE *Avg. = 501*	
1 China (Shanghai)	556	China (Shanghai)	600	China (Shanghai)	575
2 South Korea	539	Singapore	562	Finland	554
3 Finland	536	China (Hong Kong)	555	China (Hong Kong)	549
4 China (Hong Kong)	533	South Korea	546	Singapore	542
5 Singapore	526	Taiwan	543	Japan	539
6 Canada	524	Finland	541	South Korea	538
7 New Zealand	521	Liechtenstein	536	New Zealand	532
8 Japan	520	Switzerland	534	Canada	529
9 Australia	515	Japan	529	Estonia	528
10 Netherlands	508	Canada	527	Australia	527
17 **United States**	500	31 **United States**	487	23 **United States**	502

Source: Organisation for Economic Co-operation and Development (OECD), Programme for International Student Assessment.

Interestingly, in comparisons with the United States, two of the chief reasons given for the difference in results were the amount of work done and also that the Chinese students were much more attentive in class. The PISA report states: "Typically in a Shanghai classroom, students are fully occupied and fully engaged. Non-attentive students are not tolerated."[13] As I share in this book, technology can promote both time-on-task and student engagement.[14]

Technology and the Need for Metrics

Before we even step into the classroom or debate the merits of online learning, computers can be used to streamline the process by which we analyze data and offer objective metrics for judging employee productivity. The education system has traditionally responded to each student performance challenge by hiring more adults. Only now are leaders within the system beginning to understand that expanding the workforce doesn't translate to reducing the problems.

In 1950, for instance, US school districts were hiring one instructional employee (including teacher, administrator, or guidance counselor) for every nineteen pupils.[15] By 2005, the ratio had shrunk from 19:1 to 8:1. "If class-size reduction were the solution to America's education crisis," said Paul Peterson of Harvard's Kennedy School of Government, "that crisis would have passed long ago."[16] The large number of adults added to the system has resulted in lower compensation and miniscule investment in technology—and likely lowered average teacher quality.

Peterson pointed out that the number of other school employees—from clerks to aides to bus drivers—has also grown. There are now twenty-seven pupils for every support staffer, compared to fifty-eight in 1960.[17] It is difficult to make the case that this increase in staff has improved student learning. In fact, the opposite likely occurred as low wages shrunk the human capital pool.

Had there been increases in pupil achievement (including better graduation rates and better college attendance numbers) to match these staff increases, it might be money well spent. Instead, there has been a steep decline in education productivity, and educators have been underpaid. Additionally, almost every state is now in a fiscal crisis.

Part of the problem has been the inability to accurately measure both student achievement and teacher effectiveness. There are often strong objections and a lengthy process involved when laying off teachers, because teachers think it is usually a purely subjective decision—and they have a point. The absence of rigorous gains data that measures how much a child learns in a year versus what the child should learn in a year means decisions are subjective. With the right metrics on student performance, decisions could be based on facts and not merely opinions. This would also allow states to avoid costly, ineffective policy initiatives like class size reductions, which cost a fortune and provide little to no benefit.

As test metrics move from static scores to gains, we will be able to measure teacher and program effectiveness much more clearly. Strong school management and improvement will also become attainable with good individual student growth metrics. Using single-point test scores for schools with high student growth or high student turnover is almost useless. Instead, we need to examine how much each individual student learned compared to what they should have learned for each year. (This turns out to be more complex than it sounds, as the expected learning for each student is not necessarily the same.)

Fortunately, the country is now seeing more sophisticated growth models emerge, but these growth models have a long way to go. Adaptive testing is capable of measuring gains, but states have not adopted it yet. With computer adaptive testing, there only needs to be a single test for grades K-8, as the test would be able to pinpoint what a student knows and indicate how much the student progressed in a given time period. The adoption of the Common Core State Standards also promises greater unity and consistency in assessing student learning in the United States.

I once discussed this issue with the head of the union of a large district. She had no objection to removing bad teachers but was adamant that it not be done in an arbitrary way. The fear was that teachers would be fired simply because the principal did not like them. If metrics were available showing that the students in two third-grade classes gained a full year while students in another third-grade class did not gain at all, there would be a good case for giving that teacher some professional development, and if there were no improvement in scores the following year, asking the teacher to leave. Test scores could and should be one of several measures used to evaluate a student and teacher.

Even without the data, teachers usually know who among their colleagues are effective and who are not. When parents ask me how to identify the best second-grade teacher at a school, I tell them to go ask the third-grade teachers which second-grade students come the best prepared. It always amazed me when I toured schools how unanimous the teachers were when asked this question.

Children in grades K-5, particularly at-risk children, cannot afford to have one year with an ineffective teacher because language arts and math are cumulative. If students don't understand yesterday's math lesson, they won't understand today's lesson either, and they will fall behind tomorrow. Before long, they drop far enough behind that they can't catch up to their peers, and they're likely to lose interest in the subject. Children from affluent families or educated families can intervene with tutoring or by changing schools. Families in poverty rarely have that luxury. One bad year can ruin a child's lifetime prospects. Fortunately, technology offers the potential to eliminate this problem through better monitoring and increasing teacher effectiveness. The best way to remediate a child is to ensure that the child never falls behind.

In New York City, Mayor Michael Bloomberg, who was granted control over Gotham's public schools in 2002, managed to work successfully with the education establishment. His success stemmed, in part, from developing sophisticated metrics for measuring school and teacher progress—to make the evaluation system less capricious. Those metrics include measurements of student performance over time, the actual test scores, attendance figures, and satisfaction surveys of parents, teachers, and students. In high school, factors such as graduation rates and performance on state Regents exams are also figured into the grades given to each school.[18]

While there are a whole host of reasons why American schools have fallen so far behind, the encouraging news is that the trend can be reversed. Technology can spark the change that will improve American education by improving curriculum, assessment, instruction, information access, and data analysis. While the potential of technology has not yet been tapped, that is changing, as innovators figure out how to harness the power of computers and the internet. By loading computers with sophisticated software and introducing them into schools, the status quo can be shaken up and American education can make a quantum leap forward, just as it did over a century ago when education became compulsory. If education in Shanghai can come so far just decades after the Cultural Revolution, American education should be able to do even more.

3

THE COMPUTER IS NOT YOUR FATHER'S TV

*H*aving worked in education for almost fifteen years, I have seen many memorable things. I once sat in on a closed-door meeting with a Texas legislator who told me that he didn't care how good online education was for children, he could not support it, even if there was perfect evidence that it was better for students. He simply believed that there shouldn't be any competition for the local brick-and-mortar school, and education should remain the same as it had always been. It was quite shocking and illuminating. At that moment, I understood why it took such a long time for the overhead projector to make it from the bowling alley to the classroom: politics and lack of competition stifle innovation.

To be immersed in education is to live life in the slow lane. At a time when everything from car manufacturing to corn harvesting incorporates the computer into the daily drum of its operations, the favored teaching technology in our schools remains pencils and paper, bound books, and the chalkboard.

There are a variety of reasons why schools have been reluctant to embrace the computer. The failure of the television to revolutionize the classroom has not made it any easier to introduce computers to the learning process. The example of television is also a reminder that, no matter how good or productive the technology, there will always be excuses not to welcome it or to misuse it. The failure of computers to do much more than sit idle in the backs of classrooms (or be used as sophisticated typewriters to teach keyboarding skills) has not made the case for their ability to revolutionize the education system.

But it's not the computer's fault.

Critics of technology love to cite Thomas Edison's famous remark that "the motion picture is destined to revolutionize our educational system and...in a few years it will supplant largely, if not entirely, the use of textbooks" to make the point that we've heard these promises before.[1]

Before television became a "vast wasteland"—a term coined by FCC Chairman Newton Minow in a 1961 speech to the National Association of Broadcasters[2]—it was supposed to revolutionize the classroom. Beginning in the 1960s, every classroom got its television, the futuristic teacher's aide, installed in a high corner at the front of the room. It frequently sat silent, as if waiting for someone other than Mister Rogers to appear. While educational television has gone beyond Captain Kangaroo, and some shows have demonstrated real educational value, it has hardly revolutionized education.

The challenge is articulated in questions posed recently by the respected policy journal *Education Next*: "Can new education technologies short-circuit change-resistant politics, lengthy sales cycles, limited budgets and remake our schools, or are well-intended advocates once again over-hyping the ability of electrons and processors to solve thorny problems of teaching and learning?"[3]

I think the answers to those questions are yes and yes. The new computer-based technologies will undoubtedly remake education, and in the remaking process, there will undoubtedly be some overhyping. The internet has already had more impact in a few years than television or motion pictures have had in decades. The ability of technology to now be interactive and facilitate communication makes it dramatically different from film, television, or even personal computers that sat in the back of classrooms.

The illustration for the *Education Next* story was inadvertently revealing. It depicted a road leading toward the horizon until coming to the proverbial fork: to the left was a computer, to the right, a textbook. Which will it be? What will be the road not taken?

The problem, of course, is that decisions are not so simple—at least not at this moment in history. Long before coming to the fork in the road, American education will be using computers and textbooks (although most textbooks will soon be digitized and read on eReaders).

Todd Oppenheimer, author of the bestselling 2003 book *The Flickering Mind: Saving Education from the False Promise of Technology*, spoke in stark either/or terms. He cited the Chinese definition of *crisis*—a combination of two characters, one signifying danger and the other opportunity—to illustrate what he believed were the stakes at hand: "politicians and education leaders in nearly every community in the world have been making their largest investment ever in state-of-the-art technology."[4]

This is a false dichotomy—and a false premise. Can we blame the computer for being misused? Or for being "oversold and underused," as Larry Cuban, a Stanford professor of education, titled his 2001 book?[5]

Oppenheimer was technically correct in stating that there is more spending than ever on technology for use in schools, but he was wrong to imply that such investment is in any way sizeable. As Frederick Hess, director of education policy at the American Enterprise Institute, pointed out, public school expenditures on technology went from virtually zero in 1970 to more than $100 per student in 2004.[6] Yes, that's the "largest investment ever," but given that this represents around 2 percent of the money spent on education, the amount is paltry. I believe we should be spending significantly more on technology, which is far less expensive than additional human capital and scalable.

Though Oppenheimer's long treatise on technology in the classroom is packed with useful information (the chapter "Education's History of Technotopia" is excellent), his premise that technology is fool's gold—a "false promise," he called it—is as "fevered" an argument against computers in the classroom as he believes the arguments promoting technology to be.[7] The truth, as usual, lies somewhere closer to the middle of the road—and we haven't come to a fork yet.

The New Pony Express

Though I often talk about the technology of online learning as a window to content, I also understand it as a delivery system. The World Wide Web is as agnostic about content as was the Pony Express or the Railway Express—as is Federal Express.

Indeed, the predecessor of the virtual school—or online learning—is not a piece of technology in the classroom but a correspondence course. Every generation has had its distance learning, delivered by the latest communications devices, including the horse, the railway, Edison's motion picture device, the radio, the telephone, and the television. Even now, the computer is a multiplatform device that can just as easily operate a railroad as an iPod.

Perhaps people didn't begin to confuse the medium and the message until television. When the mailman arrived with your set of auto-mechanics course manuals, you didn't have any expectation that the postman was the teacher. Nor did you one day decide that because the postman was driving a car instead of riding a horse, your mail had suddenly become educational.

The hype that accompanied educational television engendered the expected antihype, specifically the now famous "vast wasteland" speech given by Newton Minow in 1961 while he was chairman of the Federal Communications Commission.[8] Televisions in the classroom were an educational bust, but educational television still exists (think *Sesame Street*). The television evolved into its highest and best use: a one-way medium. The computer began as a glorified typewriter, but we now know that it is much more than that (though not a magic box that will get your kid into Harvard). Indeed, the early attempts to put computers in the classroom were marked not just by the promises of overly optimistic dreamers but by a fundamental misunderstanding of the machine's capacity and purpose.

Perhaps what is most striking about the ongoing technology revolution—and I include in that the many subsidiary revolutions, including the silicon chip, the internet, Google—is how pervasive it now is and how very different it is from what preceded it. Yes, we tried to carry televisions in our pocket, but we didn't build them into our washing machines and calculators. We didn't mix solar panels into our paint.

To argue against the computer or the internet now seems as sensible as arguing against the rising sun. To give the critics their due, just as there are good and bad days, there are good and bad technologies. Railing against the automobile is, however, now a quaint exercise, even though protesting the dangers of the combustion engine has had a revival.

As with so many arguments about the direction and speed of change, we need first to know where we are and where we want to go. We need to have a good idea of what is really wrong with public education before we suggest solutions. Shooting the messenger is not the solution.

A Window to the Future

Criticisms of technology in education reach back many years, and many past criticisms were valid, as technology was being forced into trying to be a replacement for content rather than a window to the content or its delivery mechanism.

Gradually, educators are beginning to understand that computers are not the objects of education; they are the means to one. They are to modern schools what chalk—and chalk dust—were to schools of the nineteenth century. The computer, in short, is a tool. The internet is an even more powerful one because it is interactive and allows two-way communications. The web can provide access to an almost unimaginable array of content and also put an individual in contact with an extraordinary number of people. Facebook taken as a country would now be the third largest and will likely soon be the largest country in the world. It is not even ten years old! The speed of adoption has increased significantly over the past century.

Despite resistance, online education has already made amazing inroads into American K–12 education. Both customer satisfaction surveys and educational gains have demonstrated its value—and its untapped potential. Online education has been able to break through this resistance because parents and students want it.

The International Association for K–12 Online Learning (iNACOL, formerly the North American Association for Online Learning) reported a hectic pace of growth in the online education world: in 2000 there were fifty thousand full- or part-time enrollments; in 2005 there were five hundred thousand; by 2007 there were one million.[9] By comparison, it took fifteen years for charter schools, which started in 1991, to enroll over one million students.[10] (To put these numbers in perspective, the National Center for Education Statistics, which is part of the federal Department of Education, reported that in the fall of 2008, a record 49.8 million students enrolled in public elementary and secondary schools nationwide;

an additional 6.2 million students attended private schools.)[11]

In another view of the online world, according to the US Department of Education, during the 2002–2003 school year, 36 percent of US school districts (5,500 out of 15,040) had students enrolled in distance education programs, and 38 percent of public high schools offered distance education courses. The DOE study also showed that 328,000 students in 8,200 public schools were enrolled in distance education courses.[12]

The growth of online learning enrollment in the last ten years, according to *Forbes*, has been 30 percent annually, which is why the business magazine estimated that the market was worth $300 million in 2008 and today exceeds $1 billion.[13] While still a blip on the radar of the $500 billion public school universe, we at least know that we can educate successfully online.

There are several reasons why online education has expanded far more rapidly than other education reforms. The most important factor has been the proliferation of public charter schools. Public charters enable groups of private citizens to form public schools that are run with far fewer bureaucratic restrictions than face most public schools. Forward-thinking groups could create online schools and contract with outside providers, such as K[12], to provide the systems and curriculum for these schools. K[12] has invested over $300 million (and growing every year) in the curriculum and systems to deliver an online education—an amount no district could afford to spend, nor could they spend it as efficiently as a private sector Silicon Valley–type company could. In this way, private education companies are similar to companies building fighter jets for the military. Had each of the fourteen thousand school districts had to invest in this technology and content, online education would not be nearly as advanced as it is.

The explosion of online education in charter schools, led by parents, has made districts and states offer online education far faster than they would have without this external influence. Online education is also scalable, which means that once the content and systems are built, they can serve millions of students. That has prompted "customers"—parents—to demand access to online courses. Every year K^{12} receives thousands of emails from parents asking when K^{12} will be in their state.

With many children using the internet before they enter preschool, their parents are demanding online education—and the education establishment is beginning to provide it. Parents in states without public virtual academies have a difficult time understanding why they do not have them in their state when over thirty states have them. Parents in states where the public virtual academy has an enrollment cap have an even more difficult time understanding why they cannot attend a public school that wants them and costs the taxpayers less money. The irrational denial of access for these families has created a strong choice movement and empowered parents and students as education consumers. More and more, parents are refusing to take no for an answer. They no longer want to be told which school their child has to attend but want to make the choice of public schools themselves. It is difficult to come up with a good reason why they should not be able to do this.

Disrupting Class by Ignoring It

Disruption is a key theme of Clayton Christensen's recent book on online education. On the one hand, there is an obvious demand for online education; on the other, the dominant system is resistant to—or ignorant of—such innovation. According to Christensen, the key to unlocking the schoolhouse door is to "let it compete against non-consumption at the outset, where the alternative to taking a class from the computer is nothing at all."[14]

Convoluted as the language may be, this is how online education is beginning to take root in the traditional system (as opposed to full-time online charter schools): by offering classes that were not available elsewhere. These classes could include the Chinese course that your rural school couldn't afford to provide you or the calculus class that your inner-city public school didn't offer. Additionally, online classes are less expensive to deliver than face-to-face courses, and the school system could make better use of the $300 million invested by a private company. My own son took Chinese online over the summer, which is allowing him to learn two languages rather than just one during high school. Every student should be able to do this if they desire.

As I explained in the introduction to this book, an attempt to supplement my daughter's math instruction led me to create a company that offered a comprehensive K–12 curriculum online. The alternative, at the time, was nothing at all. Christensen called these market niches "areas of nonconsumption."[15] At the beginning, those niches were inhabited by courses that schools couldn't provide and were used by homeschoolers, students wanting to do extra work, or those trying to make up work they missed. As we now know, and as the numbers cited earlier demonstrate, the niches are growing. Christensen predicted that online learning will be mainstream within the decade. The current fiscal crisis will likely accelerate this trend as districts and states look to do things differently and more efficiently.

I was lucky that someone like Bill Bennett understood the potential of online education in 1999, when the field was anything but avant-garde. In fact, Google wasn't launched until 1998, and the dot-com bubble burst in 2000. Bennett provided K[12]—and online learning in general—instant credibility. Fortunately, there were people like Governor Tom Ridge in Pennsylvania who instantly grasped the idea and the power of online education and allowed it to happen in Pennsylvania. Individualized education was soon a reality.

"I've been a critic of educational practice in this country a long time," Bennett told the *Milwaukee Journal Sentinel* when K[12] launched the Wisconsin Virtual Academy in 2002, "and I decided to stop cursing the darkness and light a candle."[16]

Goals of Online Education

The purpose of an education is to prepare a student to live a successful and fulfilled life. All children should earn a high school diploma, and when they graduate they should be equipped to pursue whatever they want to do in life, whether that means becoming a physicist, an actor, an entrepreneur, or an electrician. American schools have frequently been institutions that constrict choices and cut off options, as students fall further and further behind in academic achievement until they drop out of school, sealing their fates, in too many instances, for a lifetime.

We now know we can deliver a world-class curriculum and a first-rate education—online. It is not a fad. We know we can deliver it in traditional environments, our hybrid schools, and even brick-and-mortar schools, and as I'll soon share, we can deliver it much more efficiently.

As Susan Patrick of iNACOL put it, "The biggest challenge at the moment is misunderstanding. People still think that a computer is teaching their kid. They don't understand that there are teachers hired and trained to use computers to teach their kid."[17]

It cannot be stated strongly enough: *technology is not going to replace teachers anytime in the near future; it will help them do their jobs more efficiently and effectively.* Over the next ten years, there will be an increasing amount of technology in all aspects of education, and teachers will love it. We will soon come to the fork in the road, with students carrying their textbooks on an interactive mobile that fits in their pockets or backpacks. At a minimum, textbooks will be delivered on Kindle or iPad-like devices within the next decade.

The education labor pool will indeed shrink but by attrition, not firings. The predicted teacher shortage will not occur—the computer and internet will deliver the productivity gains to avert this looming crisis. A good portion of the savings achieved by introducing more technology is likely to be used to pay teachers more. When salaries for teachers rise, more people will want to teach, and that will bring higher-qualified teachers into the education system. In the process, everybody wins: taxpayers, teachers, parents, and students; a more globally competitive country is a country positioned for a more competitive and dynamic future.

Teachers Are Eager to Use Technology

In 2012, the Manson Northwest Webster (MNW) school district in Indiana decided to migrate from a traditional textbooks-and-hardcopy approach to a sleeker, more online-based learning model in its "goal to bring cutting-edge technology into the classroom," wrote the education journalist Joe Sutter. This included a variety of upgrades to the teaching materials and programs available to students—new laptops for fourth through seventh grades, Google apps to inexpensively store and share documents, and taking on the K^{12} curriculum. In an interview with Sutter, Superintendent Mark Egli explained how K^{12} is bringing the MNW classrooms into the twenty-first century:

> With MNW's new contract with the online service K^{12} Learning, teachers will be able to use materials from the online classes as a part of their classes. Egli said many of the high school classes will be phasing out textbooks in favor of online content from K^{12}.
>
> Students will complete quizzes and respond to questions as they study, he said, rather than just reading out of a book. Teachers can then see how much time each student spends on an activity and how well they understand it.

"We believe this will increase the amount of reading the students do, and the amount they know when they come into class," Egli said. "Not only are we lightening the student's backpack, which has always been my goal, we also have access to content presented in a format that helps the student learn."

Using the system, students will have access to a greater variety of classes. Egli said Spanish, Japanese, Mandarin, German and Latin will be offered as online classes, in addition to MNW's French classes. About fifteen students are signed up for Spanish this year. The program will also allow homeschooled students to get K12 online classes through MNW, and offer new options for the alternative school.

Egli said the upgrades were funded by the Physical Plant Equipment Levy.... These changes in no way replace teachers...they replace textbooks and give teachers the chance to work with students who have better understanding.

Egli said companies with millions of dollars are able to hire the best minds and teachers in the world and create multi-media to make content more engaging than what local teachers can make on their own.

"It's becoming apparent that corporate-developed courses are likely more engaging and perhaps more academically sound than anything we try to create ourselves."

Source: Joe Sutter, "Teachers Are Eager to Use Technology," the *Messenger News* (August 2, 2012).

4

THE VIRTUAL SCHOOL AND INDIVIDUALIZED LEARNING

*P*hil and Sue Jones had to nurse their son to life before they even thought about school. Mark was just five when he sustained a spinal cord injury in a car accident. He was in a coma for seven weeks. Doctors didn't expect him to live.

"He kept surviving," said his mother. "Doctors said he would be a vegetable the rest of his life and recommended that we put him in a nursing home."[1]

But the Joneses insisted on bringing Mark home, where friends and relatives cared for the young boy day and night, praying over him and reading to him. Much to the surprise of his doctors, the boy's mental capabilities kept improving. He began to speak a little, and it was clear that he also comprehended what was being read to him.

"One day we got a card in the mail about an online education program," recalled Sue, "and we decided to check it out." They signed Mark up for K[12]'s second-grade curriculum. "He flew through it," said Sue about Mark, who was still completely paralyzed from the neck down, on a ventilator, and wheelchair bound. "He really got the math."[2]

Despite never having set foot in a traditional school, five years later, Mark was testing at grade level—thanks to online education, which was able to make individualized education accessible for Mark.

Homeschooling, Charters, and Online Education

In many ways, the individualized education movement owes its existence to a small army of pioneer parents known as homeschoolers. They were sufficiently frustrated to leave the traditional education system and brave enough to attempt to educate their children at home. They advocated for the right to homeschool their children, and some of them spent time in jail. They eventually prevailed, and the right to homeschool now exists in all fifty states.

Over time, homeschooling became the fastest growing segment of education. There were perhaps ten thousand homeschooled children in 1975. Today there are over two million.[3] Originally, religious reasons motivated the majority of families. That changed about ten years ago, and today the majority of homeschooling families cite reasons other than religion when asked why they chose this option for their children.

Innovators themselves, homeschoolers were often early supporters of online education. They were the true advance guard of the disruptive innovation that would become online education—and they were familiar with the process of turning a part of their homes into a classroom. As computer technology innovations fueled the growth of online education, more traditional students were tempted to try it at home.

As the online education world grew, so did the number of homeschoolers. Their success in national spelling bees and other competitions popularized the belief that children could receive a quality education being homeschooled. Some of the most rigorous curriculums in the country were being taught through homeschooling. Yet that was by no means ubiquitous. There were no teachers, no standardized tests, and no control over the curriculum being used in these homes, which made it impossible to guarantee the quality of the education or even measure it. The quality was inconsistent. In summary, home-schooling was delivering some of the best and the worst education in this country.[4]

Public charter schools were the other significant movement in education that would eventually accelerate virtual education. The movement began in 1991, when Minnesota passed the first charter school law in the country. California followed suit in 1992, and by 1995, nineteen states had laws allowing for the creation of charter schools. Today, forty-two states have public charter school laws, although some of these laws are so weak that these states might as well not have a law.[5]

The public charter school movement shares with the homeschool movement a desire for something different from the local school down the street but doesn't want to leave the public school system. Public charter schools are public schools. I am always amazed when I hear people contrast charter schools and public schools; they are both part of the same system.

Public charter schools are a subset of public schools. Virtual public charter schools might even be the most public of all schools, as they are not limited to a single geographic area and often take any student in a state who wants to enroll. Though each state law differs slightly, charters are very much part of the public education system: they are publicly funded and free to all students, the schools cannot select their students or charge tuition, and their students are required to show up for school and follow a curriculum that meets the state standards (they also have to take all the state tests in a proctored setting). What makes them different is their organizing model: each charter is independently run by a nonprofit board, not subject to local district control and often exempt from the some of the bureaucratic regulations that govern traditional public schools.

Number of States with Signed Laws Allowing for the Creation of Charter Schools (including DC)

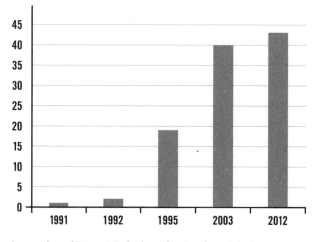

Source: Advanced Science & Technology Education Charter Schools.

These schools are generally funded at lower amounts than traditional public schools and have to find their own facilities. Despite these hardships, the movement has survived and thrived. Public charter schools impressively achieve similar academic results and much higher satisfaction results with substantially fewer dollars to spend than do their traditional public counterparts. A recent Cato Institute study of spending in several urban school districts would suggest that the cost differential is much larger than states realize.[6] Most states could save billions of dollars simply by making all schools charter schools.

Number of Students Enrolled in Charter Schools in the United States

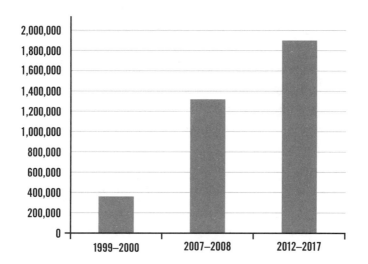

Source: Advanced Science & Technology Education Charter Schools.

Charter schools create choice within the public school system. They cater to a variety of interests. Some specialize in particular subjects (art, music, science, foreign language) or offer different educational philosophies. Others are single-sex schools or serve at-risk children. For the first time, private citizens can form public schools. These schools have tremendous accountability in that they have to recruit students in order to be economically viable. If they don't serve the students' needs or the charter's mission, they go out of business. By competing with traditional public schools for students, charter schools improve, and traditional noncharter public schools improve as well. For the first time in history, traditional public schools face competition for students. In the private sector, competition delivers better products for consumers and forces producers to be more efficient. While there are varying interpretations of whether or not public charter schools deliver better outcomes than traditional public schools (and the data is too complex to discuss here), there is no doubt that competing with public charter schools makes public schools strive to be better and more responsive to their customers. There is also little doubt that public charter schools are more cost-efficient and have more satisfied customers.

While charter schools created choice for some students, location dictated their ability to take advantage of this choice. The schools could not create individualization either. These limitations were removed when charter schools discovered online education—and online education discovered public charters.

A Serious Academic Alternative

Ann Alonzo of Fond du Lac, Wisconsin, was typical of many parents in traditional schools. Her youngest child "floundered," but she was not ready for the responsibilities of homeschooling.[7]

That is when she heard about the Wisconsin Virtual Academy (WIVA), an online K-12 charter school launched in 2002. Like all charter schools, WIVA is a state-chartered public school that operates outside of a traditional classroom and is open to all children in the state. There is no official schedule—online schools are open 24/7—and students are encouraged to progress at their own pace (another major advantage of the new technology). Many families appreciate the self-paced, asynchronous nature of online education. As public school students, however, children are expected to spend a certain amount of time each day engaged in schoolwork and to take standardized tests mandated by the state of Wisconsin.[8]

WIVA established specific benchmarks for gauging progress in time as well as in subject areas. Attendance can be easily monitored, as each student has to log in and log out of the site. WIVA students also have district-approved graduation requirements, aligned to meet state university admission standards. Experts developed the curriculum to meet or exceed those standards, and it proved to be one of the top-scoring online school curriculum programs in the nation.

Ann Alonzo's son quickly went from floundering to thriving. Despite years of class size reduction in traditional schools in order to give students more attention, part of the reason her son was succeeding was due to the individualized attention he received. "When he needs a teacher," said Alonzo, "they are there for him, despite being physically miles away."[9]

WIVA has a teacher–student ratio higher than most public schools, but because teachers and students work at home, WIVA doesn't need to worry about classroom discipline, hallway monitoring, bus duty, or developing classroom lessons. Teachers can therefore spend more time working directly with students on their academic progress. Additionally, the curriculum is engaging and interactive, which lets students learn with less teacher time.

Students also benefit from not having the distractions that accompany brick-and-mortar schools, enabling them to get their work done in much less time. Though attendance, planning, and assessments are all recorded online, only 25 to 50 percent of the student time is actually online, with the percentage higher for high school, as students work at more of a collective pace online in conjunction with the teacher. The rest of the K[12] curriculum relies on printed and hands-on materials, including meticulously crafted textbooks, paint, math manipulatives (e.g., blocks and cones for math class), and microscopes. Students spend some time online and some time doing offline activities, which are especially important for students learning to read and write. As a student moves up, the amount of time spent online naturally increases.

The creation of the K[12] curriculum was a large effort that involved teams of subject matter experts, writers, animators, educators, and instructional designers. Often ten or more experts would work for over a year on one subject. Almost always, the curriculum used the insights of cognitive neuroscience to make it more effective.

The instruction of handwriting illustrates the importance of incorporating cognitive neuroscience into curriculum. It would be tempting to stop teaching cursive writing in the era of keyboarding; one could argue that handwriting is no longer necessary. There is evidence that suggests taking such a step might be a mistake, however, as writing may have other benefits to brain development. Reza Shadmehr and Henry Holcomb of John Hopkins University published a study in *Science Magazine* showing that their subjects' brains actually changed in reaction to physical instruction such as cursive handwriting lessons. The researchers provided PET scans as evidence of these changes in brain structure. Further, they demonstrated that these changes resulted in an "almost immediate improvement in fluency," which led to later development of neural pathways. As a result of practicing motor skills, the researchers found, knowledge becomes more stable.[10]

Recent studies at Indiana University also suggested there is value to learning handwriting. Students who wrote letters showed more enhanced neural activity in an MRI than those who were merely shown letters. "It seems there is something really important about manually manipulating and drawing out two-dimensional things we see all the time," said Karin Harman James, assistant professor of psychology and neuroscience at Indiana University, who led the study.[11] Another study, at the University of Washington, showed that children in primary school wrote more quickly, used more words, and expressed more ideas when using handwriting than when using a keyboard.[12]

Thus, we probably don't want to stop teaching handwriting, and any decision to do so should be backed by substantial research demonstrating there are no adverse effects to doing so. At K[12], we try to make sure everything we do is backed up by research and cognitive neuroscience—we never want to get in the habit of moving forward just because it is different. It needs to be better.

Alonzo also learned that worries about socialization were unnecessary. Students at the Wisconsin Virtual Academy have the opportunity to participate in many academic and social outings. These outings and activities include trips to museums, zoos, clubs, student government, dances, and even graduation ceremonies. Additionally, the children are involved in numerous activities outside of school, during which they interact with other children. At K[12] we have over one hundred thousand full-time students, and not a single parent has told me they would like their child to be a hermit. In fact, many of these families enroll their children in virtual schools to avoid some of the negative socialization that occurs in traditional public schools. These might include drugs, alcohol, and swearing. Recent studies show that virtual school students are as socialized as their public school counterparts, and their socialization skills do not decline the longer they spend in virtual schools.

For Mark Jones, the wheelchair-bound boy who is now ten years old and uses a mouth mouse with his computer, participating fully in extracurricular activities will always be difficult. For the Joneses, however, just getting the schooling for Mark was significant. He is now testing at a fifth-grade level.

"For Mark it was a miracle," said Sue, his mother. "The school program was awesome—history, math, English, science—everything. The curriculum is so well laid out and it is self-paced. When you get something, you move on; when you don't, you have time to get it. It is all interactive and very engaging, and a certified teacher calls regularly to check in with us and the kids."[13]

Who Are the Online Students?

The Joneses' and Alonzos' experiences are typical of the growing on-line virtual school movement. Using the new charter school laws in the United States, which gave public school students the opportunity to attend nontraditional schools, full-scale, state-certified online schools in Pennsylvania and Colorado were established in 2001, serving one thousand children in grades K–2. In 2002 Ohio, Idaho, California, Arkansas, and Minnesota were added, serving approximately six thousand students.[14] That number has grown to thirty states in the last eight years, and the number of full-time students served is over one hundred thirty thousand in K[12] schools alone.[15]

When WIVA opened, we offered all parents in the state the opportunity to enroll their children in the school (serving kindergarten through fifth grade). We had nearly one thousand applicants and enrolled six hundred. Even though the school is technically chartered in Wisconsin's Lake Mills School District, a majority of WIVA students reside outside the Northern Ozaukee School District and attend WIVA under the state's open enrollment program.[16]

The number of reasons students enroll in online schools is quite large and still growing. What all these students share, however, is this: the local brick-and-mortar public school is not meeting their needs. It could be because of inadequate teachers or because of a bad fit; not every child learns well in the traditional classroom. Many of our students say they felt trapped in their local school because they were not at grade level, while others felt held back because it was not challenging enough.

Today, students attending public school are simply assigned to their local school. If their parents have the money and can move to an area with good schools, the child has a greater likelihood of having access to a reasonable education through their local public school. However, students from poor families, or those living in an area with bad schools, are stuck. Until the advent of online public schools, most students were trapped and had no choice. Online schools can serve children anywhere in the state, are tuition free, and have no geographic boundaries, which makes them the most public of all schools in the state. For the first time in the United States, every public school student can have a choice! I have been doing this for twelve years, and the variety of students in online schools never ceases to amaze me.

These students tend to fall into one of six general categories:

1. **Gifted and talented:** These are students who are working far ahead of their grade level. They are often bored in their regular school, which has a hard time accommodating them. Sometimes online schools are also for students with a very strong talent—chess, car racing, swimming, acting—because regular school hours are too inflexible to allow these talents to be developed. Many top athletes and children in the entertainment industry are in public virtual schools. Additionally, these students benefit from taking individual courses not available at their local schools.

2. **Special needs:** These are children who have special learning needs, physical handicaps, autism, Asperger's syndrome, hearing disorders, attention deficit disorder, etc. They comprise over 10 percent of the children in full-time public virtual schools today.[17] The percentage of special needs students in virtual schools has been increasing recently.

3. **Social conservatives:** These children and their families feel that the current social milieu at the public school is unsatisfactory. They are often religious but not always. They don't find that the morality in the public schools is aligned with their values, and they worry about negative peer values. This category of conservatives includes evangelical Christians, Muslims, and Jews. They want the rigorous content without the negative socialization. Virtual schools give them the opportunity to have the best of both worlds: sound academics and the freedom to be protected from what they perceive to be negative social values.

4. **Behind grade level:** These are the students who are one or more
    grade levels behind. They are sometimes high school students
    who are about to drop out, children who need extra time to
    learn the material, or students who are enrolled in an underper-
    forming public school. This group is a large percentage of the
    students in middle school and high school and has been growing
    rapidly.

    The parents, desperate to bring their children up to grade
    level, send their children to virtual schools. If certain children
    need five extra minutes to master a concept, they can get it in
    a virtual school; teachers in a brick-and-mortar classroom can-
    not give this five minutes, as they cannot afford to wait for that
    child. Once children fall behind in math or language arts, they
    have difficulty catching up. Fortunately, online schools can
    help—when students like these can fully engage with them.
    Online schools now offer individualized learning programs with
    extensive online intervention and tutoring sessions to bring
    these students to grade level.

5. **Wanting more rigorous education:** While not true of most vir-
    tual schools, this standard is certainly true of the virtual schools
    that use K¹² curriculum. The curriculum was designed to exceed
    the most rigorous standards and teach what the best schools in
    the world teach in every subject. This includes the core subjects
    (math, science, language arts, and history) as well as art, music,
    and foreign language.

    The efficiency and individualization of online education
    makes this possible. Everything in the K¹² curriculum cannot fit
    into a traditional eight-hour school day, because in classrooms
    there is too much downtime. The instructional modality in
    virtual schools is much more effective. Even though it may not

be in the best business interests to build the product this way, K^{12} did so because it is the right thing to do for children. From a business point of view, K^{12} could attract more customers by dumbing down the curriculum (a curriculum that only taught state standards in the tested subjects would probably produce higher state test scores), but taking this path would only short-change students.

6. **Rural and expatriate students:** There are many students who face a long commute to school each day. Online schools can save these students several hours per day of commuting time. Additionally, there are over 250,000 expatriate children living abroad. Many of them cannot get access to a high quality, American education. The ability of a student to live anywhere and *still* receive a high quality, accredited education is empowering and revolutionary in what it does for families who previously had to move or separate from their children in order to get this. In K^{12} private online schools, there are now students from six continents.

Thus, online schools serve a broad spectrum of kids: the gifted child who is bored, the athlete who has to study at odd times, the child actor, the autistic child, the rural child, the physically handicapped child, the migrant child, the dropout, the military child, the expat. While the number of students going to school full-time online might eventually be only 5 to 10 percent of school children, for those children, virtual schooling will be a powerful option that helps them get the education they want and need.

I recently met Zach Veach who, at sixteen, is an up-and-coming driver for Andretti racing. His discipline, maturity, and motivation to succeed were impressive for a person of any age, let alone a sixteen-year-old. The first thing his dad said to me was "Thank you. If not for what you do, my son could not do what he is doing." He then went on to tell me the family had tried another virtual school first, and the quality of it was not sufficient. When they found the K[12] school, they realized Zach could pursue his dream, which is more than a full-time job, and still get a fantastic education. In essence, this captures what K[12] and virtual education are all about: allowing students to pursue and achieve their dreams, whatever they may be.

"Virtual schooling may not be best for every student," said the *Wisconsin State Journal*. "But it is for many, and those children deserve to learn in the environment that they and their parents believe works best for them."[18]

Most of the students in K[12] virtual academies come from traditional brick-and-mortar schools. The economic spectrum is wide, but in most states there tends to be a higher percentage of children below the poverty line than the state average. Most public virtual schools provide the student with the curriculum, materials, and a teacher and lend them a computer and pay for the internet.

The state of Arkansas conducted a study that showed high numbers of poor people were signing up for virtual schools. The added benefit is that parents are learning technology. As Sharon Hayes, who runs our hybrid online school in Chicago said, she's "capturing two generations in one school."[19] And children in racial minorities were, in some instances, out-performing the Caucasian children in the Arkansas virtual schools. They are the true public schools—the most public schools in every state in which they operate—and they allow students to learn without any preconceived stereotypes or geographic bounds. Additionally, they allow the individualization of education for all children. In fact, technology is the only cost effective way to achieve individualization in education.

How It Works

To better understand how online education works, consider this example from Wisconsin.

As a story in the *New York Times* put it, "Weekday mornings, three of Tracie Weldie's children eat breakfast, make beds, and trudge off to public school—in their case, downstairs to their basement in a [Milwaukee] suburb…where their mother leads them through math and other lessons outlined by an internet-based charter school."[20]

Each WIVA student receives a computer, printer, software, and hardware to connect to the internet from his or her home, which is the new classroom. Depending on grade level, each student also receives several boxes of textbooks and manipulatives (the latter for math and science courses), used to supplement the challenging, comprehensive, and interactive curriculum that our company developed. They also have a certified teacher. Parents, who act as Learning Coaches (especially for the younger children), receive detailed instructions on their children's coursework, including suggested daily schedules.

Telephone assistance, both technical and instructional, is available twenty-four hours a day, and the certified teacher on the WIVA staff can also be contacted via internet or telephone. Teachers contact all students weekly, checking on progress, answering questions, discussing tests and grades, and reporting on attendance. The school's principal initially was surprised by the way the school uses teachers. They are "a vital part of the educational equation in the Wisconsin Virtual Academy," he said. "They work with families to make sure that the educational program is tailored to the individual child. That's one of the things that makes this new school so exciting: a customized educational program for each child."[21]

The *Wisconsin State Journal* has written about the benefits of online education:

> Virtual schools combine the best aspects of home schooling, the loosely regulated network of parents who teach their own kids, with distance learning, the computer-based courses popular among adult students.

The attractiveness and innovation of this style of education should be obvious:

- Virtual schools offer a ready-made, state-sanctioned curriculum, in contrast to homeschooling, which lets parents invent their own coursework under lax regulation.
- Students can learn at their own pace and receive individualized instruction that regular public schools will never be able to match.
- Online schools are more accountable than traditional home schools: students take state-mandated tests and complete daily attendance logs, among other requirements.[22]

WIVA has met federal testing requirements and, as the *New York Times* has reported, "Many parents, including Mrs. Weldie, expressed satisfaction with the K[12] curriculum, which allows her children to move through lessons at their own pace, unlike traditional schools, where teachers often pause to take account of slower students. Isabel Weldie, five, is in kindergarten, 'But in math I'm in first grade,' she said during a break in her school day recently."[23]

"That's what I love most about this curriculum," Mrs. Weldie said. "There's no reason for Isabel to practice counting if she can already add." [24]

After seeing what an online school could do for their disabled child, Sue and Phil Jones enrolled two of their other children, ages six and eight, in full-time K[12] coursework through the Ohio Virtual Academy (OHVA), another state-chartered network of online learners. Though the Joneses' experiment with online schooling was born of a tragic car accident, they realized that if such a school could help their disabled son, it could surely work for their other children as well.

5

COMING FULL CIRCLE: TECHNOLOGY HEADS BACK TO THE CLASSROOM

The Philadelphia Story—Online

The children streamed out of the old brick school building on Philadelphia's West Dauphin Street in orderly fashion—by middle-school
standards—and the line of giddy preteens soon stretched the entire
block. It was a cool April morning in 2004, and teachers herded the five
hundred students of William H. Hunter Elementary School by class
while principal Olivia Dreibelbis walked among them, quietly encouraging everyone to behave.[1]

It was not a fire drill. It was a big good-bye, a very big day for the children, the teachers, and for Dreibelbis, who soon gave the order to march,
and off everyone went, toward their new school—toward the future.

A native of Colombia, Dreibelbis came to Philadelphia as a child
and worked her way through the city's public school system, one of the

ten largest in the country. She had been a student, teacher and, for the past six years, principal. Today, she resembled a Pied Piper, leading her young charges east along West Dauphin to North Front Street—barely four blocks away—to a brand-new school building. Parents and residents of the impoverished Norristown section of the city lined the streets, as if watching a Fourth of July parade, and cheered.

They all knew the struggle—and were rooting for change. Yes, the kids in the K-4 school were poor (the overwhelming majority qualified for the free or reduced-price lunch program) and faced heavy odds against learning, given that poverty and academic achievement seem to walk in lockstep.[2] In addition to being from low-income homes, 86 percent of the Hunter kids were Latino, and many of them spoke English as a second language, which often meant they did not speak English at all.[3]

Indeed, despite herculean efforts by staff over the decade prior to the move, students at Hunter performed poorly, even after the introduction of many new programs—e.g., team teaching and theme teaching, Small Learning Communities, Children Helping Children, Hands of Learning, Extended-Day Program, Read to Succeed, and Reading Excellence. Most of the school's students scored far below grade level on standardized tests; and for the second year in a row, the school had failed to meet the new federal (No Child Left Behind) standard for Adequate Yearly Progress.[4]

Additionally, there was the problem of the school building: it was over one hundred years old and had been heated by coal until 1990. It would have been condemned if the school district had someplace to put the kids. "In one room you could grow orchids," said one teacher, "and in the next the kids had ski jackets on."[5]

But on this April morning, as students and staff poured out of their old brick structure, they did have a place to go: a state-of-the-art building just four blocks away. It was reason to cheer.

Turning "Weaklings into He-Men"

In an earlier era, the iconic bodybuilder Charles Atlas touted a program that promised to "turn weaklings into he-men." While it's unclear whether the program delivered on its promise, I believe online education could transform the weaklings of the U.S. public school system into the educational equivalent of he-men. Indeed, this was what Paul Vallas, then Philadelphia schools superintendent, wanted to do for traditional brick-and-mortar schools when he called me in early 2003 to ask if we could put our online school in a regular classroom. (Paul Vallas is one of the nation's most visible and innovative superintendents, having now served in this position in Chicago, Philadelphia, New Orleans, and Bridgeport, Connecticut. In all of these cities, he has led major reform efforts.)

Vallas knew that K[12] combined a content-rich curriculum with the latest technological innovations. He also knew that little was working in the city, as the school system was in free fall. A report commissioned by the State of Pennsylvania said the district had spent more than $10 billion "with no clear accountability for the results."

> The school district finds itself overwhelmed with considerable, institutionalized issues across many critical functions, including a dizzying array of curricula with little centralized district control over them...and a poor and uncoordinated [information technology] system that leaves the District powerless to understand and use both student and educator performance data.[6]

Many of the city's 178 schools were substandard and 50 percent of its 215,000 students (almost 80 percent of them poor) dropped out before graduating from high school. The district was also deeply in debt (its deficit was over $200 million), and in December of 2001, just hours after the students left for their Christmas vacation, the state took it over.

It was "the largest such action of its kind," said the *New York Times*.[7] The state suspended the city's board of education and replaced it with a five-person School Reform Commission (SRC). The SRC, at the urging of the then governor Tom Ridge, brought in several for-profit education management companies to run many of the city's schools and then recruited a new superintendent, Paul Vallas, who had recently done an outstanding job as CEO of Chicago Public Schools.

Vallas had been a top finance aide to Mayor Richard Daley before Daley took control of the Windy City's troubled school system and appointed Vallas superintendent of schools in 1995. "Teacher strikes had become common, the district was on the brink of ruin financially, academic performance was abysmal, and school facilities were crumbling," wrote Alexander Russo in the policy journal *Education Next*.[8] Over the course of the next six years, Vallas instituted a shotgun blast's worth of reform initiatives for the city's public schools, "bringing order and energy to Chicago's moribund school system," according to Russo, and quickly becoming "the nation's most sought-after superintendent."[9]

Philadelphia got him. Vallas was a major figure, a game changer—one of the best large-district superintendents in the United States and among the most innovative. He scaled back many of the contracts to let private companies run schools, but he also expanded the menu of innovative educational reforms—dubbed the diverse provider model—and, among other things, invited K[12] to create what he envisioned as a model twenty-first-century school.

The idea was to take what was a truly needy school—Hunter—and put it in a brand-new building with all the latest pedagogical and technological innovations, and the people who knew how to use them. K[12] had a good track record with virtual academies like those in Wisconsin and Ohio (and six other states, including Pennsylvania). Vallas wanted to find out if we could make a rich, technology-based curriculum work in a traditional brick-and-mortar environment.[10]

This was new territory for K[12], since the company was built as an online venture that primarily catered to people one-on-one, via the internet, who were not getting the education they wanted from traditional schools. The curriculum had been designed for one-on-one, individualized learning, not one-on-many. The setting had one advantage over virtual schools—a controlled learning environment—but the control was only partial, as we would have no control or influence over staffing at the school.

K[12] knew it would lose money on the Hunter venture, but it was the perfect place to test the theory that we could reform our public education system without killing it or even restructuring it. Could technology-based curriculum make ordinary schools better?

As an entrepreneur, I know my instincts are to find every possible place in the education system where innovation can help. If technology-based learning is to provide a world-class education to every child, then it must be delivered to the fifty million children in our traditional schools. The ability to do this without changing staff is the only way to improve our schools. If society is going to rely on having a great teacher in every classroom, we will still be having this discussion one hundred years from now.

The Vallas proposal was part of an experiment to bring data-based education to what veteran *Washington Post* education reporter Jay Mathews called "a very old and tired city."[11] It was an incredibly attractive offer because we knew that if we could figure how to deliver to the inner-city classroom what we had been delivering to homes across the country, we could potentially help every child.

Drilling for Online Education

The parade to North Front Street by the children of Hunter Elementary was a march to the future. Kids, teachers, and staff were told they couldn't take anything with them from the old school—no desks or chairs or books or curriculum material. They left behind, quite literally, the old education system, its bricks and mortar and chalkboards, and entered a new world, a new century, a shiny steel-and-glass building with SMART Boards and laptops—and wired to the world.

"We are the most advanced school in any setting, private or public, in the metropolitan area in terms of technology," a beaming Principal Dreibelbis told the local press.[12]

Dreibelbis is an effective principal who welcomes change if it gets better educational results.

Changes were made, beginning with curriculum. It was the first time, despite all the reform strategies attempted up to then, that Hunter had a comprehensive and consistent curriculum in any subject.

Unlike the sleek and technologically sparkling High School of the Future that Microsoft would build for Philadelphia on Parkside Avenue several years later, the new Hunter school was focused on using technology as a window to content. The vision at Hunter was to see how a true technology-based basal curriculum, with the right training for teachers, could affect the achievement of the most disadvantaged students. Peter Stewart, senior vice president of school development at K^{12}, recalled:

> K^{12} was already up and running in Pennsylvania, doing online education, and had a desire to do more of these pilot programs—[to] go into existing schools, retrofit the classes, install SMART Boards and projectors, and try to put our model into helping teachers teach more effectively. We didn't want to run the school; we were interested in working with the existing collective bargaining agreement, [putting] a trainer in the school who would have access to the administration and teachers on a regular basis to help them improve math and science scores.[13]

Stewart, a former head of school, teacher, principal, and curriculum director who had worked in urban, rural, and international schools, did a lot of background work on the Hunter project in 2003. He also dispatched our senior director of classroom academics to move our successful virtual school program to Hunter (what we called the discovery model), essentially setting up a virtual school within a traditional brick-and-mortar school.

Our normal online discovery program, used in our virtual academies, consisted of a complete package of instructional materials, for a grade-level appropriate curriculum in all the core subjects. It included textbooks and manipulatives and hands-on science kits that were fully integrated with online coursework. K[12] would adapt this program to Hunter and use their existing teachers rather than our own.

K[12] started the training instruction in January of 2004 (nine months before the new building was to open), while staff and students were still in the old Dauphin Street building. K[12] personnel journeyed to Hunter for two days each week for many months, working closely with Principal Dreibelbis. K[12] hired a full-time staff trainer to be the onsite monitor for the program's implementation, doing professional development for the teachers, getting parents involved—anything involved in the day-to-day implementation of the curriculum. She had several interactive whiteboards installed in the old building so the orientation could begin before the move.

The onsite monitor, Sue Furick, explained, "A crucial part of what we did was intensive professional development...We created for each teacher a personalized professional development plan. By using some informal methods, and getting feedback from them about what they wanted to work on, we customized some things."[14]

"The Students Were Entranced"

It was not a smooth transition, since few of the teachers were comfortable with technology, and most had never used an interactive whiteboard before. In 2004, this was all quite new. This technology allows the curriculum to be delivered via the web to a large group of students and is significantly less expensive than each child having their own computer. It also facilitates group, interactive instruction. These interactive whiteboards are now commonplace in many schools.

The idea of a comprehensive subject-area curriculum was also foreign to most of the teachers. The K^{12} curriculum was rigorous; the lesson plans for the teachers were already developed, giving them clues about where kids would struggle and what to do about that, and the interactive lessons engaged the children.

"We had no curriculum before K^{12}," recalled Barbara Foster-Dolt, a teacher at Hunter. "None at all. And we had no textbooks. We would have to make copies of pages from books and hand them out."[15]

Foster-Dolt began using the new curriculum with her fourth graders at the old Hunter, including introducing to students an interactive whiteboard, which was connected to the internet via a laptop.

> The kids were entranced by it. We had links to interactive websites. The first one I did was the Underground Railroad. We went to a National Geographic site, where the kids were able to make decisions: should we run, or should we hide? You'd hear dogs barking, [and] you'd click on hide. And then you'd see what would happen while you were hiding. Should you go to the next house, or should you stay? The kids loved this. It got their attention, and they were involved in it.[16]

Foster-Dolt joined the parade to the new school, and like most of her twenty-five teacher colleagues, was excited about the future. The full curriculum program was now rolled out. It was a demanding and comprehensive program of science, math, history, and art. (Because of the school's large Latino population, the school had already instituted a specialized English language arts curriculum designed for English as a second language [ESL] students.) The curriculum came with textbooks and a rich assortment of math manipulatives and lab kits. In addition, each classroom was now fully wired and equipped: interactive SMART Boards, ceiling-mounted data projectors, and laptop computers for each child. K^{12} also hired a second teacher trainer.

One of our mottos at K^{12} is use technology in a purposeful way. One way we want teachers to use technology is as a presentation device—a presentation of rich content. The more comfortable the teachers are with the technology, the more comfortable they are with the curriculum. We've designed it to be multimedia. Our students move to the whiteboard and move things around on the screen. There are also times when they are away from the computer and away from the interactive whiteboard, doing science experiments with dirt or seeds or using blocks and cubes to learn math—or reading from a history book.

Students arrived with test scores, of course, but as in many states, such assessments are taken only annually, and the results are notoriously late in coming; months go by between the test and the results, with teachers not knowing what guidance a student needs.

Hunter tested each child at the beginning of the year using software that gave us immediate profiles of each child in each subject area. The children were tested again in the winter, then in the spring. This way we knew immediately what they had mastered and what they needed to improve.

Each child also took a placement test to determine which course was the best match for their skills and abilities. The course didn't have anything to do with a student's grade level or even what learning standards the child needed to cover. It meant that a fifth grader could be following a third-grade math program, because that was the level of the student's proficiency. Thanks to these assessments, coupled with the laptops and interactive software, children in the same classroom could be working quite comfortably at various levels of proficiency while still being exposed to the appropriate grade-level concepts. Thus, we could close the skills gap and still give students a chance to succeed.

K[12] created a schoolwide, two-hour math block and divided it in half. During the first hour, every student at Hunter took math. That means that we used every teacher on staff for math and regrouped kids according to their math proficiency. A fifth grader, for example, would be regrouped with other kids at the third-grade instructional level. We took into account the age of the child and made every effort to be sensitive to that in the regrouping. For one hour a day, the children were able to work on remedial skills within the third- and fourth-grade content levels. For the other hour of the day, they returned to their homerooms and their regular homeroom peers and worked on the appropriate grade-level content.

Support the Teachers

To further refine the assessment process, teachers gave their students a pre-test assessment and a post-test assessment—every week and in every subject. That way, teachers knew exactly what the children knew and what they needed to work on.

Many Hunter teachers told us that in the past they were just given books and told, "Now get these kids up to speed," but because they didn't know what skills the kids lacked, they didn't really know where to start.

"We constantly had data coming in, and that was an important part of the culture change," noted Sue Furick. "We had a conversation about data rather than a conversation about the success or failure of certain teachers and certain kids."[17]

The intensive teacher training included lessons in classroom management skills, which many of the teachers lacked, and planning for lessons, which many were not doing. Furick continued, "We did a great deal of day-to-day coaching and looked for ways to help with the finer points of teaching, such as how to do related questioning activities, grouping within the classroom, differentiation in subject areas—that kind of thing."[18]

The teachers caught on because the program was so carefully structured, and the actual teaching became more enjoyable. Learning became easier too—as the students were more engaged. While outsiders sometimes see a comprehensively organized curriculum and guided pedagogical techniques as inhibiting a teacher, the teachers simply didn't have the capacity to make professional instructional decisions in every subject. Realizing this, we gave the teachers the tools to make these decisions and then showed them how to use these tools.

Deborah Williams-Gordon, a literacy coach who had worked at Hunter for twenty-five years, thought it would take three years to test an academic program, but she saw improvement almost immediately. "This company has brought in a program that has caught the attention of the kids," she told the *Philadelphia Daily News*. "When the teacher first turned on that interactive whiteboard and it [was] interactive and kids [could] participate, [the kids got] real excited with that."[19]

Third-grade teacher Marquita Washington told the newspaper that she used the SMART Board to teach a lesson about money, with students taking turns touching and dragging images of coins on the screen. "I feel like a kid in a candy store," Washington said of her new resources. "These children are doing math, and they're doing a great job and they're learning. They want to be math masters, and that's what we want them to be."[20]

Foster-Dolt, who began her teaching career in a Catholic school (from 1972 to 1985), was an immediate fan of the new program:

In the old Hunter, you didn't know what you were going to do from day to day. You had to do your own lesson plans and you had to find things to put in the lesson plans because there were no books, no teacher guides. It was a disaster. I don't know how

I survived.... At the new Hunter, we had plenty of supplies, we had an interactive curriculum, we had teacher guides, we had masters for copying. We had everything all of a sudden. And it made a big difference how you went about teaching every day. The kids did better. They were more engaged in the learning. I found it easier. I wasn't constantly looking for outside ways to explain something or to give them examples. I wasn't always going to the store, looking for Unifix cubes for counting and other supplies. Everything was there. It came with the program.[21]

What impressed me when I visited the school was how well-behaved and engaged the kids were—quite a change from the old Hunter, according to the teachers—and how engaged they were by the technology. I was also amazed by the enthusiasm of the teachers, who embraced the curriculum and taught it effectively.[22] As education technology continues to become more engaging, these effects should increase even more, and the data-driven instruction that took place at Hunter is becoming more commonplace in schools today.

Parents and Performance Count

The K[12] team also introduced a very active parent program at Hunter; we *encouraged* parents to call. Every student and their parents also had a username and password to log on to their computer, enabling any family with internet access (70 percent of them had access) to check the site and see the lessons the students were doing that day—or going to do. This connection started to draw parents back to school as a place where they could be helpful. They began to re-engage with the school, playing a constructive role in the education of their sons and daughters.

As Foster-Dolt concluded when the year ended, "There was no chance that the state scores wouldn't go up."[23]

When I received the results from the statewide Pennsylvania System of School Assessment (PSSA) tests for Hunter, I couldn't believe it. Performance had not only improved, but had exceeded our highest expectations: the school's third-grade proficiency levels in math had jumped from 40 percent to 86 percent, and for fifth graders, the math leap was from 23 percent proficient to 45 percent.[24]

Hunter School Achievement after One Year of K12 Involvement

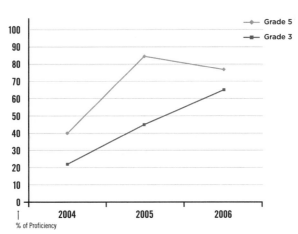

Source: K12 data and resources (www.k12.com).
Note: After just one year of using K12, the Hunter school achieved impressive gains on the Pennsylvania System of School Assessment (PSSA) state math exams.

We would have been perfectly happy with even half of these increases. I called Peter Stewart five times that first night. "Are you sure about this?" I asked. I made a point of visiting the following academic year to better understand how the school was achieving such progress. Moreover, the results continued to get better. In the second year, 66 percent of fifth graders achieved proficiency in math. In two short years, without changing the staff, the proficiency rate had improved 43 percentage points. By way of comparison, reading is the one subject we did not offer to Hunter, and the improvement in math dwarfed the improvement in reading. The message is crystal clear: technology, when used properly, can be a transformative force in education. This is true not just in virtual schools but in the classroom as well. In some ways, the ability to control the learning environment makes the classroom even more manageable.

Hunter is no one-hit wonder. K[12] has now led seven of these installations, and each one has had significant improvements in test scores without changing the length of the school day, the administration, the faculty, or the collective bargaining agreement. These schools have been located in rural areas and in urban areas. Two of these schools are worth singling out.

The first one is Draper Elementary School in Washington, DC. This is a school with almost 100 percent of the children eligible for free or reduced lunch. It is located in Anacostia and generally considered one of the most troubled schools in the district. K[12] was given permission to install its science program in this school. In Washington, DC, schools administer science testing in only one grade—fifth. In the first year with this science curriculum, 100 percent of the fifth graders were proficient in science, including all of the children with special needs. This compares to a district average of 29 percent. Even after experiencing the success of Hunter Elementary, these results stunned me.

Results of the DC-CAS Fifth-Grade Science Test

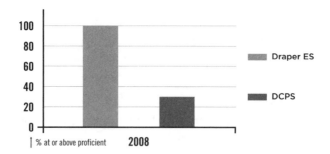

Source: K[12] data and resources (www.k12.com).
Note: District of Columbia Comprehensive Assessment System (DC-CAS), elementary school (ES), District of Columbia Public Schools (DCPS).

The second school is Como Elementary School in rural Mississippi. In November 2007, the *Washington Post* published an article reporting that this school was the worst-performing school in the lowest-performing state.[25] The state, which had taken over Como Elementary, asked us to put our math/science curriculum in the school to see if we could achieve the results that had been achieved at Hunter. This was perhaps even more challenging because of the remote location, but in the end, the results were even more impressive. In just two years, math proficiency improved from below 30 percent to above 70 percent—proof of how technology-based content can work in coordination with almost any other school-improvement program.

Percentage of Students Proficient or Better on the MCT2 Math Test

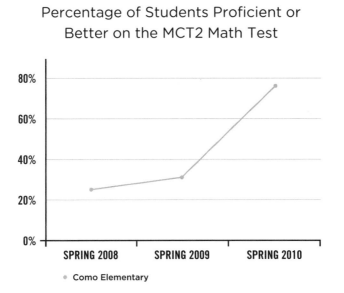

Como Elementary

Source: K[12] data and resources (www.k12.com).
Note: Mississippi Curriculum Test, Second Edition (MCT2), developed by the Mississippi Department of Education.

6

A FLEXIBLE MODEL:
ONLINE HYBRID SCHOOLS
AND FLEX ACADEMIES

*I*n 2004, the winds of change were also blowing across Lake Michigan and right into the city of the big shoulders. Chicago, with the third largest public school system in the country (some 420,000 students), was wrestling with some of the same problems as Philadelphia—although, having already had Paul Vallas as its superintendent, it was much further along the reform trail than Philadelphia.[1]

According to Brian Jacob, an assistant professor of public policy at Harvard University's John F. Kennedy School of Government, Chicago had introduced "a comprehensive accountability system," ended the practice of "social promotion," and mandated summer school for low achievers. It was one of the first major city school systems to hold schools accountable, closing or "reconstituting" those that showed insufficient progress.[2]

In fact, Chicago was embarking on a second level of school improvement with the then Mayor Richard Daley and the new superintendent (and the future US secretary of education), Arne Duncan, collaborating on an educational Marshall Plan called Renaissance 2010. Chicago was fortunate to have two of the nation's finest urban school superintendents back to back.

Launched in June 2004, Renaissance 2010 promised to close underperforming schools and open one hundred small, autonomous schools, both charter and noncharter.[3] According to the Chicago Public Schools (CPS), "Student achievement, increased demand, and strong parent satisfaction" in Chicago's charter schools "set the stage for the Renaissance 2010 initiative." Based in part on the success of independent private-school operators, CPS also announced plans to pursue more of such partnerships as part of its school turnaround strategy.[4]

"Chicago demonstrates a reinforcing loop," observed Julie Peterson and Jordan Meranus, of the New Schools Venture Fund, in a 2008 article. "Entrepreneurial activity informs changes in district policy, which in turn unlocks new opportunities to transform district structures and develop school systems that look more like diverse 'portfolios' than the one-size-fits-none approach. It's clear that charter schools can, and do, serve as both independent alternatives and agents of systemic change."[5]

Renaissance 2010 drew fifty-seven different applications for new schools in 2005, including proposals for an all-girls high school focusing on math and science; a number of performance schools; and thirty-nine privately run public schools, two of which would be "no failure" schools. "Instead of giving [students] an F," explained the proposal's author, "we will give them an incomplete and work with that student until that student is up to par."[6]

More than Virtual and Less than Brick-and-Mortar
That, in fact, was one of the advantages of the proposed Chicago Vir-

tual Charter School (CVCS), which was utilizing K¹²: there would be no failures, but there would also be no excuses. Arne Duncan, with whom I had met when Paul Vallas was in Chicago, knew that K¹² had applied its curricular and technological expertise to a traditional school in Philadelphia with some success and was supportive of K¹² creating something similar in Chicago.

Duncan supported innovative models and wanted to make sure students in the city had a variety of choices. Most importantly, he wanted to make sure schools performed. He was intrigued that our rigorous, technology-based curriculum worked for children in inner-city Philadelphia and liked the idea of a hybrid in Chicago: combine the online study at home (our traditional "virtual academy" model) with an actual physical meeting place, where families and students could receive face-to-face instruction as well as extra support.

As an entrepreneur, I was excited by this new hybrid model. It would offer face-to-face contact more than a virtual academy (we would have a central meeting place) and less than a typical brick-and-mortar school (meeting would not be an everyday affair). We applied to work with a new charter school—CVCS—and it was surprising that anyone would oppose such an innovative concept when a large portion of the country was already doing full-time virtual learning. After an arduous process, which involved a contentious meeting with the state board of education, the school was approved—thanks in no small part to the strong support of Arne Duncan and the staff at the Chicago school district. The hybrid model in Chicago marked the beginning of a hybrid or blended learning movement that is now quite significant.

Doubting Sharon

By coincidence, we had been contacted by a retired Chicago Public School principal, Sharon Hayes, who was doing some consulting work for CPS and had heard about our work in online education. "I was always looking for ways to keep kids from falling through the cracks," she recalled.[7]

Hayes had, quite literally, spent most of her life in CPS—starting as a student in kindergarten, graduating from Calumet High on the South Side and spending more than thirty years as a teacher and administrator in CPS. She opened Thurgood Marshall Middle School on the North Side and finished her career at Parkside Community Academy, also on the city's predominantly African American South Side, where she was principal for eleven years. Hayes has, as she said, "a real passion for urban education."[8] While she had her doubts about online education, she proved to be open-minded and a quick study.

"I really was not comfortable with the idea of a virtual school for an urban community," recalled Hayes. "I couldn't wrap my brain around the idea of meeting the needs of a city like Chicago using virtual education. There are too many different learning styles, too many life styles—just too many different things to see how learning could be done virtually."[9]

When Hayes visited K[12] headquarters in Herndon, Virginia, and got a chance to see how a virtual school worked and the attention that was paid to curriculum and teaching, she became interested. When she heard that the decision had been made to make the school a hybrid and that children and parents could come to a learning center, she was fully on board—and agreed to serve as the head of school.

Maiden Voyage

From the moment Hayes joined the Chicago Virtual Charter School, it was full speed ahead to acquire a charter (from the Illinois State Board of Education), find a location for the learning center, and enroll students—all three at the same time. Arne Duncan demonstrated tremendous leadership, convening teams of CPS educators to help in the effort. The school received one thousand applications for grades one through eight. This was nearly eight hundred more than the school could handle that

Impact of Technological Advancements on the Productivity of Employees in the Steel Industry

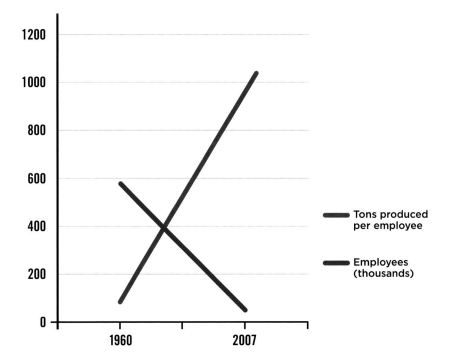

A

US Dropout Rate in 2005

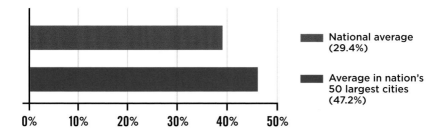

National average
(29.4%)

Average in nation's
50 largest cities
(47.2%)

Highest Dropout Rates in US Cities in 2005

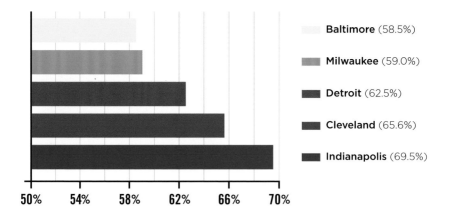

Baltimore (58.5%)

Milwaukee (59.0%)

Detroit (62.5%)

Cleveland (65.6%)

Indianapolis (69.5%)

Total Government Spending: $6.3 Trillion for Fiscal Year 2012

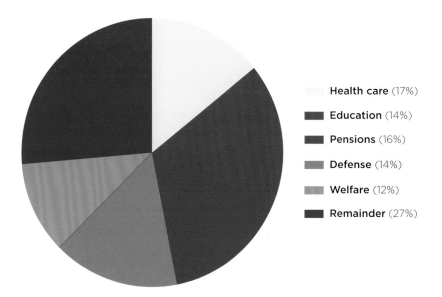

- Health care (17%)
- Education (14%)
- Pensions (16%)
- Defense (14%)
- Welfare (12%)
- Remainder (27%)

Average Undergraduate Tuition, Fees, and Room and Board Rates for Full-Time Students

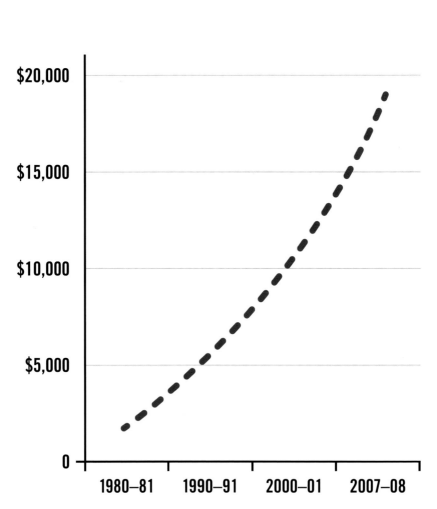

What Asian Families Saved for in 2012

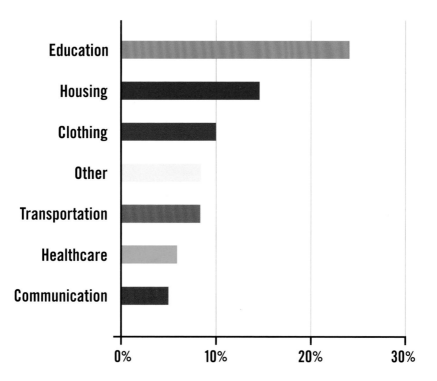

2009 PISA Test Scores

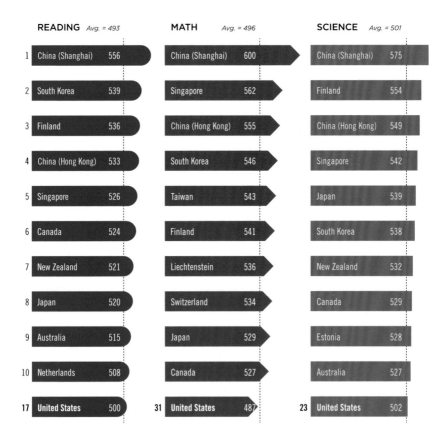

READING *Avg. = 493*

1	China (Shanghai)	556
2	South Korea	539
3	Finland	536
4	China (Hong Kong)	533
5	Singapore	526
6	Canada	524
7	New Zealand	521
8	Japan	520
9	Australia	515
10	Netherlands	508
17	United States	500

MATH *Avg. = 496*

1	China (Shanghai)	600
2	Singapore	562
3	China (Hong Kong)	555
4	South Korea	546
5	Taiwan	543
6	Finland	541
7	Liechtenstein	536
8	Switzerland	534
9	Japan	529
10	Canada	527
31	United States	487

SCIENCE *Avg. = 501*

1	China (Shanghai)	575
2	Finland	554
3	China (Hong Kong)	549
4	Singapore	542
5	Japan	539
6	South Korea	538
7	New Zealand	532
8	Canada	529
9	Estonia	528
10	Australia	527
23	United States	502

Number of States with Signed Laws Allowing for the Creation of Charter Schools (including DC)

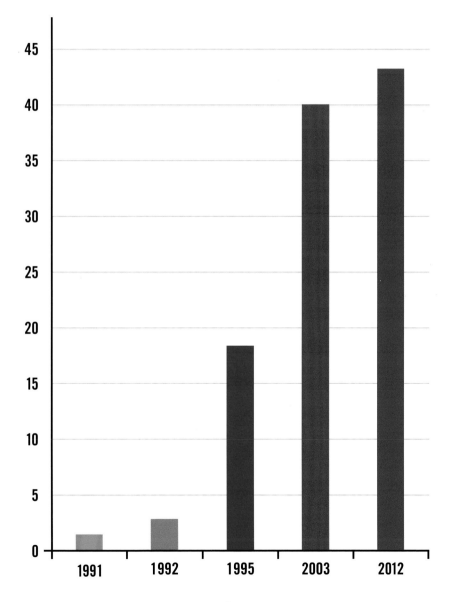

Number of Students Enrolled in Charter Schools in the United States

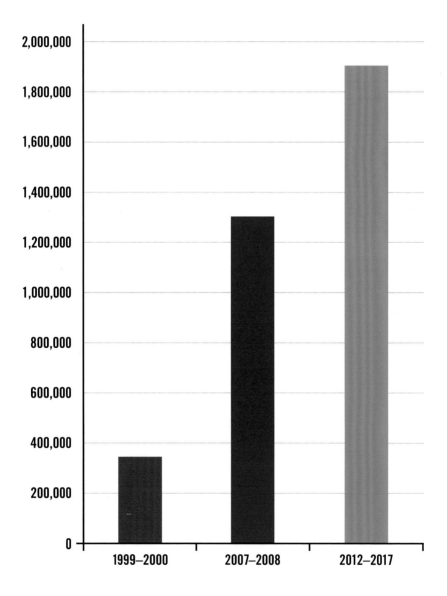

Hunter School Achievement After One Year of K¹² Involvement

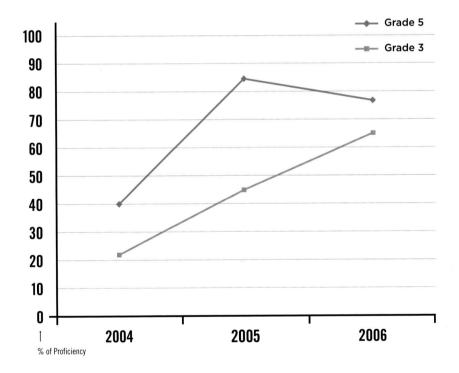

Results of the DC-CAS Fifth Grade Science Test

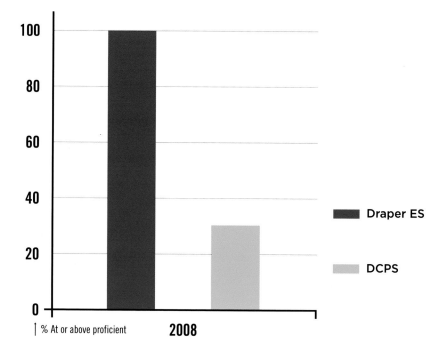

100

80

60

40   ■ Draper ES

20

0

↑ % At or above proficient   2008   ▨ DCPS

Percentage of Students Proficient or Better on the MCT2 Math Test

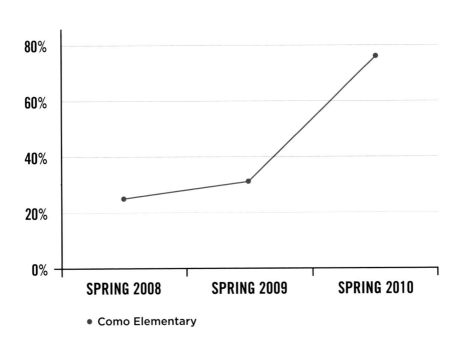

● Como Elementary

K

K–8 Parent Satisfaction at CVCS in Spring 2012

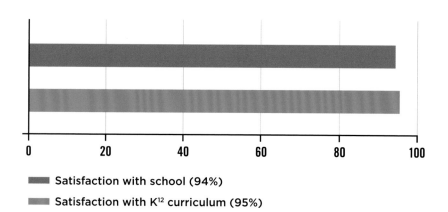

0   20   40   60   80   100

■ Satisfaction with school (94%)
■ Satisfaction with K^{12} curriculum (95%)

Decline in Student Performance After the Removal of K¹² Involvement

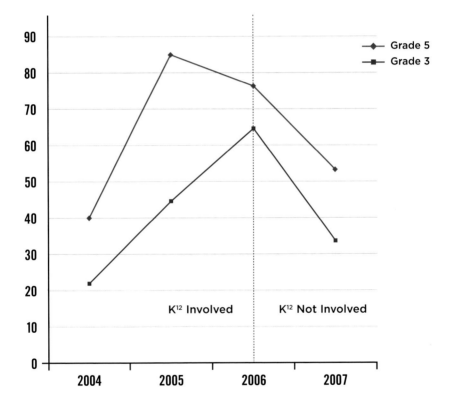

Number of Farmers in the United States

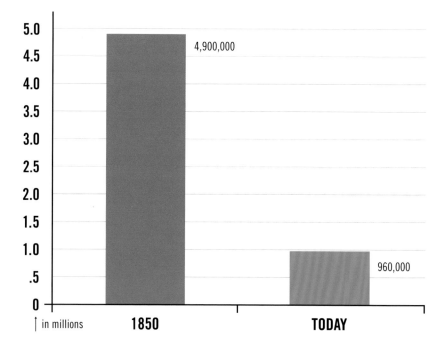

5.0
4.5
4.0
3.5
3.0
2.5
2.0
1.5
1.0
.5
0

4,900,000

960,000

in millions   1850   TODAY

N

K¹² Gains Relative to 2010-2011 Scantron Norm Group

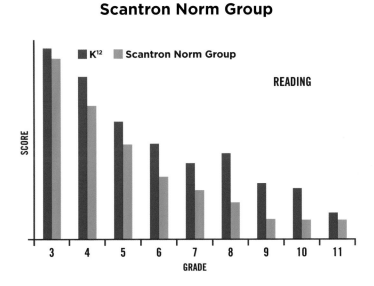

K¹² Gains Relative to 2010-2011 Scantron Norm Group

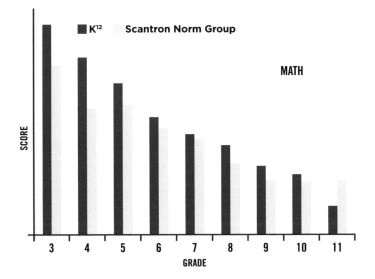

K¹² International Academy Scantron Performance Series Gains Compared to the National Norm Group in Reading, School Year 2010-2011

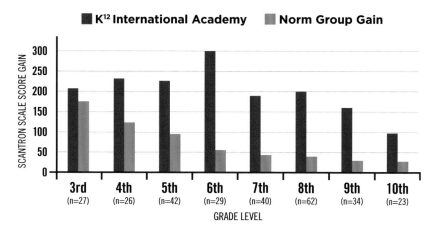

K¹² International Academy Scantron Performance Series Gains Compared to the National Norm Group in Math, School Year 2010-2011

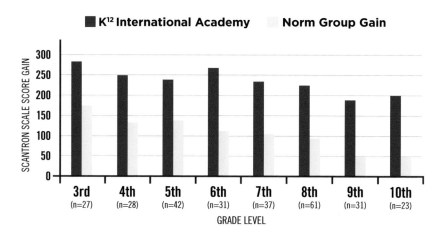

first year, and it eventually enrolled two hundred fifty. "It was a diverse group," said Hayes, "in every way—socioeconomically, [by] education level, and culturally. We had all kinds of parents. Some didn't have a high school education, some were lawyers and MDs."[10]

That first year, CVCS was 50 percent African American, 30 percent Caucasian, and 17 percent Latino—very close to the demographic of the city of Chicago itself but quite different than the CPS demographic, which was over 70 percent African American and less than 10 percent Caucasian. By offering a school that was innovative and rigorous, it became possible to pull students who had previously enrolled in private schools or been homeschooled back into the city. The families that enrolled were believers in public education, but the system had not offered an option that appealed to them until CVCS.

The school opened in September—two weeks late because the state board of education didn't approve the charter until late August—and was housed in rented quarters at DePaul University's downtown campus. In January, it moved in with the Merit School of Music, also in downtown Chicago, which has been home to the school ever since. Since CVCS was a hybrid, students (and parents) came to the learning center just once a week, on a rotating basis (to fit the schedule of parents and students). That meant we needed much less space than a traditional school. CVCS thus used fewer classrooms, including one designated as a parent room, for students, their parents, teachers, and staff.

Can It Work in Chicago?

"As an urban educator," said Hayes, "my big question was how to make sure that these parents are following through and implementing this wonderful, rigorous curriculum with their children four days a week. We had to make sure that the parents were going to follow up, that they were going to do all the things necessary for their children to make progress.

I invited the parents to come into the learning center while the children were in class, during the brick-and-mortar part of the program. We then gave training to the parents in the parent room. K[12] already had numerous parent workshops designed, and we could do those virtually or as a group in the parent room. This parent room helped parents feel like the important part of the school that they are. They could congregate there while their children were in school. In a big city like Chicago, which is built on community relationships, we wanted a climate in the parent room where as many parents as needed to could come in there and form a bond and...a strong sense of community.[11]

Hayes realized that she would have an opportunity to pull the parents in, work with them closely, and provide support where needed. She knew that the teachers could go online and identify whether or not the students had been on the computer and how much progress they had made. Face-to-face monitoring was also an option when the student came to the school one day each week. As Hayes recalled:

Those were some of the things that convinced me it could work. I was fearful of the kids goofing off, even if they had the best of intentions. But with this model, the parent makes a commitment. They sign a "contract" that says "I understand and agree"—and they have to initial each thing on the list. When I opened the school, they had to do that with me face-to-face, one-on-one.

I admit that when I went through that list, my expectations for those parents were low. We did, of course, have parents who did not really want to do that, but we knew that pretty quickly and were able to urge these children to go elsewhere. I must say, with my background working with these students and parents in the regular Chicago schools, I was surprised that we had so few problems—the issue of families who didn't grasp the program. I learned that if you meet with them at the beginning and make clear what the requirements are for the program, then you can bring those families along.

I recall a parent coming to me and saying, "Ms. Hayes, I just gotta tell you this. Not many people know this, but I never graduated from high school. And I have learned so much from working with my niece and working with this program that I decided that I'm going to take the GED test. And if I don't pass, I'm going over to Daley Junior College and I'm going to enroll in a class so that I can take that part of the test over again."

So I'm in urban education heaven right now. I have grabbed two generations at one time and changed their attitude about education. Her niece was a major discipline problem in the traditional school setting. They were calling her up to the office on a daily basis. This girl was suspended, ditching school, all kinds of things. Now everyone was enthusiastic about learning, and I had several families where that happened. When I started getting those kinds of parents and those kinds of stories, then I was hooked on K^{12}.[12]

Using Class Time Differently

Our Chicago Virtual Charter School beat the CPS average on test score results that first year, expanded enrollment the second year, and had a 90 percent retention rate.[13] As we move to the future, a significant portion of learning in grades K-12, as well as in college and professional development, will be blended, or hybrid. The school now has a long waiting list and will need to move facilities so that it can expand to meet the large demand. It was named by *Chicago* magazine in September 2012 as one of Chicago's best high schools. Clearly, there is enormous demand for brick-and-click schools. They may be used one day per week, two days per week, or even five days per week, but online learning is being merged with brick-and-mortar schools, and the pace of this merger of old and new is accelerating.

Susan Patrick of iNACOL (International Association for K–12 Online Learning) agrees, and she should know. As director of the Office of Educational Technology with the US Department of Education before coming to iNACOL, Patrick wrote the 2004 National Technology Plan. Patrick said:

> We're not going to call it blended learning, but we're going to use class time differently. We're going to use the space differently. We're going to use online resources and teaching tools. The curriculum that K^{12} has is excellent. Why not give all kids access to those resources? They are so much more dynamic than a textbook.... What you can do in the blended environment, like they're doing in Chicago and Philadelphia, is make the best of the face-to-face environment but also use the class time differently. You can have more discussions and more robust interaction while having full access—thanks to the internet, to the content at school and at home. And you can also see how kids are doing immediately, digitally; how they're interacting with the curriculum, where they're getting stuck. You know that right away, whereas in the traditional classroom, you're just guessing at it.[14]

The parents at CVCS have continued to remain very active in the school and provide suggestions on how to make the school even better. While I visited with an education officer for Chicago schools, he told me he had never visited a school where the parents loved the school more than did those at CVCS. I joked with him, "Are these the same parents who just told me how many things we could improve?"

These parents and their suggestions are part of the reason the CVCS continues to advance and why K[12] continues to advance. K[12] now operates these types of schools in Indianapolis and Muncie, Indiana, as well as Honolulu and more than thirty additional site locations. In some of these, physical attendance is mandatory and in others, optional. These schools, which are independent charters, have generally shown good academic gains every year, despite unfavorable demographics and a rapid increase in the number of pupils. These schools also enjoy high parent satisfaction, and continue to benefit from helpful suggestions from these parents.

K–8 Parent Satisfaction at CVCS in Spring 2012

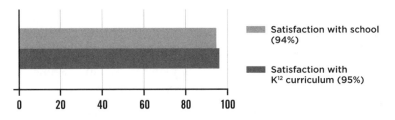

Satisfaction with school (94%)

Satisfaction with K[12] curriculum (95%)

Source: K[12] data and resources (www.k12.com).
Note: Chicago Virtual Charter School (CVCS).

After Chicago, we opened up mandatory-physical-attendance hybrid schools in Indiana and Hawaii. All of these schools were soon full—with waiting lists—and each school model functions differently. In Indiana, the school meets two days a week, and each class is split so that the student does part of the instruction online and a portion in class. Other models have a student taking an entire course or courses online and taking the rest of the courses entirely in a brick-and-mortar session. The online course could be at home or it could be in a computer lab, with the teacher in the lab or online. The permutations for how the days and instruction can be arranged are numerous and constantly expanding, making one optimal solution unlikely. Instead, and in tandem with the students and their different needs, the optimal school model should offer different solutions, depending on the student mix.

Flex Schools:
The Ultimate in Individualized Learning

In the fall of 2010, in the heart of downtown San Francisco, a new type of school opened—one that combined the social and custodial elements of brick-and-mortar schools, the benefits of face-to-face tutoring, and the engaging and individualized benefits of public virtual schools. This school, appropriately called the San Francisco Flex Academy, was located in the Old Press Club building downtown and had a series of workstations, where students work online in the same courses and individualized manner that students in the virtual schools do, as well as breakout rooms, where the students get one-on-one tutoring from certified teachers who staff the school. This school accommodates parents who have a difficult time enrolling their children in full-time virtual schools because there is no one to watch the child and provides the benefits of individualized learning that full-time virtual education offers all students. Students who want individualized instruction but also want to go to school with large groups of students can now do so.

This model differs significantly from the model used at Hunter Elementary in Philadelphia. In the Hunter model, teachers instruct the class at a synchronous rate, using the K^{12} curriculum as the core curriculum. In the Flex Academy, students go at their own pace so that each student has an individualized learning program. While Hunter is set up for grades K-5, the Flex Academy is designed for students in grades 6–12. While all teachers are present at Hunter, only the core teachers are present at the Flex Academy. The elective teachers are online.

As with the public virtual schools, the variety of students who come is amazing. The school is racially, economically, and academically diverse. In the first year, we had students who were serious athletes and needed more time to train. There have been students who wanted to finish high school faster than four years and enroll in college, as well as students who were about to drop out of high school and turned to Flex as the only option left for them. Incidentally, many of these students are now thriving, enjoying school for the first time and planning to attend college. In other words, these schools are transforming lives.

While it might seem odd to see a classroom with every child doing something different, this is an extremely efficient solution. Children learn at different paces and have different strengths. This school automatically customizes the learning to the student. How amazing that this is happening for perhaps the first time! If we were to step back from the traditional classroom paradigm that we are all accustomed to, the idea that we deliver information at a constant rate to a group of thirty students who have very different strengths and needs seems almost ludicrous, and certainly antiquated, when we can now customize schooling for every child. In a normal classroom, some students can learn much faster while some cannot keep up. In the normal classroom, advanced students can be frustrated by frequent interruptions and questions. Even more problematic, students who need more explanation and guidance may refrain from asking questions for fear of embarrassment.

The Flex Academy removes these issues—every student can learn each subject at their absorption rate and get one-on-one help when needed. We eliminate the problem of children who fall behind and stay behind for life and also stop boring the students who can learn more quickly. The education becomes individualized—a quantum breakthrough.

This lack of individualization in the traditional model may be causing a significant issue with high-performing kids, according to a recent study by Fordham Institute and Northwest Evaluation Association.[15] The study found that many high-achieving students struggle to maintain their elite performance over the years and often fail to improve their reading ability at the same rate as their average and below-average classmates. This may be occurring because all of the emphasis is placed on all children being proficient as opposed to allowing advanced learners to move ahead even faster. It may also occur simply because teachers cannot move fast enough for these students, who will then naturally regress to the mean. This is not an issue in virtual schools or flex academies, where students can move as fast as they can and are not held back by the teacher needing to slow down for others. We have some students who progress two grade levels per school year.[16]

The Passport Model

As I mentioned earlier, the high school dropout rate in this country is a national tragedy and something that troubles me greatly. I worry about this for the children who drop out and lose their chance at the American Dream, and I worry about it because it foreshadows trouble for the US economy. The problem deeply troubles me.

There are numerous reasons for the dropout problem: socioeconomic factors, poor schools, lack of motivation by students, to name a few. One could write a book on this alone. The relevant question for this book is: can technology correct the problem? I think the answer is yes. Technology, wisely implemented, can improve K-8 education, making school far more interesting. It can also create more engaging and flexible high schools. In Chicago, we set up a school designed to attack a specific problem and answer the question: can we bring the dropouts back?

The school we set up is something we call the passport model, and a student has to be dropped out for more than a year in order to enroll in this school. Set up with a few technology-equipped classrooms in a community college, the students spend fifteen hours a week in the center and do the rest of their work online. Their teachers are also online, and each student works independently while at the center. The center is staffed so that students can get face-to-face help if needed. Many of these students have jobs, and this type of model allows them to keep their jobs.

There are two things about high school dropouts that should be emphasized but are often not understood: (1) students drop out of high school for the most absurd reasons, and (2) once they drop out, they have difficulty getting back in. There are many students who fail a course like ninth-grade English but pass tenth- and eleventh-grade English. They are told in their senior year they will not graduate with their class, and they just drop out as a result of discouragement. Once this happens, they can't really go back, because these students don't want to be in classes with fourteen-year-olds, and parents and high school administrators don't want twenty-year-olds in class with fourteen-year-olds. There are also teen mothers who were excellent students before they became pregnant, but how do they go back to school when they have a baby at home? Again, online education offers a promising solution.

Many of these students have been out in the world and realize that their opportunities are limited. Once the light clicks on, and they have something they want to do that requires an education, their motivation goes through the ceiling. It gives me hope to witness the bright intensity of their newfound motivation. Ideally, online education soon will be able to turn this light on long before these students drop out.

From the passport school experience, one thing is now abundantly clear about dropout students: there are many who want back in, and if a solution works for them, they are motivated. The results of the passport program demonstrate that beyond a shadow of doubt. This school is now graduating a significant majority of these dropouts, with many going on to postsecondary education.[17] Hybrid and online education allows the student to come back into the system in a flexible way without any embarrassment.

To summarize, the various types of blended learning can be classified into broad categories:

Blended Learning Models

Type	Description
Flex	In a brick-and-mortar school, children use technology to work at their own pace in individualized programs.This model functions like a full-time virtual school, but children attend it together in a brick-and-mortar setting where they can also get face-to-face instruction. Flex schools may be embedded within traditional brick-and-mortar schools.
Group Didactic (Discovery)	In this model, the teacher teaches to a group of children, but the lecture sessions are aided by collaborative learning software and an online multimedia curriculum, with such tools as interactive animations, videos, simulations, and learning games. This model fosters peer-to-peer learning among students, and students also have access to the curriculum at home.
Flex Permutations	This model can be combined with project-based learning and traditional methods. For example, one-third of students could work independently, one-third on a group project, and one-third with teachers. Many permutations are possible.
Split Calendar	Students spend entire quarters or semesters doing full-time online instruction and spend other quarters in brick-and-mortar classes. A school district that moves to full-time online instruction for summer school is a good example. Expect to see a great deal of this model at the graduate-school level and maybe the undergraduate level.

Source: K[12] data and resources (www.k12.com).

Blended Learning Models, cont.

Type	Description
Split Course Load	Students attend school less than full-time with some courses being entirely in person and some courses being entirely online. The online courses can be done in a computer lab or at home. This model could also include students who pay for additional courses not offered in their school. This model has the potential to reduce the need for more brick-and-mortar facilities.
Split Individual Courses (Hybrid, Passport)	Students attend school less than full-time, and the individual course is taught partially in person and partially online. Hybrid and passport schools fall into this category. Students might meet for instruction or tutoring one, two, or more days per week.
Combinations	Most, if not all, of these models could exist in a single school.

Source: K¹² data and resources (www.k12.com).

7

BUMPS IN THE ROAD

*P*ublic education is subject to the slings and arrows of politics—
and school districts are subject to more political intervention than
most government entities. Any reform in education, including technology, must work its way through this complex political maze in order
to succeed.

Our introduction to the complex politics of Chicago came with
the filing of a lawsuit by the Chicago Teachers Union against CVCS
before the school even opened its doors. In Philadelphia, despite nearly
unanimous teacher buy-in to the K[12] program and its extraordinary performance, there was a movement against allowing private companies to
be involved in the education system.

We were aware of these problems, of course, and had been able to
work our way through them in other locales to establish public virtual

academies. The more success online education achieves, the more threatening it becomes to many educational interest groups. This was disappointing—but not surprising. Too often in education, the more successful an innovation, the more resistance there is to it. In all sectors of the economy, entrenched interests try to find ways to stave off new competition. What's different in education is that the entrenched interests so often succeed at the expense of children and educational liberty.

The battle for education transformation and liberty has been long and difficult, but the battle must be fought and won if we are to reach the point where every child has an opportunity to succeed.

Victory in the Badger State

In Wisconsin, the state's largest teachers union, the Wisconsin Education Association Council (WEAC), sued to prevent virtual education almost before it had even begun. They didn't like the idea that parents would spend a significant amount of time working with their children, even though research shows that schools and children would do much better when there is parental involvement. WIVA (Wisconsin Virtual Academy) had twenty certified, unionized teachers, but the unions chose to sue anyway. It didn't seem to matter that the teachers in the virtual schools were union members or that there was very high demand for these teaching positions (there were often ten applications for each available teaching position).[1] (In 2011, K^{12} received approximately forty-five applications for every teacher position.)

The *Wisconsin State Journal* called the move a "war on innovation":

> Hidebound union officials see jobs under threat. WEAC, which has demanded that Northern Ozaukee jettison its plans, now has tried to shut down two of Wisconsin's virtual schools (the other is based in Appleton). Critics of virtual schools worry that for-profit companies are muscling into modern schooling. The business model puts customers first—and those customers,

Wisconsin families, so far are very satisfied with the product....
A clearheaded Dane County judge dismissed WEAC's previous
attempt to shut down a virtual school. Union leaders deserve
detention for failing to learn their lesson the first time.[2]

A state trial court dismissed the case, but in December of 2007, an
appeals court said, among other things, that the academy was violating
a state law requiring that public school teachers be licensed.[3] This was a
curious finding. WIVA had fully licensed teachers who taught students
and supported parents in their role as Learning Coaches. The ruling,
when taken to its logical conclusion, seemed to imply that if parents were
to help children with their homework or volunteer in a classroom, then
the parents had to be licensed. It conflicted with everything we know
about parents and education—the more the parents are involved, the
better the student does.

The ruling incensed parents like Bob Reber, an insurance salesman
who lived in Fond du Lac and whose eight-year-old daughter was a
WIVA student. "According to this ruling, if I want to teach my daughter
to tie her shoes, I'd need a license," Reber said.[4]

Holding signs that read "Don't kick me out of school—I didn't do
anything wrong!" and "This vote will go on your permanent record!"
Reber and more than one thousand other parents and students from
online schools rallied in Madison, the state capital, urging lawmakers to
save their schools.[5]

"In school, you study history," Rose Fernandez, president of the
Wisconsin Coalition of Virtual School Families, said to the boisterous
crowd. "But today, you're making history."[6] She went on to say:

While the Supreme Court decides whether to take up the
appeal in the virtual school case, there are several well-
intentioned legislators looking for a legislative fix. We have

union dues paying teachers, parents, kids, school administrators, and those well-intentioned legislators on our side. The teachers union, which wants to close these schools, stands alone with their allies at the State Department of Public Instruction. We hope this massive civics lesson today will help bring even more allies our way. AB697 is the only legislation out there that will keep these schools open—3,000 kids could be kicked out of the public school that works best for them if this legislation doesn't pass. I want those who oppose this bill to look these little ones in the eyes and say, "Tough luck, kid, I have to side with WEAC on this one. Now hit the road."[7]

It's heartwarming to see parents and students standing up for a high-performing school that is delivering the education they want. Watching this transpire, I wondered how powerful our educational system would be if all parents had this passion for the schools their children attended.

Faced with the prospect of a court-ordered closure of half a dozen online public charter schools in Wisconsin, the group rallied in support of a bipartisan bill, which had a public hearing later in the day. The rally attendees did not return to their hometowns when the speakers were done, however. The group went to the legislative committee hearing to register their support and then spent the afternoon visiting their lawmakers.[8]

Other advocates took to the media. One wrote, in a letter to the editor of a local paper, "Why restrict learning choices for children who don't fit the cookie-cutter style of traditional schools? If WIVA closes, my child could again flounder, but this thing is no longer about just my child. It is about future students who may need another option in education."[9]

The press weighed in as well. Editorial headlines ranged from "DOYLE, WEAC WRONG TO TRY TO SCUTTLE VIRTUAL SCHOOLS

COMPROMISE" (*Sheboygan Press*) to "STUDY BUT DON'T CAP ONLINE SCHOOLS" (*Wisconsin State Journal*) and "AN UNNECESSARY CAP ON ENROLLMENT" (*Milwaukee Journal Sentinel*).[10]

By this time, K[12] alone was serving students in forty-six states and several foreign countries. And Susan Patrick, head of iNACOL, was receiving calls from reporters overseas about the Wisconsin brouhaha. "They didn't understand what the problem was," said Patrick. "Most European schools and students have been wired for years."[11]

In January 2008, legislators reached agreement on a bipartisan bill that would allow the schools to stay open, conditioned upon online teachers keeping in close contact with students and coupled with increased state oversight of the schools, including a statewide enrollment ceiling. The state's governor at the time, Jim Doyle, signed the bill in April 2008. It made changes to the laws governing charter schools, open enrollment, and teacher licensing—and it allowed virtual charter schools in Wisconsin to operate with public funding.[12]

The new law was a milestone for the children of Wisconsin and laid the groundwork for a renaissance in the state's schools. By early 2012, the caps on virtual school enrollment were lifted and the open enrollment window expanded. This was a remarkable expansion of educational liberty that few could have foreseen in early 2008.

The Story of a Michigan Family

It had been an arduous 2007 for Sandy Smith and her family. That October, both Sandy and her six-year-old son, Andrew, the youngest of three, were diagnosed just four days apart with different types of cancer. Sandy's breast cancer had a favorable prognosis. Andrew's rare brainstem cancer, unfortunately, did not. But they did their best to fight their illnesses over the next two years. Tragically, Andrew died of his cancer in December 2009.

The Smith family had become interested in K¹² in 2008, but no K¹²-powered, public partner school was available in Michigan at that time. Sandy wishes it had been, because "given that we were in survival mode as a family, I was concerned about the academic consequences."

The Michigan Virtual Charter Academy (MVCA) didn't open until the fall of 2010, after their ordeal had ended. Nonetheless, Sandy said they decided to "try it for a year" in order to help their daughter Charis catch up, especially in math, and to see if the program would appropriately challenge their eldest, Stephen, who had always been off the charts; for example, he began reading at age two. One year was followed by a second, and then they signed up for a third. So far, Stephen has finished 10th grade, and Charis has completed 7th grade. *Overjoyed* is not too strong a word to describe their experience.

During her schooling, Charis took advantage of MVCA's participation in the National Math Lab initiative and went online to attend one-hour sessions four mornings a week. This was in addition to her regular math course. From a student who was struggling in math, now she "loves it so much." In fact, she loves all of her MVCA courses, from writing to history to geography to French. She's even "blossomed into a student leader in the virtual learning environment," said her mom. In addition, Sandy noted, participating in an online school at home has meant that as the learning coach, she's been able to affect Charis's study habits, which had declined during their family's disruptive years.

As for Stephen, any concern about whether he'd be bored in an online school has been completely alleviated. He's been taking all honors-level classes and "really appreciates the attitude of the teachers, is very happy with their encouragement, and the one-to-one time they spend with him." Said Sandy: "The teachers truly care about Stephen and are having a good impact on his character." Meanwhile, with Stephen's test scores in the 99th percentile, major universities are already recruiting him.

As to whether an online school isolates children socially, there's no worry on that score for the Smiths. Both kids excel musically, and they perform in the Mid-Michigan Youth Symphony. They also volunteer: Stephen at a local hospital and Charis with a nearby family. They participate in church activities in addition to the time they spend just hanging out with friends.

Coming through such a difficult time would be a mountain to climb for any family. For the Smiths, having the choice of Michigan Virtual Charter Academy has been part of their healing process, allowing greater family togetherness while individualizing—and accelerating—their children's academic progress. As Sandy summed up, "We have just been thrilled."

Source: Author interview and correspondence (January 25, 2012). For the full testimony, visit: http://www.youtube.com/watch?v=TTiq2RAaZg0.

Problems in Chicago

We encountered problems in Chicago similar to the ones we'd had in Wisconsin. Shortly after the Chicago Virtual Charter School opened its "doors" in September of 2006, the local teachers union sued the Illinois State Board of Education. The union alleged that CVCS didn't provide sufficient direct instruction by certified teachers, and thus it amounted to homeschooling at taxpayers' expense. The union filed this suit even though the school had been approved by Chicago Public Schools, its school board, and the Illinois State Board of Education. Initially, the union had tried to stop the school from opening, but it failed amid the strong support from Chicago schools and the city's innovative super-intendent, Arne Duncan, as well as the strong voices of parents who couldn't wait to enroll their children in this exciting new school. A law-suit was nonetheless filed, and attempts were made in the legislature to close the school.

The recollections of Sharon Hayes crystallize the challenge:

When I received a call to tell me that this bill to close our school was out there, and they needed me to go to Springfield to testify, I went into the parent room and said to the parents, "You're not going to see me for a couple days because I'm going to Springfield." I explained to them what the bill was about and that it would mean that our school would be closed if the bill actually passed.

One of the parents said to me, "Ms. Hayes, both of your kids have graduated from college. Why are you going to Springfield to fight for our kids' school [when] we're not there to support you?"

As a Chicago Public School principal, I didn't get active politically or involve parents in this way, so I had no experi-ence [with either possibility].... I went back to my parents and told them that they could come with me to the hearing, but they had to be silent. It was a very formal procedure, and their silence was going to speak more loudly than anything they could possibly say. So these parents got together, put their money together, and filled two busloads—parents and chil-dren—for the trip to Springfield. They all wore their Chicago Virtual Charter School shirts. I had to call both buses and tell them at the last moment that they couldn't bring signs or ban-ners, and they said, "No problem, Ms. Hayes. We'll leave them on the bus." I really stressed to them the importance of being very quiet.

After they arrived, we met and everyone wanted to know what they could do: "How will anyone know that we're there for you?" So I said, "Well, the only thing I can think of is—if you can do this in complete silence!—maybe you can stand up when I speak."

I didn't think anything more of it until I was at the table in the front of the room, facing the committee.... I started talking, and I got to the second or third question that they were giving me when the chairman said to me, "Mrs. Hayes, are they going to stand up during your entire testimony?"

I did not even hear them stand up. I turned around, and I saw this sea of CVCS shirts—all standing, all silent. And I stood up and looked at 'em and said, "My team, you are so wonderful. Thank you so much. You may be seated." It was just so impressive. These parents came together from all walks of life to save their school.

Very quickly the bill went from something that would have killed CVCS and ended funding for online education in Illinois to something that said, "We will form a committee to study the effects of virtual education." That was very exciting.

The chairman of the committee later said, "I was so moved by the parents who wanted the school that I don't think it is right to deny parents their choice." It turns out a new political force was emerging—parents who wanted a great education for their children—and it was going to lead education into the twenty-first century regardless of the obstacles put up by entrenched interests. This should not be surprising, however. If parents are asked, "Do you want the government bureaucracy to choose the school for your child, or do you want to choose your child's school?" I believe most parents would want the latter.[13]

Staying Focused—On the Kids

Public virtual schools have been subject to several lawsuits. The students and parents who wanted greater educational freedom have prevailed in the lawsuits that have threatened this liberty. While the suits were painful in the short run, they proved beneficial in the long run, as the publicity surrounding them drove enrollment growth and increased awareness and support. Many parents said they heard about the school from newspaper articles that covered the lawsuit: "I read about the lawsuit in the paper, and the school sounded great to me, so we enrolled." In this way, the suits were a blessing in disguise.

Parents and students should never take no for an answer; too much is at stake. Virtual education should be in every state so that all children have the option of pursuing online learning. When there's a solution that benefits the children, we have to do whatever it takes to make sure the children are served. Innovations that threaten established interests always face resistance, so we have to persevere and refuse to be intimidated. Education entrepreneurs, like all pioneers, run into many obstacles, but they keep going.

As time passes, K[12] and its technology are being embraced as individuals throughout the education system realize that online education does not compete with the system but helps the system fulfill its promise of offering a quality education to every child. K[12] simply provides a service to the public school system, much like a textbook company provides books or Apple provides computers.

Making progress takes patience, of course. We're running a marathon, and we have to run it at a hundred-yard pace. So we have to be infinitely patient—but also infinitely *impatient*. That is one of the core values at K^{12}.

A Different Story in Philadelphia

While the students and families eventually prevailed in Wisconsin and Chicago, they faced a bigger fight in Philadelphia. One lesson learned is that navigating big-city governments can be more complicated than navigating state governments, and strong support of the mayor, which existed in Chicago, is often critical. That wasn't the case in Philadelphia. The mayor was under tremendous pressure to preserve the status quo, and many private vendors were forced to leave, regardless of their success.

K^{12} had delivered a quality product that clearly helped many students, teachers, and parents. After the decision to discontinue K^{12} involvement was announced, Mensah Dean, a reporter for the *Philadelphia Daily News*, wrote, "If you randomly call Philadelphia elementary schools and ask principals and science teachers about K^{12}, Inc.'s science curriculum, some won't know where to begin with the praise."[14] The same article quoted the principal at Hunter, Olivia Dreibelbis: "The curriculum is innovative, the kids like it, it's very demanding... To change a curriculum company midstream... is devastating for a school. I'm nervous about the impact that would have on this school."[15]

When creating the science curriculum for Philadelphia, we included scientists of different ethnicities and eras—not just George Washington Carver, who seems part of history, but those making history, like the African American chemist actively doing research for a pharmaceutical company or the Latina woman working for a defense contractor. We wanted inner-city children to have role models (most of Hunter's had never met a scientist) and to see that there were real jobs related to what they were learning. They needed to understand that improving their academic performance would give them opportunities to go to college and get a good job. While there are many reasons why students drop out of high school, one reason is that they don't know the value of an education.

Dreibelbis was right to be worried: a year after we left Hunter, test scores dropped close to their pre-K[12] level. I felt physically ill when I saw them. How someone could do that to the students of Hunter is unfathomable to me. A school on the verge of greatness was brought down for no reason other than politics. We had clearly seen how students could benefit from a technology-based curriculum, with the proper teacher training. The sad part is that we also learned what happens when technology is taken away.

Decline in Student Performance
After the Removal of K[12] Involvement

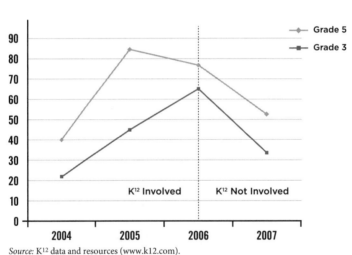

Source: K[12] data and resources (www.k12.com).

From a data point of view, the termination of the program allowed us to isolate the effects of the program. Because a technology-based reading program was not used, we could pinpoint the successful results of K[12]'s technology-based program. We knew our program could provide both local and state superintendents with the tools to improve underperforming schools.

The second test came in Washington, DC, and had even more impressive results, albeit on a smaller scale. K^{12} was allowed to offer its science curriculum in an underperforming school that served students from low-income families. For the second time, the results exceeded my wildest expectations.

One year after K^{12} offered the curriculum and trained the teachers, 100 percent of the fifth-grade students tested proficient in science and *every special needs student tested proficient in science*. The results crushed the district average, and it was achieved without changing the staff.

This experience in Philadelphia and Washington, DC, gives K^{12} confidence that we can raise student achievement in underperforming schools. In fact, K^{12} is so confident that it has told school districts that if it does not improve the results, they don't have to pay.

8

EDUCATION PROBLEMS AND THEIR SOLUTIONS

High school students who couldn't take Regents Examinations because of today's snowstorm will not have a chance for makeups until June, according to education officials. And those taking the two-day Comprehensive English test will have to scrap the first part, which was administered Tuesday. "They are out of luck, so to speak, because they are going to have to take the whole exam again in June," said state Education Department spokeswoman, Jane Briggs.

—*Albany Times Union*, January 28, 2009

*S*now days. If political obstacles to school improvement aren't enough, there are meteorological ones. Usually, snow days are celebrated by students, and any student who lives north of the thirty-fifth parallel knows the drill. High school students in upstate New York learned all too painfully in early 2011 that there are significant academic disadvantages when high-stakes tests, prepared for with intensity, are canceled.

An online test might have helped; online curriculum would have helped even more. Snow days might become obsolete in the near future as classroom curriculum moves online. With online education, students will be able to keep going to school after hurricanes or other natural disasters.

Most education problems can be solved by computers and online education—if not now, certainly in the near future. Meteorological challenges are no exception. If a hurricane hits, and the students are dispersed, they can continue with their education as long as they are somewhere with electrical power and a phone line. If a pandemic like the 1918 influenza outbreak ever comes again, students will not be able to go to a brick-and-mortar school. However, if a state has a virtual school, children can be educated almost seamlessly—and not just a few students but every child in the state.

This is just one reason why online education is such a valuable supplement to America's education system. Online education also offers:

- Courses that regular schools cannot provide
- Credit recovery courses to improve graduation rates
- Ability to provide quality teachers to more students
- More engaging learning experience in classrooms and virtual courses
- Tools to create a technologically proficient workforce
- More individualized learning
- More flexible time schedules
- Dropout recovery
- Greater cost efficiencies
- Affordable and flexible summer school
- Expanded choice for students
- Parent empowerment
- Private sector involvement in course creation and management of schools, which creates a competitive dynamic and rapid innovation that is without precedent in public education
- Expanded vocational education
- Opportunity to complete college courses in high school
- High quality education available to *every* student in the United States and throughout the world
- Easy horizontal and vertical curriculum articulation

- Accessible education for the incarcerated
- Separation of educational opportunity from geographic limitations
- Reduced need for new physical buildings

Thus, online education expands educational opportunities and improves teaching quality while enhancing the remedial education that prevents students from dropping out. The Southern Regional Education Board (SREB) reported that many local schools are simply "too small to offer all of the courses that students need today to prepare for college or careers. Cost is a major factor, especially if only a handful of students want or need a particular course."[1]

Even large schools can't offer students all the choices they desire and deserve. With online education, however, there is no limit to the number of courses a school can offer. I expect that within the next ten years, the number of online courses offered to high school students will be greater than the number of courses offered today in large brick-and-mortar universities. Also, many if not most electives will be taught online, as this reduces the cost of delivering these electives, expands the number of electives available, and allows schools to better use their physical real estate and concentrate on the core subjects. Once this occurs, some schools might choose to run two shifts and potentially double capacity.

Good teachers aren't often attracted to out-of-the-way or unsavory locales, contributing to a vicious cycle for students attending schools in remote rural areas or dangerous inner-city neighborhoods. Many schools lack the ability to offer all of the courses their students need to qualify for good colleges or to meet changing high school graduation requirements. Growing numbers of schools cannot afford to provide a quality fourth year of mathematics, multiple years of even one foreign language, or two or more advanced placement (AP) courses.

Online education enables schools—and students—to overcome these challenges. It can deliver a world-class education anytime, anywhere, and to anyone. Once the constraints of geography, demographics, and calendar are removed, a whole new world of education opportunity opens up. That was the vision underpinning the founding of K[12] in early 2000—and that vision is steadily becoming a reality in American education.

Can Learning Be Customized?

After K[12] launched a virtual academy in Idaho, a committee in the state legislature held a hearing that covered online education. Some of those who testified provided compelling stories about the power of virtual education. We heard from a woman whose child with severe special needs learned to read through the virtual school after having difficulty in brick-and-mortar schools. Soon after, we heard from a young polymath who said this was the first time in his school life that he had been challenged. The two children, with very different abilities, were using the same curriculum—one working years ahead and the other several years behind—and they were both getting what they needed. The power of online education to serve a broad spectrum of children was never clearer.

High quality online education, whether accessed through a virtual academy, a flex academy, a hybrid school, or a traditional brick-and-mortar school, combines high academic standards, compelling content, and a great teacher. It also offers an individualized, self-paced learning program that allows gifted students to excel while students having difficulty can spend more time where needed and receive more individualized small-group instruction when needed. Content is delivered in an adaptive way that fits a student's learning needs and preferences.

In the past, such customized learning would have been considered an expensive luxury—if not impossible—as there were not enough teachers to provide individual attention. Schools were built, and then administrators tried to shoehorn the kids into them. Something better is no longer a luxury, yet we continue to treat it as such—unfortunately. One size doesn't fit all, and countless teachers end up teaching to the middle level of the class. As a result, fast learners are bored and slower learners are often lost. In cumulative subjects like math, where students cannot master today's lesson without having mastered yesterday's, the results can be disastrous, particularly for at-risk children with no safety net. If they have one poor year of instruction in math, they are unlikely to ever recover.

Technology will put an end to one-size-fits-all schooling. Computers, for example, facilitate both interactivity and individualization. Moore's Law, postulated in 1965, says processing power continues to grow exponentially. Such power was on display in May of 1997, when an IBM computer (Deep Blue) defeated the world chess champion, Garry Kasparov, in a six-game match—a feat that could not have happened a decade earlier. Within thirteen years, a computer then beat the best *Jeopardy!* players in the world—a feat that is exponentially more complex than chess and would have been impossible ten years ago. This improvement in computational power and software leads to continual improvement in the online learning experience. When combined with higher bandwidth and greater investments in content, online lessons will improve dramatically in years to come. As private companies gain scale, they will be able to make the necessary investment in online learning to develop these intensive, interactive courses. Education will be more individualized and engaging than ever before.[2]

The experience at the Hunter school showed how technology could improve academic results in ways that would have been technologically impossible a decade earlier. Its instructional program for math was changed almost overnight to meet the needs of teachers unaccustomed to teaching with technology, and it was customized to meet Pennsylvania's learning standards.

Gaining Mastery

We were also able to institute a culture of data gathering and computer-aided decision making at Hunter. We used assessments and benchmark testing to give us a sophisticated view of what individual children were (and were not) learning. As we continue to refine our ability to provide adaptive content, thanks to the computer, we can instantly assess a student's responses to content queries and adjust content delivery to facilitate maximum mastery of the subject.

At Hunter there was constant and instant assessment followed by constant and instant adjustment. While there's nothing new about student assessments, it has often been inadequate. In fact, it has frequently led to children being incorrectly evaluated because of a single high-stakes test or a less-than-effective teacher.

Customization should not be confused with the kind of personalized learning that became popular in the 1970s, when children were encouraged to use classrooms as forums for unguided self-expression. This type of personalized learning often meant no learning at all. Today's quality online education is performance based, competence based, and knowledge based. We can create assessments fine-tuned enough to gauge a child's progress on a daily basis, and by adjusting the content based on those assessments, we encourage children to gain competency in a subject. It is not a free-for-all; it is the opposite. Online learning and curriculum allow schools to provide an education that is much more consistent than traditional classroom instruction and provides a great deal of flexibility for both students and teachers. This system also ensures that students receive and master the content required by state standards, while the use of the internet allows further exploration of topics far beyond the lesson for students who are capable and interested. The adoption of Common Core State Standards will make online education even more powerful, because curriculum will no longer be so fragmented, allowing for deeper, more focused explorations.

By the same token, traditional schools are hamstrung by an antiquated system that sometimes pushes students forward (in grade level) even though they have not mastered a subject—or it holds them back even when they have. Sorting students by grade level is not always the best way to facilitate learning. A significant percentage of children in virtual schools are at a different grade level in math than they are in language arts. This is difficult to accommodate in a traditional classroom but clearly demonstrates the need for individualized education. Why shouldn't students be able to work ahead in areas where they excel? Similarly, why shouldn't students have more time to master a subject that takes them a little longer?

Thanks to computers and increasingly sophisticated assessment software, grade-level designations can be all but eliminated. Computers direct our subject-matter energies at the individual child, with a teacher there as a guide, so that each child has a chance to learn—and master—the material without being pushed beyond his or her level of proficiency or being held back. It will be a significant improvement when we think of education as a continuum rather than in the discrete chunks that we currently call grade levels.

In the not-too-distant future, lessons will be customized to best address each individual student's strengths and weaknesses, with multiple lesson for each topic so students will be able to try different approaches until they master the material. Some of this customization is already occurring. For example, in mathematics, K^{12} can deliver an automated test that accesses what a child knows and then match the result against the relevant skills for math. Soon we will be able to use this data to generate a customized set of instructional materials specific to the needs of the individual student, providing extra explanation and practice to make up for skill and knowledge deficits or accelerating when a student demonstrates mastery and is ready to sprint ahead. This concept was the original impetus for K^{12}. We're also working to refine adaptive learning so that when students take a test, they will know immediately where they are, and the next lesson will be automatically adjusted to take account of their competencies and deficits. Remediation can be done simultaneously when a student takes a course because the computer can diagnose background deficits and give the student the basic skills they need for the lesson. Technology is even at the point where it can measure how much time students take on a question to determine how well they understand the material: a student who can correctly compute "6 x 8" in less than a second has a different mastery than a student who takes twenty seconds. Thus, the determination of mathematical fluency recaptures accuracy and speed. Good adaptive learning incorporates multiple variables.

Adaptive Learning Tools

Learning experiences can be made more efficient and effective by building in the logic an expert teacher or tutor uses to differentiate instruction in the course, automating individualized learning; adaptive learning tools do just that. Based on assessment results or individual activity, many K[12] courses automatically route students to an alternate explanation or additional practice or remediate on some prerequisite skill to a key concept until the students master it. Our courses also accelerate students past previously mastered concepts, leaving more time for challenging work. In addition, students have the ability to choose their own learning path, such as selecting which of six novels they wish to read, while moving at a pace that adjusts to the rate at which they are gaining mastery.

Another tool is adaptive testing, a customized form of assessment that changes the difficulty of questions based on how the student answered the previous questions. This allows the assessment to be much more precise, and it involves fewer questions. Adaptive testing is probably the best way to measure a student's knowledge because students from any grade can take the identical test and still produce precise measurements of their learning gains.

From curriculum to testing, adaptive learning tools offer the customized, individualized edge that can bring students in the United States to a previously unattainable level of learning efficiency.

Location, Location, Location—Cutting the Ties to Place

In addition to the computer's ability to tailor content to an individual student's abilities at any given time, online learning can go where traditional schooling cannot go—and it can go anytime. While many online courses offered today are little more than glorified correspondence courses, today's high quality online courses are an order of magnitude better and are far more engaging and effective than any correspondence course. They are also accessible to anyone who can access an internet connection. To take full advantage of this tremendous flexibility, many states need to change their laws to allow school attendance on weekends, expanding school hours and the school calendar beyond what is offered by brick-and-mortar schools. In the first few years of K¹², I was amazed by how often regulators tried to apply brick-and-mortar rules to online schools even though the rules were often written before the internet was created; charter laws were supposed to allow freedom from these rules. Changing these archaic rules was and still is quite difficult, because those who oppose innovation and competition in public education use the rules to protect their turf. Eventually these archaic regulations will disappear, and online education will be allowed to do everything it has the power to do. Online learning will continue to improve rapidly. While we shouldn't judge the automobile by the first cars built in the early-nineteenth century, we shouldn't judge online learning based on what we have today. That being said, online learning is already a powerful form of education for many students.

Arizona Virtual Academy is an example of how online learning can meet the needs of hard-to-serve constituencies. The school and K[12] have partnered with Project PPEP (Portable, Practical, Educational Preparation, Inc.), a forty-two-year-old program to try to improve the quality of rural life for migrant farm workers. John David Arnold, the founder of Project PPEP, launched it "aboard a 1957 Chevy bus named 'La Tortuga'," as the program's website puts it, and today Project PPEP is introducing the internet to its distance learning program. Migrant workers can now get a twenty-first-century education as long as a mobile device can bring the internet to them.[3]

Other beneficiaries of the flexibility offered by online education are teen mothers. Many of these girls never go back to school after giving birth.[4] In one urban district I visited, only 19 percent of girls who became pregnant graduated from high school. With online education, however, these girls can stay home with their babies, find time to study, and (hopefully) graduate. Perhaps they can come back a year later and not be behind. An online program for teen mothers can also save taxpayers a substantial amount of money, as these girls can now be home with their children, reducing the need for government-funded childcare. Often excellent students, many of these young mothers are in our dropout recovery school in Chicago. Online education will enable them to complete high school, and they should be able to complete college online, which is moving online at an even faster pace than K[12].

Many schools have tried to set up alternative learning programs as a safety net—or last stop—for students with disruptive behavior and as a way of safeguarding the learning environment for other students. Instead of being consigned to a room with a ratty textbook and an unhappy teacher's aide, they can go to that room and continue their studies online.

Speaking of being confined, we all know that people with college degrees or even minimal experience in higher education are less likely to commit crimes. Studies also show that prisoners who pursue education while serving time in prison are less likely to be reincarcerated.[5] Online education should also be offered in America's jails and prisons. It might even make sense to offer reduced sentences for nonviolent criminals who complete a high school diploma or associate's degree while incarcerated. Their employability will increase, and recidivism is likely to decline.

Even in traditional school settings, children do not need to be relegated to specific grades. A twelve-year-old boy might be a sixth grader who needs to take fourth-grade math, but none of his classmates need to know where he is in his studies, so there's no stigma attached. Online education makes it possible for students to move ahead in their strong subjects and catch up in their weak areas.

As previously mentioned, education should be thought of as an ongoing stream of learning, from kindergarten to college. Students will be at different places along that path and traveling at different speeds, depending on the subject. Since online education is available to everyone, students in Scarsdale and in the South Bronx have the same educational opportunities, although perhaps not the same family environments. By increasing the educational opportunities available to at-risk students, individual economic futures improve as well. The next century is the century of human capital, and a person's skills and work ethic will determine their economic situation. These skills will likely have to be upgraded continually throughout a lifetime as the pace of societal and technological change continues to accelerate. Nothing other than online learning will allow this continuous education to occur.

Online education has shattered the nexus between geography and educational quality. This is the twenty-first-century education revolution. Public virtual schools are the great equalizer, representing the true democratization of education. Students may go to a brick-and-mortar facility to receive an online education, and they may sit in a classroom with a teacher instructing them using a technology-based interactive curriculum. In all cases, the educational experience will be more engaging, more consistent, more individualized, and more effective. Most students will continue attending a brick-and-mortar school for the foreseeable future, so technology must be able to enter these schools. When it does, the improvements in student achievement will be ubiquitous.

While the power of full-time virtual learning is great, it should be noted that it is not for everyone. There are students for whom full-time virtual learning may not work due to environment or motivation issues. As online learning continues to evolve, it will become better at addressing challenges like these and will work for an increasing number of students.

Other Problems We Can Solve

Technology can combat the major problems facing the educational system in the United States and in countries throughout the world. Some of these problems will be solved using online courses, others will be solved using technology in a classroom, and still others will be solved using online learning in a supplemental fashion. Mobile technology and online learning will allow developing nations to leapfrog brick-and-mortar schools in the same way they skipped over landline telephones. The following sections identify these problems and describe how a well-crafted online program could solve them.

Summer Regression

It's well documented that American students fall behind during their summer vacations. The extended break from school is a throwback to the times when most American families resided on farms. Today, this applies to only about 2 percent of students.[6] While fixing the problem by moving to year-round schooling seems simple, there are cost implications to this change as well as powerful forces that are protective of this agrarian schedule.

Number of Farmers in the United States

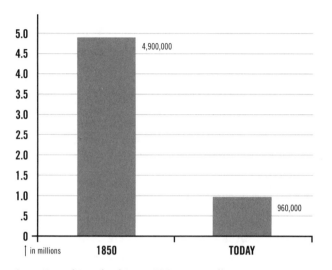

Source: National Agricultural Center, US Environmental Protection Agency.

When students return from their summer vacations, they are a few months behind where they were when the school year ended. This effect is even more acute in children who are at risk, likely because they are living in households where education is not the norm, and they do not attend summer camps as middle class children often do. Moreover, these children often come from families without an adult who is home during the day, which creates another set of worrisome issues.[7]

The academic component of the summer regression problem can be ameliorated with the same technologies used to promote academic mastery. Because servers can run twenty-four hours a day, students can go to school whenever they want to. Being freed from the traditional school schedule combats not just the summer regression problem but also the social promotion problem. Schools can move away from the agrarian calendar once and for all in an affordable manner, simultaneously solving the days-of-instruction problem and the credit recovery problem. With around-the-clock access to quality curriculum and online teachers, students can continue to learn regardless of the time of day or the time of year. Children can move ahead during the summer and even be exposed to subjects that the normal school year may not have time to offer. For example, online summer learning is allowing my own son to study multiple languages each year in high school. A student can complete an entire year of Chinese in just eight weeks during the summer! Imagine elementary school students learning a foreign language or high school students learning how to design a video game. The possibilities are endless, real, and here today for many students.

The Agrarian Calendar

I don't think there is any disputing that the number of days teachers spend in the classroom is insufficient. Today, American schools have forty fewer instructional days than do schools in Singapore and Korea. American students do not receive a great deal of instruction outside the classroom either, unlike the students in many Asian nations.[8]

It is not surprising that American students don't perform as well on international exams as these students in Asian nations do. Would professional athletes be as good if they practiced 25 percent less?

The gaps in classroom days are worrisome, particularly compared with Asia. According to comparative studies conducted by the Trends in International Mathematics and Science Study (TIMSS), Japanese students spent 243 days in the classroom, followed by 220 classroom days for students in South Korea.[9] It is no wonder that Asia is emerging as a global force. In several of these nations, families often spend more on education than they spend on housing. In Korea, the average child spends at least thirteen hours a day in the classroom when afterschool programs are included, according to the TIMSS data.[10] If you include the cram schools, where students receive extra, intense instruction for several hours per day after school, the difference in time spent learning is staggering. Interestingly, the efficiency of this time is much less than in

Finland, which performs at similar levels with far fewer hours.[11]

When one combines a quality education system with a low-tax, free-market economy, the economic transformation is almost unbelievable. Singapore, for example, has moved from a poor nation to one of the wealthiest nations in just forty years without an abundance of natural resources or obvious competitive advantages. The comparison with Jamaica in the following graph demonstrates the value Singapore has found with human capital strategies.

Singapore Success through Human Capital Strategies

	PER CAPITA GDP	
	1960	2011
SINGAPORE	$2,271	$41,953
JAMAICA	$2,255	$5,032

Source: Milken Institute (www.milkeninstitute.org).

Increasing time in the classroom is quite expensive, requiring a small increase in facility costs and an enormous increase in personal costs. With online education, however, teachers can continue to have their summers off while students learn at home or at designated online learning centers. Online courses could be offered to children during the summer that might push them ahead in language arts and mathematics or allow them to explore electives. These courses could be offered to students on an individualized basis for math and language arts. If the technology can increase productivity during the school year, the net cost of implementing this change could be zero. In many areas, families would be happy to pay for a quality (online) summer education, because they are often searching for ways to make certain that their students advance in the summer. Solving the summer regression problem also solves the agrarian calendar problem.

Time on Task

Altering the agrarian calendar will increase instructional time, but it's also important to lengthen the school day. Online education makes it possible for students to work on their courses for hours after the school day ends. If the software is powerful enough, only a few teachers are needed—for custodial reasons and to answer students' questions. K[12] has a remedial reading course designed to bring a child who is three years behind to grade level in only eighteen months and more than half the time requires no teacher. This is the power of technology—enabling integration of the various learning areas: school, afterschool, and home. This gives more focus—more time on task—to each student's academic program and allows them to work independently. If a child needs help in a certain area, that message can be sent (via email, of course) to the afterschool program and home at the same time. Imagine you're the parent of a fifth grader who did not master the science lesson that day. An email could be sent to you that allows you to work on the lesson at home with your child. The afterschool program could do the same thing. This integration of the home with the school and afterschool programs, using a technology-based curriculum with a daily mastery approach, will help ensure that students don't fall behind.

Creating a cost-effective model that lengthens school days and keeps children on the school campus will also reduce crime. Police studies have shown that most crime by minors is committed between 3 PM and 6 PM— precisely the hours when many children are unsupervised.[12] The value to our economy of using these hours for something productive is almost immeasurable—it will produce better human capital because fewer students go awry.

A technology-based curriculum also allows substitute teachers to be far more productive. Instead of being left at the mercy of substitute teaching corps who are handicapped when they are put into a classroom for one day, the schools will have online lesson plans with interactive instructional pieces for the substitute teachers' use.

The question for educators now is: how much do students learn for the amount of time they spend *trying* to learn? Maximizing this ratio should be the goal of curriculum designers, software engineers, states, districts, schools, teachers, students, and parents. I call this the Learning Efficiency Ratio (LER) and define it as:

$$\text{Learning Efficiency Ratio (LER)} = \text{Content mastered} / \text{time spent on task}$$

Creating the most educated child depends on maximizing the LER.[13] This ratio can be easily illustrated by looking at examples of inefficiency. For example, there are some animated software games that might be engaging, but kids who spend hours playing them learn just one thing. Spending hours to learn the letter *C* and its sound—when you can do it in ten minutes—is, at best, inefficient and, at worst, an obvious waste of time. This used to drive me crazy when I worked with my own children; it's a bad use of technology. (The chalkboard can also be a bad use of technology when many of the children in the class are failing with this instructional mode.)

Another extreme is just putting text on the web. For students, they might as well read a textbook. Putting text on a screen and thinking you have a web course is faulty and dangerous, as it gives people the wrong idea about online education. Web-based learning should be—and can be—better than reading a textbook and should, with today's technology, be better than sitting in a lecture hall. If the student needs to scroll down to see the text on the screen, it's worse than a textbook. The research is pretty clear that the comprehension rate for content you need to scroll down to see is dramatically less than the comprehension rate for material that is above the scroll line.[14]

Since its inception, K[12] has taken cognitive science and academic research quite seriously, incorporating both into our lessons. Understanding how the brain works is still in its infancy, and I expect every year that we will learn more about how the brain learns. High quality online learning will continue to incorporate this data to give the online learning experience an even higher LER than we can imagine today. As mentioned earlier, this efficiency concept can be applied to nations as PISA attempted to do when it looked at performance versus classroom hours.

Course Quality

The internet has simplified the task of creating content that meets state standards, delivers questions similar to those found on the specific state's assessments, and makes the lessons come alive. It also allows us to instantaneously go to the web and conduct research in hours that might have taken weeks twenty years ago. One of my children asked me the other day how I did homework before Google. It was certainly more difficult than it is today, when information on anything and everything is available in a matter of seconds.

While it may sound easy to deliver high quality lessons that meet state standards, it is not. Every state has its own standards, and state tests do not always align with those standards. Common Core State Standards should simplify this once they are implemented. However, even with these, there will still be some local state variation. Textbooks are only updated every few years and are not generally written to meet the standards of every state. Teachers in most of the country are forced to adapt their lessons to match their own standards, and some do this well while some do not. Even if the instruction is aligned to the standards, the types of questions on the state exam can be very different for almost identical standards. High teacher turnover compounds the problem. Matters are further complicated when states change their standards or assessments.

Using a web-based curriculum makes it far more possible to develop state-specific courses and change them when standards change. It also supports new teachers coming in and succeeding; they need to spend very little time—if any—doing lesson plans. Moreover, there can be access to lectures by engaging experts. Engaging speakers can be broadcast to millions, not just twenty or thirty. Flash animation, simulations, videos, and games—all offer the means for engaging students both at home and in the classroom.

This interactivity and engagement in courses will increase dramatically over the coming years. As students become more engaged as a result of rich media, they most likely will perform better. As courses become better and more specialized, online education will succeed with more and more students.

One of the big problems in schools is that different third-grade teachers within the same school cover different material, which is often not aligned with what fourth-grade and second-grade teachers are teaching. In educational jargon, this lack of coordinated curriculum within a grade level, and with grade levels above and below, shows a lack of horizontal and vertical articulation, and the deficit is one of the reasons students tend to have gaps in their education. With online curriculum and assessments, however, this problem disappears, significantly reducing the odds of a child missing something or having a bad year. Students who move between states will also have fewer problems than they have had historically when online curriculum is combined with Common Core Standards.

Teacher Shortage, Teacher Quality, and Teacher Pay

Two of the common misconceptions about online learning are that it supplants teachers and that teachers are not important. Technology doesn't replace teachers; it allows them to be more effective and better leveraged. The best teachers can be made available to thousands or even millions of children through online lectures, which leads to better-educated students. A significant part of the didactic instruction can be conducted through these sessions as well as through interactive animations, videos, simulations, and learning games. Collaborative learning software fosters peer-to-peer learning in much the same way that going to the library has done for college students for centuries. The teacher can then concentrate on helping struggling students or facilitating discussions that challenge the students. Teachers' roles may change, but teachers themselves will continue to play a central role in student learning—at a more effective and efficient level.

The end result of this increased leverage and effectiveness should be more highly paid teachers, because teachers will be serving more students. To see this, imagine a teacher who can now teach thirty students with the aid of technology as effectively as the same teacher could previously teach twenty students without. The amount of money being spent by taxpayers on that classroom in a public school (or by parents on a similar classroom in a private school) has now increased by 50 percent. A significant percentage of these funds would be best spent on improving teacher pay and performance.

Online learning programs could also address a teacher shortage that the US Department of Education says could run into the tens of thousands. As more students move to online classes, where higher ratios can be maintained, the number of teachers required will gradually decline. Indeed, with national teacher turnover rates and retirements averaging about 15 percent, the nation's public schools could accomplish a relatively seamless ramping up of online education simply by replacing teachers at a slower rate.[15] Online learning and improved teacher leverage is unlikely to result in any teacher layoffs ever.

The demand for specialized teachers in subjects such as advanced math, the sciences, and foreign languages will continue to outstrip supply, especially in rural areas. In many regions, there are no highly qualified physics teachers. Online learning will allow these qualified teachers to serve students regardless of where they live and level the playing field so that every student has access to an accomplished teacher in every subject.

This improvement in teacher productivity will come quite naturally. As students begin to learn in interactive classrooms with content designed for these classrooms, and with access to the online lessons at home and in afterschool programs, student achievement is destined to improve even as the student-to-teacher ratio increases. Additionally, teachers will have an array of tools to help them explain concepts and to administer and grade assessments.

The classroom experience will be more individualized, effective, and efficient as teachers concentrate on teaching. As technology allows students to master the material with less lecture time, teachers can then spend their time fostering higher-level discussions and helping students overcome obstacles. This is known as a flip classroom, which will become increasingly common. The improved learning experience will be more efficient and productive for both teachers and students, averting any teacher shortage while increasing teacher pay.

Student Motivation

One of the most consistent comments made by veteran teachers who have used new online software is that kids are much more engaged in learning. That engagement leads to quieter classrooms in which students pay attention to the teacher.

In today's world, student engagement is more important than ever. Outside of school, today's youth are accustomed to an extremely high level of stimuli (they are sometimes referred to as the Xbox generation). When I was a child, Pong was a big deal. Today's video games are so vivid that I sometimes think there is an actual football game on television when my sons are playing the latest football video game (in their allotted and limited video game time).

After a child has spent an evening or an entire weekend playing video games, listening to a teacher lecture in a classroom can be boring and difficult. One hundred years ago, the same lecture might have been preferred to working on a farm in 100-degree heat. Stated differently, the classroom has not changed much, but the distractions available to children have grown exponentially in both number and engagement. The good news is that educational software has traveled light years in sophistication in just the last ten years. While it does not yet match the bells and whistles of the latest computer games, the gap is closing—and will continue to close.

Computers can simulate chemical reactions at a molecular level, and these simulations can give children insights that they could never get from a textbook or a single experiment. Software can make quadratic equations visual and interactive. Technology can bring high quality Shakespeare productions into the learning process and make the nation's top experts accessible to every student and classroom.

Technology has the ability to make content more engaging through interaction and simulation—and this process is just in its infancy. In a decade, we will wonder how we ever learned without it in the same way my children wonder how we lived without mobile phones, Google, or MP3 players.

Online courses can even change a student's aspirations and motivations. By creating courses that help students find their pathway and understand the value of an education, the students become more motivated. K^{12} has a six-week online course called Finding Your Path. At the beginning of the course, 67 percent of the students said they planned to attend college. At the end of the course, 76 percent wanted to attend college. Perhaps every student in the world should take this course. With online learning, they can.

The Benefits of Video Games

Are there benefits to video games? This is one of the most common questions asked by parents, especially by parents whose children—usually boys—spend countless hours every day playing these games. Video game research is still in the early stages, but it appears that there are benefits to playing video games, along with some drawbacks. Recent studies have provided some evidence that playing video games can increase creativity and hand-eye coordination. There is also some evidence that video games could potentially increase aggressive behavior or obesity, but the evidence is mixed at best.

A 2011 study on information technology use and creativity done at Michigan State on about five hundred twelve-year-old students provided some evidence that students who play video games score higher on the Torrance Test of Creativity. The study showed a positive relationship between video game playing and creativity in girls and boys. Additionally, the results held for all types of video games, and the possible benefits of video games on hand-eye coordination were documented and discussed.[1]

Another study on surgeons confirms this. In a study conducted by Beth Israel Medical Center and the National Institute on Media and the Family at Iowa State University from May to August 2003, researchers examined if video game skills translate into surgical proficiency, and the study suggested that doctors who spent at least three hours a week playing video games made about 37 percent fewer mistakes in laparoscopic surgery and performed the task 27 percent faster than their counterparts who did not play video games. While the sample size was only thirty-three physicians, it seemed to indicate there might be benefits.[2]

Another study conducted by researchers from the Centre for Vision Research at York University indicated that when gaming experience was given to people who had not previously played video games, there was increased activity in the parietal cortex, which is usually associated with hand-eye coordination. Experienced gamers showed increased activity in the prefrontal cortex of the brain. By extensively practicing the visuomotor tasks associated with video game play, the gamers changed the way their brains handle such activities.[3] Visual processing may also be augmented. Researchers at the University of Rochester in New York demonstrated action video games can train the brain to better process certain visual information. A paper in the May 29 issue of *Nature* showed action video gamers can process visual information more quickly and track 30 percent more objects than those who don't play.[4]

On the negative side, many have suggested that video games can promote obesity or increase violence, but the relationship between these activities is weak and may not exist at all. Playing video games doesn't necessarily lead to a more sedentary lifestyle. Interestingly, there is not a strong correlation for watching television as well. With regard to violence, Lawrence Kutner and Cheryl Olson from Harvard Medical School suggested in *Grand Theft Childhood: The Surprising Truth about Violent Video Games*, no correlation exists between violence and video games.[5] They did show, however, that students who play mature-rated games were more likely to have been in a fight in the past year. Cause and effect were hard to separate.

Given all of this, what should parents do? Like so many things in life, it probably is better to do whatever in moderation. The real danger in video games seems to be doing them in exclusion of other activities, such as reading, writing, playing a musical instrument, or doing nonsedentary activities like athletics. Playing a few hours of video games per week may provide some benefits without detrimental effects. Just make sure children are doing all of the other things and treat the game like you would a movie. Choose one that is age appropriate and doesn't expose the child to things you do not want them exposed to. There is no evidence that violent games have more benefits than nonviolent ones, so why let your child play them? Other games are just as engaging and provide the same benefits.

While I don't claim to have the ultimate answer on this topic, and there is no magic number of hours, I limit my own children to weekends only and never more than two hours per weekend. They spend far more time reading than they spend playing video games—a rule I think every parent should follow, at least until research shows otherwise.

1. Linda A. Jackson et al., "Information Technology Use and Creativity: Findings from the Children and Technology Project," *Computers in Human Behavior* (2011), doi:10.1016/j.chb.2011.10.006
2. James C. Rosser et al., "Are Video Game Players Better at Laparoscopic Surgical Tasks?" Beth Israel Medical Center and National Institute on Media and the Family, Medicine Meets Virtual Reality Conference, (Newport Beach, CA, 2009).
3. Joshua A. Granek et al., "Extensive Video Game Experience Alters Cortical Networks for Complex Visuomotor Transformations," *Cortex* (2010), doi:10.1016/j.cortex.2009.10.009.
4. Daphne Bavelier et al., "Enhancing the Contrast Sensitivity Function through Action Video Game Playing," *Nature Neuroscience* (2009), doi:10.1038/nn.2296.
5. Lawrence Kutner and Cheryl Olson, *Grand Theft Childhood: The Surprising Truth about Violent Video Games and What Parents Can Do* (New York: Simon & Schuster, 2011).

Credit Recovery and Remediation

One of the major causes of students dropping out of school or not graduating is their inability to pass a required course. In most districts, a large number of students drop out after failing algebra multiple times. Since the course is usually only taught once a year, a failing grade dooms the student to repeating an entire year of school just to make up for a single failure. Few adolescents, especially those already struggling, have the patience to repeat a grade, and few school districts have the resources to provide private instruction to help the student recover quickly from the failure. Online education offers a solution—and one that could be even more effective than classroom teaching.

Since algebra is the single biggest point of failure, let's look at how credit recovery could work for this course. It's rare for students to fail algebra because they don't understand it; usually, they've failed fractions or other math skills that are necessary for algebra. Online learning can address this far more efficiently than can a classroom. It is possible to test students in algebra and quickly assess which concepts the student doesn't understand. Just as quickly, the software can then compile lessons that teach the algebraic concepts the student has mastered in addition to the basic math necessary to grasp these concepts. These lessons can include video lectures, interactive flash pieces, real-world examples to give relevance, and sample problem sets done on a whiteboard, with audio and perhaps a simulation game. Students could work through those lessons necessary to master the material and not waste their time with what they have already mastered. Even better, this customized, individualized course could be taken over the summer, with a teacher available to answer questions. This teacher-on-demand model is highly efficient when compared to today's lecture-a-day, one-size-and-pace-fits-all model. Customizing the curriculum to fit the individual student helps solve the dropout problem.

Students' deficiencies should be addressed before they ever take algebra—something online testing and learning tackles easily. As stated earlier, the reason many children fail algebra has nothing to do with algebra; they don't have the foundational math skills to do algebra. They might not understand negative numbers. So let's have the students who fail algebra take a diagnostic test that covers all the course skills necessary for algebra. Such a test would uncover precisely what students need to learn in order to master algebra, and the missing skills would likely be different for each student.

A significant motivating factor for students who have failed a subject is being able to move at their own pace and feel they have one-on-one access to the teacher. This customization doesn't mean that it's a free-for-all; students are still going through the pacing charts, but it's perfectly acceptable for them to work ahead. They aren't sitting around bored, waiting for everybody else. Often, gifted students who already know what the teacher is teaching become the behavioral problem because of boredom. Online education should create a learning environment where no student is ever bored. The self-paced nature and interactivity of high quality online learning create an engaging, individualized environment that allows students to not only complete classes more efficiently but also take individualized remedial programs.

The Achievement Gap

"The gaps between African Americans and whites are showing very few signs of closing," Michael T. Nettles, a senior vice president at the Educational Testing Service, said in a paper he presented at Columbia University.[16]

African American and Latino children have historically scored lower on standardized tests than have Caucasian and Asian American children. This is true in math, the language arts, and science. There are a number of possible explanations for this achievement gap, including school performance. The achievement gap cannot, however, be solely explained by the schools these children attend. African American and Latino students almost always achieve lower test scores when they are in the same schools. This appears to be true even when they have the same teachers.[17]

One noticeable exception to this is the Arkansas Virtual School. In 2006, when the results came back for this school, children of racial minorities outperformed their Caucasian counterparts. This was probably not a simple statistical anomaly; it was the product of learning in a colorblind environment where students were not stereotyped or plagued by the self-esteem and confidence issues associated with this approach. According to research conducted by Metis Associates from 2005–2006 (which was contracted by the state of Arkansas), the findings within the virtual school model were interpreted as follows:

1. Female students are associated with higher literacy performance than male students.
2. Minority students are associated with greater achievement in literacy than nonminority students.
3. Students with higher levels of engagement/interest in school (according to parents' perceptions) are associated with higher performance.[18]

The Arkansas Virtual School shows how online learning may reduce or eliminate the achievement gap. It also shows that statewide virtual schools give students (and their parents) the opportunity to escape underperforming schools and get a first-class education—a long-term benefit for students, parents, and the country in which they live. Lastly, it stated the obvious: the more students engage, the better they do.

The Disappearing Boys

If you can create engaging content, kids will spend more time learning. Rather than playing on their Xboxes, they'll be going to school on their Xboxes. And why not? They'll be learning high quality content while being fully engaged. If you can expand the total number of hours that children spend learning and increase the Learning Efficiency Ratio, they will learn more. They'll spend less time watching television and playing video games. They will still be learning what we believe are the essentials of a good education, but they will enjoy doing it.

This is why online education offers one of the best ways of solving the current "boys crisis." The issues with boys have become quite troubling. Boys are significantly more likely to be held back a grade than girls. By high school, almost two-thirds of all special education students are boys. Boys receive the majority of school suspensions and are much more likely than girls to be diagnosed with attention deficit disorder.

The great efforts that have been made to make schools more girl friendly—introducing new math and science curricula and teaching methods, for example—have worked wonders for girls but may have created a bigger problem for boys. More than ten years ago, the Providence College sociologist Cornelius Riordan observed that:

> Boys rather than girls are now on the short end of the gender gap in many secondary school outcomes. Currently, boys are less likely than girls to be in an academic (college preparatory) curriculum. They have lower educational and occupational expectations, have lower reading and writing test scores, and expect to complete their schooling at an earlier age.[19]

Some argue that the problem has gotten so far out of hand that schools have become antiboy. *Time* magazine devoted a recent cover to "The Myth About Boys." The writer painted a bleak picture of the state of boys in our current school system and recounted meeting Christina Hoff Sommers, author of *The War Against Boys*. David Von Drehle wrote:

> She ticked through a familiar but disturbing indictment. More boys than girls are in special education classes. More boys than girls are prescribed mood-managing drugs. This suggests to her (and others) that today's schools are built for girls, and boys are becoming misfits.[20]

While the reasons are likely complex and difficult to isolate, the fact is that boys are not performing nearly as well as girls. Boys have always seemed to have a harder time sitting in a "normal" classroom environment, and they are more addicted to video games than girls are.[21] After they play with Xboxes, which offer real-time global collaborative game playing, and other related distractions, we ask them to sit in classrooms, and many are bored to death. Schools need to be cognizant of these traits and use them to educate boys.

A recent study at Stanford, published in the *Journal of Psychiatric Research*, explained why boys are more addicted to video games than girls are. This study found that males have more activity in the mesocorticolimbic center when playing video games than females have. This is the region of the brain associated with reward and addiction. The researchers found that three brain structures—nucleus accumbens, amygdala, and orbitofrontal cortex—experienced greater activation in male brains than in female brains, and the activation increased as the boys experienced more success.[22] "These gender differences in the brain may help explain why males are more attracted to and more likely to become hooked on video games than females," said Allan Reiss, who headed up the research team.[23]

Are computer games the answer to the boys crisis? Not completely, but they have already proved to be able to engage students in a way that they haven't been engaged before. Many of today's games do little for students other than building motor reflexes. However, if the gaming is teaching algebra, calculus, engineering, science, and critical thinking skills, then it may not be a waste of time. Students may be able to take those stimulating game techniques and use them to promote very active thinking skills.

This generation is growing up as multimodality learners. This may or may not be a good thing, but it is likely here to stay. Children can be doing their homework while watching television, listening to their iPods, and instant messaging. We take these kids, who are highly engaged in an incredibly kinesthetic stimulating society, and all of a sudden ask them to go into a chalk-and-talk classroom. This is asking a great deal and seems to be even harder for boys than girls. The best online learning programs can provide the kind of interactive access to content that will get boys learning again by translating cognitive science into actual curriculum and lessons. Just as cognitive science has taught us that online lessons should avoid screens of scrolling text, it is teaching us more about how girls' and boys' brains are wired differently. Soon, technology-based learning will construct learning pathways and modalities to optimize each. In boys, this might mean taking advantage of that increased activity in the mesocorticolimbic center of the brain—in other words, making learning addictive.

The Dropout Crisis

The dropout rate in some of America's urban schools exceeds 50 percent.[24] This is one of the greatest problems facing the US education system, and it is a national embarrassment. In Detroit, less than 40 percent of high school freshmen graduate with a high school diploma four years later.[25] At a time when education is linked more than ever to high-wage employment, millions of children are leaving the US school system each year unprepared to enter the information-age workforce.

Many factors contribute to the high dropout rate. The nexus of poverty and broken families is a key contributor, and most students who will drop out are performing at significantly below their grade level when they enter high school. Many of these students leave high school to work and do not see the value in a high school education. By leaving high school early, however, they are greatly jeopardizing their ability to achieve upward mobility or even economic viability.

Online education can combat this problem. Its distinctive features—subject mastery, motivation, credit recovery, course selection, career preparation, and education anywhere, anytime, anyplace—can keep more students in school. K^{12} is seeing a large influx of twelfth graders enrolling in its virtual academies. When students enter the twelfth grade with less than three years of credit, most of them likely would have dropped out if not for virtual academies. In one western state, the overwhelming majority of seniors who matriculated this past fall were short on credits—many significantly short.

One of the primary problems with high school is that students enter having already fallen behind in grades K-8, and they have no understanding of the value of an education. Online learning can improve proficiency in elementary school and prepare children for high school, and the best way to fix high school is to fix K-8. The value of an education and how it transforms one's life and earning power needs to be communicated continuously, throughout a child's schooling. Many children in inner cities or rural areas don't know anyone with a college diploma, so they have little appreciation for a college education. Online learning can offer interactive sessions with engineers, scientists, lawyers, entrepreneurs, and CEOs, making school more engaging for students while showing them career paths that are possible with a college education.

Once technology-based learning allows students to enter high school close to grade level and with a desire to learn, online learning will create more flexibility and less boredom. Students will be able to choose from a greater variety of courses and choose when to take them. Students will no longer need to drop out of high school to work, since courses will be available around the clock.

Online education can prepare children regardless of their abilities and aspirations, college or otherwise. The current system is focused on getting students to college, but for any number of reasons, college may not be the right choice for every child. Many skilled professions do not require a college degree but still generate a decent living, like plumbing, electrical work, welding, etc. These jobs are not going to be outsourced overseas either. Students interested in one of these professions should come out of high school prepared for them, but a one-size-fits-all school system that doesn't convince students of the value of a high school degree virtually guarantees a high dropout rate.

As we saw with the passport school in Chicago, online education has the ability to bring back students who have already dropped out, allowing them to finish high school and to prepare for college. While all of them will not come back, there is no reason to believe a large number of dropouts would not return if a passport model existed in every city that could graduate the majority of those people who want back in.

Online education and technology-based education are powerful tools with which to combat the dropout problem. A rigorous K-8 education that inculcates the value of education—combined with ubiquitous flex academies, online academies, passport schools, the return of vocational education, the ability to work and go to school simultaneously, and specialized programs like teen mother programs—could potentially reduce the dropout rate by 20–30 percentage points, if not more.[26]

Costs

For fifty years, the cost of education has increased at a rate that outpaces inflation. Only in the past couple of years, when states cut education funding, has it increased more slowly than inflation. The increases are found at the K-12 level, though they are much more pronounced at the college level. A number of factors have driven this phenomenon: declining productivity, a lack of competition, and the expense associated with brick-and-mortar buildings.[27]

Technology-based learning can address these cost issues. As students move into virtual schools, these schools are funded at a lower per-pupil revenue than the traditional brick-and-mortar schools. The schools managed by K[12] generally receive less than 70 percent of the funding per child that taxpayers spend for the average pupil, according to

NCES statistics (though the level can vary dramatically from one state to another). A recent Cato study suggested that these numbers are understated and virtual schools might actually receive much less than 70 percent of per-pupil funding in a typical state.[28] Yet these schools deliver academic gains in most states that are similar to national norms, despite having adverse selection bias and not having complete control of the learning environment. Compared to traditional schools, the online schools we serve often receive less from the public funding streams in areas such as local property tax revenue, facilities, school lunch assistance, bond issues, and construction. Thus, even when a state delivers the same average daily attendance dollars to virtual schools, the absence of some or all of the other funding streams means the total funding for virtual education is much less on a per-pupil basis. This makes them a bargain for taxpayers.

K[12] is often asked what we believe to be the proper reimbursement level for virtual schools. This is a difficult question to answer because the cost structure varies dramatically from state to state, given different wage rates and other compliance issues. It is a fallacy to think that virtual schools should be dramatically less expensive than brick-and-mortar schools simply because they do not have buildings. Virtual schools spend dramatically *more* on student supplies than typical brick-and-mortar schools, and they provide the students with computers and other infrastructure. The sum of these additional costs is often equivalent to what some brick-and-mortar schools spend on facilities. Virtual schools also incur special education costs that are sometimes greater than those in brick-and-mortar schools, and they face additional costs associated with testing.

Employing certified teachers is the largest cost associated with operating a quality virtual school. Teachers may spend more time on individualized instruction and less time lecturing than those in a brick-and-mortar classroom, but they are extensively engaged in high quality virtual schools. K[12] alone employed close to five thousand teachers in 2012. According to a 2006 report, a full-time virtual program costs between $7,200 and $8,300 per student.[29] Today, according to NCES statistics, traditional brick-and-mortar schools spend an average of more than $10,000 per student, which is likely an understatement of what is actually spent.[30]

The biggest cost savings from online education will come not from placing children in full-time virtual schools, because only a small portion of the fifty-six million children in grades K-12 will be enrolled in such schools. The bigger savings will be derived from the productivity gains realized in the brick-and-mortar classrooms and blended environments that will address the impending teacher shortage.

According to a NCES public school expenditure report, salaries and benefits were $8,464 out of the $12,236 spent per child on public education in the 2007–2008 school year. Labor costs include teachers and every other adult employed in the system. If labor productivity (measured by labor dollars per child) could be increased by 20 percent, this could potentially save taxpayers close to $80 billion out of the $600 billion being spent on public K-12 education.[31]

Labor costs are not the only savings. The increase in productivity would obviate the need for much of the school construction that currently amounts to about $15 billion per year.[32] This savings would occur because we will need fewer new classrooms in K-8 as teacher leverage increases. Also, a higher percentage of students will go to school online full-time. Mandating that high school students take two courses per year online could significantly reduce the need to build new high schools in this country for quite some time. High schools could move from one to two or three shifts, essentially doubling or tripling capacity. Imagine a high school with eight periods and each student taking four courses on campus and two virtually. In cities like Los Angeles, comprehensive high schools can cost over $50 million. If each current high school can serve twice as many students, the need for new high schools is drastically cut.

Perhaps the largest benefit of technology-based education is not on the cost side of the equation at all but on the future GDP side. When only 70 percent of students are graduating from high school, the United States sacrifices enormous economic value since the reservoir of human capital is not being maximized. If the dropout rate could be reduced by 10 percentage points, the economic impact would be enormous. The Alliance for Excellent Education estimated in a March 2011 study that reducing the dropout rate by fifty-one thousand students would increase GDP by $681 million.[33] This represents only 4 percent of the dropouts each year. To realize these gains, the higher graduation rate must be achieved through an improvement in the educational system and an elevation in human capital—not simply by lowering the bar, which is often the temptation.

An antiquated agrarian calendar, high dropout rates, boys falling behind, teacher shortages—clearly, the major problems facing the educational system in the United States are going to require collaboration and innovation beyond virtual education alone to solve them. One doesn't have to believe that online education is the perfect solution in order to see how the computer, when well used, has the capacity to improve upon our current situation. I hope, however, that this book provides enough evidence of the benefits of online learning to eliminate some of the bias against it. Even better, I hope it proves that online learning is the multivitamin supplement that our public school system so desperately needs, now and in the future.

9

THE POWER OF TECHNOLOGY-BASED EDUCATION

*T*he number one rule of education technology is that the technology needs to be used appropriately, and K^{12} was founded with that in mind. K^{12} is an education company more than a technology company. Technology for technology's sake is not the point. When used inappropriately, it can become a diversion and actually impede student learning.

Online education is better thought of as technology-assisted education—"a customized educational program," as Lake Mills (Wisconsin) High School Principal Robert Gilpatrick said, that is "good for families and students, good for teachers, and—not least—good for the public school system itself."[1] In this way, technology should be viewed as the means to an education, not the ends. Technology will not deliver its maximum impact unless it is combined with the right content and the proper training of teachers, administrators, students, and parents.

Thus, the better the content and training, the better the outcomes.

Many educators complain that they installed interactive whiteboards in the classroom but haven't seen any improvement in student outcomes and that they have computers in every classroom but student learning hasn't improved. The lack of improvement shouldn't be a surprise. Unless technology has the right content, is fully integrated into the core instructional process, and is used correctly by teachers, it won't help much. It might actually hurt. Interactive whiteboards can serve as distractions, taking teachers and students down unproductive pathways. If technology is a distraction, then it will not benefit learning outcomes.

With that in mind, this chapter explores the power of online learning and the opportunities it creates to learn anytime and anywhere. Technology in education is not a tool for the future but a tool for *today*. It is not merely an experiment; it is an already proven solution that gets better and better every day.

The Power of Online Learning

There has never been a better time to be a student, and it's only going to get better. I envy today's youth and the opportunities that are available to them. Education is becoming more engaging, more individualized, and more accessible. Students have a wealth of choices—many more than any student in my generation could have imagined. As a result, there's no excuse for students to feel bored or left behind.

More than any other education stakeholder, today's students already live in the technology culture. In fact, most were born into it. Students have computers, iPods, iPads, cell phones, and digital cameras. They use Google to find information and Twitter to share it and spend hours on YouTube, Facebook, and Instagram. They do their homework while listening to their iPod, watching television, and chatting on video with their friends (sometimes simultaneously), multitasking without even realizing that they are doing it. Technology holds no particular novelty for them, being just part of their lives. To them, it has always existed, similar to the way most adults think about color television or a music player in the car.

When kids walk through the doors of their neighborhood school, they typically have to power down in the same way that passengers do during takeoffs and landings on an airplane. Cell phones and iPods are usually banned in classrooms, and more often than not, the teacher stands in front of—and writes on—a chalkboard. It's little wonder our schools sometimes have problems engaging students. They are competing with powerful distractions far more engaging than a one-way television broadcast.

Interactive Whiteboards Are the Beginning of the Classroom Transformation

A major problem facing students today is that the education system adopts technology slowly, if at all. Many still seem to think that using a PowerPoint presentation or writing a paper on a computer constitutes online learning.

A hallmark of online education is for the content to come alive on a computer screen or whiteboard through streaming video, simulations, and animation, while also being interactive and customized. These tools convey the content, and it's the content that's more important than anything else. Technology shouldn't replace content but engage students, enabling them to master content more quickly and to explore it in more depth. Put differently, technology helps to accelerate learning by creating a more in-depth learning experience in which content is customized and individualized. Teachers are not replaced; but are instead more engaging and more effective.

When high-tech classrooms first came into existence, computers were in the back of the room, and teachers didn't know what to do with them. Students played games on them, and sometimes they wrote papers, but there was little focus on whether the computer work was enlivening what they were already studying. Thus, it was often unclear whether the computers were fostering more learning. The surprise is not that computers failed to improve student outcomes—it's that anyone thought that they would. The result was great skepticism that technology would ever improve the educational system in a meaningful way.

When K^{12} set up its online learning system at Hunter Elementary, we installed interactive whiteboards. Teachers used the whiteboards to teach concepts by sharing instruction videos and animation pieces, as well as having the students come up to the board to solve problems. The model was still teacher-centric, with the instructor teaching the students in a synchronous manner. In general, teachers were more willing to implement this plan compared to a more individualized model because it did not require drastic changes in teacher behavior. Student engagement increased dramatically and discipline problems plunged. These children were growing up in a video game world where chalk-and-talk lectures didn't excite many of them; asking them to pay attention to stagnant lectures when their home life offered state-of-the-art video games was unrealistic. Even the simplest of technology, combined with well-trained teachers, made an enormous difference.

What makes the new technology so transformative is its interactivity, coupled with sophisticated software engines and engagement. Two-way interaction and real-time data exchange change everything. This allows education to be individualized for each student.

A few years ago, a lesson with engaging content could have been delivered using a multimedia PC, but there would have been a range of limitations: students could not take assessments that would be seen immediately by a teacher; papers could not be uploaded for grading almost instantaneously; students could not participate in group sessions that facilitate peer-to-peer interaction, nor could teachers lead Socratic discussions with students; and the software didn't exist to assess a student and then deliver a curriculum based on that assessment.

Today, all of these features are available to students, and that allows technology-based education to take a quantum leap beyond traditional education. It's possible for students to read online books and pose questions as they read. Consider the story of Alexander the Great and Bucephalus, the horse that Alexander was said to have won when he was ten, taming the animal by turning it toward the sun so it could not see its own shadow. On the screen—or the whiteboard—this story can be clicked on and heard read aloud as it comes alive with images that correspond to the storyline. Contrary to many education experts, second graders can learn real history. It just needs to be taught through engaging stories—something that online education is great at and getting better at doing all the time.

The internet has also allowed education companies and school districts to operate in new ways. In the preinternet era, it was extremely difficult to measure student outcomes and associate them with curriculum or content, and it was almost impossible to change or improve content in a short time period. Textbooks would often have information that was out of date by years, and they were rarely—if ever—changed as a result of student outcome data.

Contrast that with how K[12] works. K[12] not only writes our own source textbooks (which can be delivered in paper format, online format, eBook format, or put on mobile devices) but also creates the online lessons and interactive instructional pieces, trains the teachers, and helps manage the schools. This creates a holistic view of the entire education process—something unavailable previously—and enables prompt changes to maximize student achievement. For example, let's hypothesize that a group of students was having trouble adding fractions with unlike denominators. This would not be based on hearsay, or what K[12] thinks, but rather on actual assessment data. With this data, teachers can be trained on how to teach this concept more effectively and modify the online lesson accordingly (options include adding more video lectures, hands-on examples, animations, sample problems with solutions, and perhaps an interactive game). The source textbook can also be rewritten in a matter of months—not years—as part of an ongoing process of optimization.

In addition to modifying curriculum based on results, the curriculum can be updated continually as the world changes. For example, when Pluto was demoted from planetary status and reclassified, K^{12} updated its online lessons it within a few days. Yet it's almost certain that in five years, there will be textbooks that still have it misclassified. The curriculum can also be modified based on user feedback or suggestions. A teacher may have an idea for a better experiment or an innovative way to teach a particular lesson. Every lesson contains a feedback button, which is available to both students and teachers. K^{12} receives tens of thousands of suggestions each year and makes more than a thousand small changes to its curriculum annually. As the network of users grows, so does the power of user feedback.

Not only does curriculum benefit from this direct relationship with assessment results, but teacher training benefits as well. Two years ago, K^{12} conducted random control studies on the effect of teacher interventions with students and the types of interventions that work. Through these studies, we were able to understand the relationship between these teacher interventions and student outcomes. (It is very powerful for teachers to be able to see the results from these one-on-one sessions.) Then the findings were built into the professional development programs for teachers. One lesson we've learned is that teaching online takes certain skills, and some teachers are better prepared than others.

In online education, those teachers who are not succeeding can be identified very quickly and given more training; if they don't improve, they can be dismissed. By basing online teacher training programs on actual results, as opposed to theory or what worked in the classroom in earlier eras, student outcomes will benefit.

Returning to the interactive whiteboards, there is now significant doubt about whether these devices have improved student outcomes. The evidence suggests that they have not helped, which seems at odds with the K^{12} experience of significant student achievement gains in seven out of seven schools. While this might seem paradoxical, it is actually quite easy to explain. When interactive whiteboards are used with the core curriculum and teachers are trained to use the technology with the core curriculum, the results are quite positive. When the interactive whiteboards are used merely for supplementary or entertainment purposes, they often become a diversion that takes away from core learning and student achievement.

The Importance of the Curriculum

Horizontal and vertical articulation in the design of curricular content is fundamental. (This, you recall from chapter 8, refers to the consistency of curriculum taught within a grade level [horizontal] and with the grade levels above and below it [vertical].) In the absence of horizontal and vertical articulation, gaps in knowledge arise, and these inevitably create gaps in achievement. Consistency is very important, and technology fosters consistency in ways previously impossible. By having assessments delivered on a weekly or even a daily basis and coupling them with high quality lesson plans and interactive, engaging instructional activities, large school districts can monitor classrooms and ensure that each one is meeting certain benchmarks. This monitoring can be unobtrusive, and teachers don't have to be given a prepackaged script to follow every day. Teachers dislike highly scripted curriculum, and that's understandable. Technology gives teachers the tools to teach more effectively without stifling creativity.

Computers and the internet now allow schools to add a layer of integration that links the classroom, the afterschool program, and the home (not to mention the world). Computers and the internet also free teachers to teach and expand upon the lesson without fear that they have missed teaching something. This has given rise to a new social context where learning and social networks converge. K^{12} has built an internal social network into our learning system, and the usage is quite impressive. Parents, teachers, and students can all get to the content faster, which creates a feedback loop that reinforces the learning, and they can seamlessly interact with each other. Parents get daily updates on their child's progress and work with their child on any lessons that their child didn't master. With online curricula, parents can work with their child on exactly the same lesson the child did in class that day.

K^{12} curriculum is created by a team of experts that often involves more than ten people working for at least a year or more to create a single course. This team could include an instructional designer, a project manager, writers, editors, teachers, subject matter experts, a video crew, actors, animators, game designers, college professors, and assessment experts, and the courses are generally built to exceed most rigorous state standards.

The best online curriculum includes thousands of lessons and assessments in the core subjects of math, English/language arts, science, history, art, and music, along with a suite of electives, including foreign language and AP courses for high school students. This curriculum brings lessons to life with a rich mixture of online and offline teaching tools, including interactive animations, award-winning printed books with beautiful illustrations and narratives, original CDs and videos, and materials for hands-on experiments—and it does all of this without losing rigor. Online content should teach *more*, not less. A higher Learning Efficiency Ratio allows more learning to happen in less time; a mastery-based pedagogy and assessment system allows students and teachers to know what the expectations are and whether they were met. By following this protocol on a daily basis, it's possible to ensure that no student is left behind.

For instance, high quality online education can do simulations of chemical reactions in ways that textbooks could never deliver. It can bring the most engaging lecturers and experts in chemistry to the fifty people who can fit in a room in PS122 as well as all 1.2 million of New York City's public school children—and many more millions around the globe. If the online lesson can make high school students understand a chemical reaction by simulating what's happening at the molecular level and showing them a video of the experiment while they develop 3-D simulation models and listen to that world-class professor—*that's* a good use of technology. Again, online education should not duplicate what happens in the traditional classroom but should improve upon it.

Automaticity

Consider a very important concept in K-3 math: automaticity. Students learn "9 x 7 = 63" or "8 + 8 = 16"—they don't think about it, they simply memorize it. Though rote memorization has taken its lumps in recent years, it is absolutely essential to learning. It needs to be developed early, so that the children's minds are freed up to think about higher-level concepts—concepts that assume a child has mastered, through memorization, basic facts. More and more cognitive research proves E. D. Hirsch right: content counts.[2] Rote memorization has been vilified even though there is no evidence that shows it is detrimental. To the contrary, we now have evidence that the more facts people have at their disposal, the more creative they can be. It turns out the mind doesn't function as a computer with a microprocessor and a memory as previously thought but instead works more like an association engine.

Imagine improving automaticity with a computer game. The child is at the computer and an equation comes up, "8 + 8 = x," and she has to target it, circling 16. She gets faster and faster, and her score goes up. She's engaged, she's learning something essential, and she's memorizing it—an entirely constructive and beneficial use of technology.

Perhaps students can compete with students all over the world in this game. It certainly beats flashcards and just about any other method in wide use. At K^{12}, we built a race car game where children learn math facts by solving math problems as the race car goes around the track. I used this with my youngest child, and it was more effective and enjoyable for the both of us than were traditional arithmetic tools.

Another way to aid the learning process is to create characters—avatars—going through a course. Isaac Newton guides students through science, and immediately the children are more interested in science because they have an interesting character teaching them. Fortunately, teachers are not competing with the characters. The composites of these luminaries are there to grab the attention of students. This will help today's teachers outperform the best teachers of twenty years ago because they will be standing on the shoulders of giants. With great historical figures to aid students, the students become more culturally literate because they now are familiar with these figures.

Technology can bring great artworks into the home and make them come alive. One of my examples comes from my own son, who was a full-time kindergartner in the California Virtual Academy. One day, while at lunch with my mother, he saw a print on the wall and asked her if it was a Picasso. Sure enough, it was. Seeing great works online at an early age is forming the foundation of cultural literacy. When combining the study of masterpieces and the creation of original artwork using techniques from the masters, the byproduct is a first-class art curriculum. Many of the parents in our online schools send emails that they are enjoying learning art alongside their second graders. We receive similar letters regarding science and history.

When I first became involved in education, there was a philosophical debate about knowledge versus skills. The debate boiled down to whether students should be taught knowledge or taught skills (which served as a proxy for creative thinking and problem solving). I remember being quite confused by this debate. I wanted my children to have knowledge and skills and didn't quite understand why they had to compete with each other. It turns out they don't compete with each other at all; they are complementary.

One of the problems with education has been the long time period necessary to gather results from studies of what works and then the confusion over what the optimal outcome should be. This has led to few conclusive scientific studies and the introduction of major shifts in instructional practices (e.g., whole language learning, new math, constructivism, etc.) without evidence that they are better than what preceded them. The double-blind, randomized, placebo-controlled studies of the pharmaceutical industry have rarely been done in education. I'm optimistic that technology will change this in the near future, as it allows measurement to occur over very short durations. It will also allow for more controlled environments and more consistent instructional quality so the results will be more meaningful.

Online *Hamlet*

Learning online doesn't mean you're not reading Shakespeare. K^{12} courses, for instance, involve far more of the bard than what's taught in many brick-and-mortar schools. We're big believers in students reading actual books; they should be reading Shakespeare, *Oliver Twist*, the *Narrative of the Life of Frederick Douglass*, and other classics. Students in modern, technology-based education should have an appreciation for—and an understanding of—the past. Good online lessons bring this learning to life and help prompt thoughtful literary analysis.

I once spoke to a group of educators in Puerto Rico, and they didn't really understand how online education worked until I showed them some sample lessons. When they saw a flash animation piece that taught subtraction with regrouping, they could see how the step-by-step visualization could be helpful in the learning process. A light bulb went on—I could see it from the podium. They not only saw how it could work from a distance but how they could use it in their classrooms. Trepidation turned into enthusiasm as they suddenly realized online education would help them, not replace them. I also showed them a simple animated submarine that took students to various ocean depths to understand the life there. It was then obvious to all how this was better than a book and better than a lecture—but still just as rigorous.

Let's return to Shakespeare and see how even the great bard can be taught online.

It's one thing for students to read *Hamlet* and discuss it in the classroom. With online education, students still read *Hamlet*, but they can also study and interact with a high school teacher on *Hamlet* or they can interact with a nationally recognized *Hamlet* expert leading a video webcast for a thousand students (that can also be made available to thousands of other students).

Now we bring in Laurence Olivier's *Hamlet* and watch him perform. We digitize those performances and have experts talk about Olivier's interpretation. In online discussion forums, students chime in with their own observations and critiques.

How do students further understand/grasp *Hamlet*? One traditional option is to write an essay. In order to learn a lot of the facts about *Hamlet* more interactively, how about playing a game show version of *Hamlet* and competing with others around the country? Students can video themselves performing a soliloquy and share it with other Shakespeare enthusiasts. Students can also compete for the best reading or open up online discussion groups in the social network. They can also write an essay as they would do traditionally. In an online environment, the possibilities are endless.

The net effect of these different options is to enliven *Hamlet* in a way that is impossible in a traditional brick-and-mortar school. Technology has not eliminated the need to read *Hamlet*; it has made the reading of it a much more fulfilling experience.

Technology creates opportunities to interact with students from around the globe who are passionate about certain works of literature— or even entire disciplines. Peer-to-peer learning and engagement is no longer limited to the classroom; students can interact on a global basis around academic interests in the same way they now interact using Facebook. They can study together just as the previous generation used to do in the college library. However, today, the library is much bigger, always open, and quiet when you want it to be.

Global Clubs

The internet provides a way for like-minded people to come together without having to rely on geographic proximity. K^{12} students come from over eighty countries, and I expect that number will rise to more than one hundred countries in the near future.

Let's return to our Shakespeare example. A normal high school might have only a few students who are excited about Shakespeare or *Hamlet*. However, in the K^{12} system, there might be hundreds or even thousands of students who like Shakespeare. This makes for a much more dedicated and interesting club membership, with the ability to create literally hundreds of like-minded clubs. In the online world, there is an affinity group for anything a student seeks.

10

HOW TECHNOLOGY
CAN HELP YOU

Technology can be used to improve learning outcomes and open up paths in ways that were impossible just ten years ago. This chapter covers how the US school system's various stakeholders—parents, teachers, administrators, and policy makers—can benefit from online education.

Parents

Technology is giving parents the opportunity to be fully engaged in the education of their children to a degree that is without precedent in the history of American education. This involvement is possible if their children are homeschooled, in virtual school, or in a brick-and-mortar classroom. Also unprecedented is that public virtual schools have given many parents a choice of public schools regardless of where they live. Parents can now make sure that their children get a great education.

Online Virtual Academies

Parents in many states can now choose public school options that include full-time public virtual schools, public charter schools, hybrid schools, and full-time public schools that use technology effectively. Parents can also buy online courses, programs, assessments, and games to supplement their children's education. They can even enroll in full-time online private schools associated with selective universities like The George Washington University.

For parents who enroll their children in a K^{12} virtual academy or a hybrid school, computer programs now take care of many practical tasks. They do the scheduling and keep track of what your children have already studied and mastered. If a family is going on a vacation, for example, parents simply enter the dates they will be gone and the software adjusts so that it knows the next lesson to give and when to do so. The software will also identify a child's skill gaps and prescribe a curriculum to fill those gaps. The software also calculates a predicted end date so that the student is not taking too much time off. Students can sign up for online one-on-one tutoring sessions. Perhaps most valuable of all, students still have access to a teacher whenever they need one.

The teachers behind the scenes at virtual academies and hybrid schools are there to help with all of a child's educational needs. They keep track of planning and progress, and if a family or child seems to be falling behind, the teachers make sure to intervene and take care of any problems to get the child up to speed. Technology helps the parents of children attending a virtual academy with the potentially daunting task of organizing the school day, the school month, and the school year. If a child doesn't understand a topic, it's the teachers who prepare customized sessions online.

A Day in the Life of a K¹² Student

A K¹² student's day has a lot in common with that of a traditional student—a variety of subjects to study, a teacher to guide learning, workbook problems to solve, and so on—but a K¹² student also enjoys schooling that is individualized just for him or her, so school days are filled with much greater flexibility.

Take Sean, a fifth grader in a K¹² partner school—the public and tuition-free Ohio Virtual Academy (OHVA). His mom, Janet, is his Learning Coach. She modifies her son's daily schedule based on his progress through the individualized Learning Plan, which has been established by Sean's teacher and the school's staff, and takes into consideration his extracurricular activities, family outings, and so on.

Sean starts his school morning in the Learning Room, a corner of the family room that's been sectioned off and contains his desk and computer. Before he logs in to the K¹² Online School, Sean looks over the day's outline of lessons and subjects posted on the wall by his mother. First on the list is language arts, a subject that Janet typically schedules early each morning because Sean loves reading and writing. He completes the reading lesson and assessment quickly, boosting his confidence.

Janet remains close by. She spends about four to five hours a day guiding his lessons. As he moves to higher grades, Janet's time commitment will decrease.

Next up is math, which is sometimes a struggle for Sean. It can take him longer to complete a math lesson, but with OHVA, he can take the time he needs and not fall behind. The K¹² Math+ program for fifth graders features adaptive learning, which identifies specific problem areas for Sean, such as multiplying fractions. The online lesson steers Sean to additional practice where he needs it most.

On this morning, Sean's teacher has scheduled an interactive session with several students who need extra help with math. Sean and his mom log in to the special website where they can hear the teacher and see her demonstrate how to solve problems on a virtual blackboard. Sean can even virtually raise his hand to ask or answer questions.

After a productive morning, Sean's mom takes him to the local park, where they've arranged to meet for lunch with other parents and kids who attend OHVA.

In the afternoon, it's time for science. Sean's mom knows he loves doing experiments. In this day's lesson, he uses litmus paper to test a solution's acidic or basic properties. K^{12} has sent Sean's family the litmus paper and other materials needed for his science experiments, along with textbooks, workbooks, and many other hands-on school supplies. After his discoveries, Sean writes down the results and moves through the lesson's assessment.

History is the main subject that remains for the day, but Sean has a chance to try out for a local soccer team. So his mom has rescheduled the history lesson for late in the afternoon.

Although Sean enjoys the variety of lessons every day, other K^{12} students may choose to focus their day on just a couple of subjects at a time—Monday may be math and science day, for example. Since K^{12} is so flexible, and since every child learns differently, why not do what works best for each?

That's one of the key aspects of K^{12}: a school day centered on the student, rather than a student bound by the school day.

Source: K^{12} data and resources (www.k12.com).

If your neighborhood public school has taken the empowering plunge into an online environment, you'll be able to track your child's progress on a daily basis and work with your child to make sure they master the material. This kind of empowerment is a major part of what online education offers—it's not simply about choice but about how the opportunity to choose benefits your child's motivation to excel. There is also significant relief on the part of parents when they are given the opportunity to move to a new school without having to move to a new neighborhood or town—a major virtue of online education. You get yet another boost of empowerment by working one-on-one with your child.

The presence of choice creates a dynamic where schools now compete for customers—the parents and students. Public charter schools usually outperform traditional public schools in parent satisfaction, for example. When schools face competition, the byproduct is higher-quality education and better service.

The Importance of Early Literacy

Parents need to know the importance of third grade. Research shows that third-grade test scores are a key indicator of future success or failure. A recent study by the Annie E. Casey Foundation found that students who don't read proficiently by third grade are four times more likely to leave school without a diploma. The number is even higher for children in poverty.[1] Some rumors suggest that states use third-grade reading levels to predict the number of prison beds they need. While this information has not been substantiated to my knowledge, there is likely a correlation between education and incarceration, although poverty and population growth are clearly strong predictors as well.

It doesn't matter whether your child is in a traditional school or an online environment—third grade matters. Fortunately, you can plan ahead to make sure your child is on track in the early grades. Good online programs provide a curriculum to keep your child at grade level and provide the kind of assessments that tell you, as a parent, if your child is falling behind. If your child is not proficient by third grade, you can then take action, such as incorporating supplemental material, hiring a tutor, or changing schools.

Public schools must allow every parent the chance to ensure that their child achieves expected proficiency by third grade. The fact that many states have already empowered parents through charter school laws and public virtual charter schools is an encouraging sign.

In all cases it is critical that you not let your child fall behind, as the mathematics of remediation are downright frightening. The table below illustrates this point.

The Math of Remediation

When a student enters a school behind grade level, it can take years for that student to catch up. For example, an incoming seventh grader who is 2 years behind in math has been making about .7 years of growth every year since kindergarten. Even if the student starts making 1.5 years of growth each year after enrolling in our school, which would be a remarkable rate of acceleration, it will still take him 4 years to be proficient on the state tests.

Years Behind	Annual Growth Rate	Years to Proficiency
1	1.5	2
2	1.5	4
3	1.5	6
3	2.0	3
4	1.5	8
4	2.0	4

Source: K¹² data analysis and resources (www.k12.com).

A child who is two years behind grade level has been learning at the rate of approximately two-thirds of a year each year. In order to catch up in four years, he would have to accelerate to a year and a half per year—more than twice his previous rate of learning. Few children ever learn at this rate. If they did, they would enter college at fourteen years of age.

It Doesn't Matter Where You Live

With online schools, parents and children have a chance to escape a school that is not working for them and do so without requiring that they pack their bags and move. For the first time, every family has a choice—not just affluent families. The separation of education from geography is powerful and did not exist until online schools were created. This separation also makes education available in developing nations and creates a more competitive environment for all children as they enter the global workforce. Nations that do not currently have a brick-and-mortar education infrastructure will likely skip this altogether in the same way they have skipped landline phones.

Supplementing Your Child's Education Using Technology

For many families, enrolling your children in a full-time virtual academy may not be possible. Many states have not allowed a public virtual academy to be created yet, and families must have a custodial situation that makes enrollment possible in the first place. Online tutoring, learning games, and supplemental courses allow you to augment your child's education even when a full-time academy is not available.

Online education also makes it possible for high school students to take elective courses that are not offered at most high schools. As a parent, you can enroll your child in these online courses, and if the course is accredited, it can be applied to high school graduation requirements. Athletes, for example, can take courses over the summer and lighten their school load during the year so that they can spend more time practicing. Many high schools will soon offer the option of online elective courses free of charge to students. In fact, Utah and Iowa have recently passed legislation mandating that students are allowed to take online courses if they request to do so. Now every child in those states can study Chinese if they so desire. They are no longer limited by the local courses offered at their high school.

Foreign language fluency is a great opportunity for parents who want to enhance their children's future learning and job options. Job candidates who can speak multiple languages are in demand by companies that are global or are seeking to be global. I am trying to raise my own children to be conversant in English, Chinese, and Spanish, all of which I believe will give them an edge in the twenty-first century. In order to hear and speak a language properly, students should be hearing and speaking it prior to the age of ten, since cognitive research shows that the receptors in the brain for language acquisition shut off around that age. Online foreign language courses are now available for children starting at six. These courses are an excellent way to begin learning another language. Many high school students want to learn two foreign languages but rarely have the schedule flexibility to do so. These students can take the second foreign language online, either in the summer or during the school year.

With this in mind, K^{12} recently entered a joint venture with Middlebury College, one of the nation's most prestigious liberal arts colleges and perhaps the best college for foreign language instruction. This venture is building immersive foreign language courses using Middlebury's time-tested pedagogy.

For the parents of children in grades K-5, online education offers an excellent chance to get quality time with your children while giving them a leg up on their education. If you are worried that they are not getting enough math or language arts in their traditional school, working through an online course in these subjects almost guarantees they will be at grade level. Online courses are also available in history, science, art, and music and provide more content than any brick-and-mortar school could ever offer in a typical school day. I was at a soccer game recently when one of the children told me he was learning far more science in his online science course than he was receiving in his gifted-and-talented magnet school.

Teachers

Technology will make teachers' lives both easier and more productive. Planning lessons and completing administrative tasks will become automated so teachers can focus on teaching. Teachers who want to modify the automated lesson plans will be able to do so, but great lessons will come prepackaged. Online content will make delivering lessons more manageable, more engaging, and more effective. Differentiated instruction and the long-awaited classroom of one will become realities. The internet has also made communication with parents much more seamless.

Yet teachers are sometimes apprehensive about technology for a variety of reasons. From a poll conducted by the Sloan Consortium for K[12], we know that the major concern of teachers about online learning is not "technological infrastructure" but "concerns about course quality."[2] This concern is probably valid for some of the courses that are being passed off as online education, but the best courses today are more than sufficient, as they provide the necessary rigor and interactivity.

While technology does many wonderful things for instructors and students, it cannot yet do the actual teaching. The human element is essential, especially for the younger children, whose work is done mostly offline: learning handwriting, doing hands-on science experiments, and working with manipulatives. In the early years, the best online learning involves offline activities. Young children need to understand that these numerals and other abstract signs represent the manipulation of concrete quantities. They should join physical objects, blocks, titles, or figurines so that they understand what that "3 + 2" on the paper means. This can be done using simulations, but there are benefits to the tactile experience for young children and the tangible representations of abstract qualities.

Think of the online learning process as a triangle. At the pinnacle of the triangle is the student. At another vertex of the triangle is the curriculum and learning systems: all the materials, workbooks, and assessments. Finally, at the third vertex is the teacher. The teacher may include, in addition to the traditional pedagogue, parents or tutors who also assist in the learning process, just as they would in the classroom or at home. If the family at home can't provide that, other options include community groups, church groups, volunteer tutors, and the like. Human engagement is still key to the learning process. Interestingly, one of the counterintuitive findings with virtual schools is that many teachers feel they have closer relationships with students in the virtual schools than they previously had in the classroom. The closer the relationship, the higher degree of student engagement.

Technology Is Not the Enemy

Teachers have a hard job—the hardest in education. There's nothing easy about teaching at a school like Hunter Elementary in Philadelphia, implementing a performance-based, online education program while outside forces try to take it away. No doubt it will take time for some teachers and political forces to understand that computer technology, far from being the enemy, frees teachers from many of the more mundane tasks of teaching.

At a time when the computer is in every industry, from car manufacturing to corn harvesting and banking, the favored teaching technology in our schools remains pencils and paper, bound books, and the chalkboard. To improve education, this needs to change. Teachers are talented individuals dedicated to helping students learn; when you are given the right tools, the effect is transformative. Indeed, I have seen this transformation take place in every school that has adopted our technology and curriculum, seeing evidence in public virtual academies and even more so in private virtual academies—especially when the student fully engages.

It Works

Students in virtual schools all over the country—and in the few online-enabled brick-and-mortar schools—are succeeding. Many students are finding that online schooling, because of its flexibility and engaging curriculum, is a great fit for them. We now have data that shows that students are gaining more than one year for every year they are with us.[3]

Measuring the academics of virtual schools is quite complex. Most states use criterion-referenced tests to determine proficiency, measuring a point in time as opposed to student gains. For schools that are not growing and have low student turnover, these tests can serve as an indicator of school performance—albeit not a perfect one. For public virtual schools, these measures are almost useless because nearly 50 percent of their students each year are new due to high growth rates and brief durations of attendance (many students stay one year or less). As public virtual schools have grown, the percentage of students who come to K[12] behind grade level has increased, as has the number of students living in poverty.

Given these facts, the average test scores of a school could decrease even though the school is doing a better job. This occurs because the academic preparedness of the entering class is worse than the previous class—a familiar situation for many of the large public virtual schools. A recent study showed that the majority of students entering the California Virtual Academy (in grades five or higher) needed to make more than one year of progress in one year in order to reach proficiency. With such a high percentage of new students and the majority of these students entering significantly behind grade level, it is not surprising to see low proficiency scores in pubic virtual schools.

A much better way to measure student performance is to use adaptive gains testing, which is starting to be used by many states. These tests are designed to measure gains rather than to interpret gains from criterion-referenced tests. The latter tests, which measure proficiency, may not measure gains accurately because they are interpreting them for two different tests. They also encourage selectively teaching to test, rather than to remediate a student by teaching the student from their starting point the skills that are most important.

Fortunately, there are now nationally normed adaptive tests, one of which K^{12} has been using to monitor learning in public virtual academies. It works to both evaluate the academic progress of these schools and to monitor how improvements in curriculum and teaching translate into student gains. The results are quite promising. In the following graphs, we can see how the gains in online schools served by K^{12} compare to national norms.

The learning gains were above the national norm in most grades. While these tests are not perfect, they are a solid indicator that K^{12}-affiliated virtual schools are delivering good results. Additionally, the power of individualized learning can be seen in the International Academy, which faces fewer issues with student engagement because parents have paid tuition for this school. The growth scores in this school are quite impressive in both math and language arts, as can be seen in the graphs on the following page.

Given that such a large number of students are new to the school, and there is normally a transition effect with students when they change schools, gains are likely to improve with student tenure. With the introduction of Common Core State Standards and hopefully adaptive testing of the standards, measuring student gains and improving student learning will become more accurate.

Susan Patrick of iNACOL (International Association for K-12 Online Learning) said:

> If we can train our teachers to teach using online courses and online resources and allow for the personalization and the customized learning for each kid, you get the best of both

K¹² Gains Relative to the 2010–2011 Scantron Norm Group

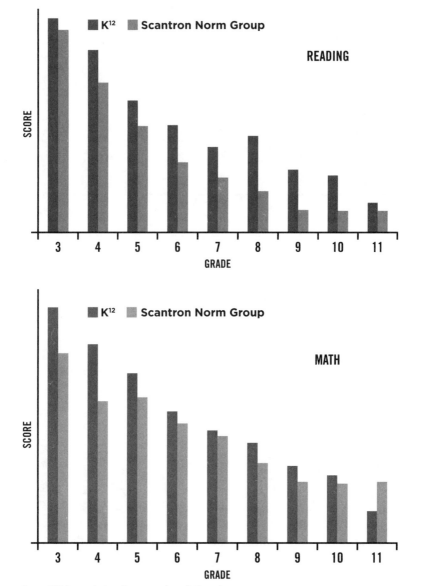

Source: K¹² data analysis and resources (www.k12.com).

K¹² International Academy Scantron Performance
Series Gains Compared to the National Norm
Group in Reading, School Year 2010-2011

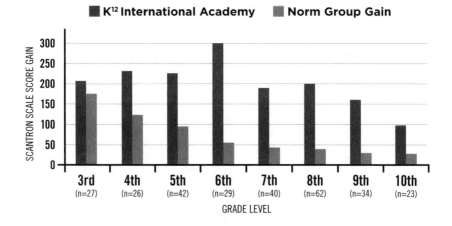

K¹² International Academy Scantron Performance
Series Gains Compared to the National Norm
Group in Math, School Year 2010-2011

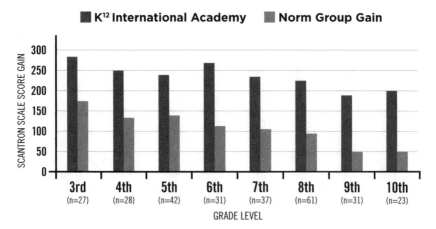

Source: K¹² data analysis and resources (www.k12.com).

worlds. You come into a face-to-face environment; the student can go at his own pace, get help when he needs it—a whole different experience for student support and student instruction. It really is personalizing learning for every kid."[4]

It is also liberating for the teacher.

Understanding Where a Child Is

As all teachers understand, knowing what children know is essential to knowing what to teach them. Computers can provide some of the best assessment measures available, making a teacher's job much easier. In addition to these assessments, the computer can provide a remediation plan and deliver the lessons. The ability to develop individually calibrated curriculum materials that can be used to remediate children will mean teachers can more effectively bring students up to proficiency. As this curriculum becomes more sophisticated, teachers will be able to work with more students. Students can work through these programs afterschool, on breaks, and at home.

Additionally, teachers can measure how much a child advances in a year by assessing at the beginning of the year and at the end. Today, teachers who inherit students who are far below grade level are penalized by the existing assessment system. Individualized curriculum based on assessment results allows teachers to bring these children up to grade level more quickly. Ideally, state assessment systems will soon allow states to measure student gains rather than absolute scores so that teachers of at-risk students will not be unfairly penalized. Teacher performance pay systems will not work until student gains can be accurately measured.

To do this correctly, computer-based adaptive tests will be required. In high school, for example, growth measures are probably not the best measure, especially for students who have been in several different schools. End-of-year mastery level tests in the core subjects may be a better measure. It is crucial that education measurements become more sophisticated so that schools can be properly evaluated. The right tests will aid in teachers with evaluating adaptive gains.

Technology can deliver tremendous benefits to teachers, including rigorous lessons with interactive pieces and built-in assessments. *Every teacher should have access to these tools, they can be the spark that ignites dramatic improvement in the quality of schools in the United States and throughout the world.*

• • •

New job opportunities are becoming available for teachers. They can now teach in virtual schools, which gives them more flexibility. K^{12} schools have multiple applications for every teaching job. Teachers love teaching in virtual schools and find, often to their surprise, that they have closer relationships with their students in a virtual school than they had in the classroom and that class discipline is no longer an issue. Additionally, teachers have more time to focus on each child and provide individualized instruction.

Administrators

Many administrators ask why education "reform" never seems to deliver on its promise. There are many great schools and stories of school turn-arounds, but nothing seems to be replicable.

"We have poured more money into schools, hired more teachers to reduce class size, expanded professional development, and retained more experienced teachers," said Jay Greene, professor of education reform at the University of Arkansas.[5] Adjusting for inflation, Greene pointed out that per-pupil spending over the past three decades has doubled. America spends more money on education than any industrialized country, with little improvement in results. The student–teacher ratio in high schools dropped from 21.7 students per teacher in 1960 to 14.1 by 1999.[6] In New York City, as Sol Stern, a Manhattan Institute scholar pointed out, there were 1.2 million students and 40,000 teachers in 1970; in 2000 there were 1.2 million students and 80,000 teachers.[7] Across the country, wrote Greene, "the percentage of teachers holding master's or doctoral degrees has more than doubled, from 27.5 percent in 1971 to 56.8 percent in 2001." In addition, "the average teacher in 2001 had fourteen years of experience compared with eight years of experience in 1971." It was an impressive—and expensive—effort. "But none of it has worked," said Greene.[8]

What's a Good Administrator to Do?

In the "war" over education reform, administrators are the ones standing squarely in the middle of the battlefield, taking fire from all sides. You take orders from boards of education and state and federal bureaucrats and tiptoe through a minefield of labor relations contracts. Often the school boards themselves are heavily influenced by the labor unions, which creates an almost impossible dynamic. Despite all this, administrators must manage staff and are expected to be leaders, delivering results.

In the end, though, progress in education is held back not by the students, the teachers, the unions, or the administrators; the real handicap is the system itself. In a meeting with students at a K[12] school, one girl in the sixth grade told me that her mother concluded that she was two years behind in math and language arts. She had been getting Bs or better in her classes, which should indicate she was at grade level, but it seemed those grades were just for showing up.

A good administrator would create options for students to prevent this scenario from ever happening. These options would include ensuring students have access to an online school and probably using technology-based curriculum to deliver rigorous content. Obviously, it would be in the administrator's best interests to have these options as part of your regular education program. A student with that aptitude and motivation—and a parent who cares—should never be behind, in any school. Furthermore, a large differential between a student's grades and test scores should be automatically flagged. Technology-based curriculum and linked assessment offer the ability to surgically repair skill gaps and remediate in a more efficient way.

The unfortunate reality is that administrators have to be proactive because many parents are disengaged from the education of their children. One of the teachers at our school in Indiana told me that in her previous school, she sent out letters to forty-six parents whose children were failing and received only one call back. This makes an educator's job much tougher.

Part of the problem is that in towns once dominated by auto manufacturing, school never really mattered. People could find employment at the plant without a diploma and lead a satisfactory lifestyle. Today those plants are all consolidating, if not closing down, but the parents in these communities don't always see the link between education and prosperity, or at least opportunity. Until this link is made, students view education as drudgery rather than a gift. It is extraordinary to see the change in students' motivation, however, once they make this connection (as demonstrated at dropout recovery schools, for example).

Technology can meet this challenge by fostering communication between administrators and parents and by making it easier to track student progress and continue lessons/learning at home. Inactive parents should not be—and cannot be—an excuse for failure. Technology can also make that link. When parents are not engaged, schools need to do everything possible to engage them. If still unsuccessful, online counseling services and courses on finding pathways need to be used to guide these students. Once the student has a goal, learning is much more relevant.

Getting—and Keeping—Good Data

One of the obstacles to long-term education reform is frequent changes in the leadership of schools and school districts. Many staff members are reluctant to devote themselves to implementing reforms when they know these reforms are likely to be reversed the moment new leadership arrives. In Philadelphia, the union didn't resist K[12] at Hunter; the teachers supported us almost unanimously. The aversion to private, for-profit management companies didn't exist at the school level or district level. However, within two years, politics had changed, and Hunter and many other schools in the city lost their private company partners.[9] We have also seen frequent incidents where leadership changes and then the districts change programs—even when their existing programs were working.

The best weapon in this particular fight is data. Schools have never had a better supply of it, and many administrators are drowning in it. Today's school administrators need to become masters of data management, as it will allow you to drive real change, especially academic achievement. Data-driven instruction will continue to increase as more useful, intuitive software becomes available. Schools of education need to do more training on data analysis and how it relates to instructional practices.

Being proficient with data doesn't mean you need to be able take a computer apart or know how many angels can dance on the head of a two-gigahertz processor. However, it does mean you need to understand data and its benefits. It also means knowing the difference between good data and bad, between significant facts and insignificant ones. As Jay Greene has quipped, "The plural of 'anecdote' is not 'data.'"[10]

Successful online learning requires a commitment to integrate computer technology into a school's culture as much as it requires installing hardware in its classrooms. Administrators must understand exactly what's under the hood: a technology that not only organizes staffing assignments and streamlines bookkeeping but also delivers a class on *Hamlet* to tenth graders. The software and content is far more important than the hardware. Many schools have recently rushed to buy tablet devices without really understanding what the benefits are.

Policy Makers

Education policy makers need to understand that the online education train has left the station, and if you aren't on it, you should start running. Online education is no longer experimental or in the pilot stage. States and districts that are not using it are risking that their students will be left behind. Technology allows policy makers to do things in a way that scales so that you can help every child in your state.

Clayton Christensen, coauthor of *Disrupting Class*, predicted that half of all high school classes will be taught online by 2019.[11] Today many academics and experts believe online education will become a major part of education. In higher education, it already has. The creation of MOOCs (Massive Open Online Courses) by the most prestigious universities will accelerate the acceptance of online learning.

Resisting the Pressure to Dumb It Down

A significant challenge for policy makers is holding the line on quality. Technology is no magic bullet and will not solve any education problem if it is misused. Poor content and technology that distracts from the learning process can be pernicious. Unfortunately, there has been a great deal of this.

Community activists have told me that kids appear to be doing fine in high school because they are getting decent grades. However, because the standards or expectations have been dumbed down, students sometimes receive a B for just showing up. This allows them to graduate even though they can't pass any kind of test or qualify for any job. This is why graduation tests are usually not at the twelfth-grade level—if they exist at all. Graduation rates can be increased by making school easier, but this helps no one.

Many students don't see the value of graduating from high school. They rightly wonder if it's a good investment of time and energy, given that there's no guarantee they will attend college or possess the skills to pass a civil service exam or become a welder, plumber, or electrician upon graduation. A high school diploma needs to mean something to employers and colleges. It is a national tragedy when 50 percent of the students entering high school in many of the nation's fifty largest school districts do not graduate.[12] The tragedy grows when one evaluates how low the bar was set for some of the 50 percent who received diplomas and how few are prepared for university.

In February 2009, the *New York Times* ran a story about a new study of college students in which "researchers at the University of California, Irvine, found that a third of the students surveyed said that they expected Bs just for attending lectures, and 40 percent said they deserved a B for completing the required reading."[13] A University of Maryland English professor told the *Times*, "I tell my classes that if they just do what they are supposed to do and meet the standard requirements, that they will earn a C. That is the default grade. They see the default grade as an A."[14]

Let's Stop Teaching to the Test and Playing Catch Up
The pressure on K[12] (and many public schools) to dumb down comes in a different way. K[12]'s curriculum is significantly more demanding and comprehensive than what's found in most states and their standards, so we are encouraged to teach only what's on the test—and not any more than that. This comes from the desire to perform well on state tests, which are often a flawed measure of schools to begin with.

Achieving good test scores becomes a challenge for rapidly growing schools in that they need to fix others' mistakes. For example, many students matriculating in the virtual schools are two and three grade levels behind, while the students who start virtual schooling in the early grades are doing better. As previously mentioned, it takes a great deal to remediate a child who is two years behind; even great schools cannot do it in one year.

When schools don't have to fix someone else's mistakes, their test scores are much improved, but schools are not measured this way. Students who have been with the school six months are measured and weighted the same as students who have been with the school five years. Clearly, this makes no sense. Policies need to encourage other schools that can remediate these students to take them, but most of the incentives created when static test scores are used (as opposed to valid gains tests) are to not take children who are significantly behind grade level. *These* are the children who need a different school the most, however, because their previous school has not worked for them. Adaptive testing for K-8 and end-of-course exams for high schools are much better solutions.

Education accountability either needs to move to a gains measure or, at a minimum, exempt students who are in their first two years in the school. A similar problem exists with high school graduation rates. We can't realistically expect a charter school to graduate a student who transfers in his senior year and is missing two years of credits to graduate in one year. While this sounds irrational, it is now happening in many states. Unfortunately, holding the new school responsible to graduate these children on time creates every incentive to not accept these children. Thus, policies need to avoid unintended consequences and make sure that schools have incentives to accept and remediate these children. If not, the number of high school dropouts will continue to grow.

In many virtual schools, the majority of students who transfer into the school in eleventh or twelfth grade are credit deficient and likely close to dropping out. Virtual school was their last option. The good news is that virtual schools, if given the opportunity to offer a fifth year of instruction, are capable of graduating many of these students who would otherwise be dropouts. The flexibility of virtual schools is tailor-made for these students who drop out to work. In addition, the societal value of this dropout prevention and the eventual contribution to the GDP is enormous.

Luddites Anonymous

John Holdren, who led the development of the K[12] curriculum, said:

> When I joined this organization I was probably the closest thing to a Luddite that they had known. I did not know a lot about technology myself. I have become more conversant about it over the years, thanks to my extremely creative colleagues showing me what could be done. As a good ol'-fashioned book person and classroom person, I was wary of the extent to which people might naively think, 'Oh, the computer will teach it.' We know that's not true.[15]

Yes, "good ol' books" are a great piece of technology in their own way and should be preserved in schools. However, it is possible to simulate certain images on a computer screen—in science, for example—that can't be simulated in a textbook. Yes, there is much to be gained by a second or third grader planting a seed and monitoring its growth, but we can also do animation on the computer screen, showing the names of the different parts of the plant and, in fifteen seconds, the six different stages of growth. Technology is taking learning to places that chalkboards simply can't go, and it is only going to get better at doing it.

Dealing with the Stakeholders for the Status Quo

Education groups who don't like change often feel threatened by the advance of technology in education, but policy makers can play a key role in leading these groups to better understand the benefits of technology.

What makes computer technology so exciting is that it allows things to be done at scale while benefiting every one of the education constituencies.

There have been other eureka moments in American history that have ultimately spurred our education system to be the best in the world: Horace Mann and the challenge of the industrial revolution (nineteenth century), the immigration school (early twentieth century), the Sputnik scare (1950s), and the *Nation at Risk* report (1983). The twentieth century was not only "the American century" but a century when America created the most inclusive and comprehensive public school system in the world.

As many nations have now caught up, America can recapture its educational greatness with the right catalyst for change. The challenge is in channeling the change so it results in effective student outcomes and students who are more prepared for success in the global workplace. Technology-enabled individualization of education is the key.

Building On Past Accomplishments—and Failures

For the past two generations, the growth rate of spending on education has greatly exceeded the inflation rate, but the higher spending has not translated to higher performance. One positive byproduct of the higher spending has been more testing and measurement, and it has laid a data trail that is perfect for computers. Many parents, too, have taken up the mantra of improving their children's learning prospects, buying tutoring for their kids at levels that they never spent before.

The problem is not a lack of effort; many good ideas exist. Teachers unions, for example, have insisted on smaller class sizes, better professional development for teachers, and more highly qualified teachers. Charter schools and voucher programs are another force for improvement, as they introduce competition, and curriculum has improved. Foundations such as Annenberg and Gates have allocated billions to public education. The Gates Foundation alone has spent billions of dollars on education in recent years (it plans to spend billions more over the next five to seven years).[16] Unfortunately, despite these focused efforts by smart, well-funded groups, the student achievement needle hasn't moved that much.

All of these reforms (charter schools, class sizes, smaller schools, more professional development) have only had a limited impact on the US educational system because they are not scalable. Some of the reforms, like class size reduction, are simply too expensive to implement with any hope of meaningful improvement. As Frederick Hess noted in his book, *When Research Matters: How Scholarship Influences Education Policy*, "the merits of reducing class size show mixed results."[17] Hess reminded us that California attempted to implement a statewide class size reduction policy "famously and recklessly" in 1996: the state spent $771 million in the first year and $1.7 billion annually through 2005.[18]

When the RAND Corporation studied the program's impact on student achievement, it found none. As Hess said, California policy makers were "inattentive to the nuances of the previous research findings," among other things. He also pointed out that the need for new teachers to achieve class size reduction created "a voracious appetite for new teachers and diluted teacher quality."[19] Class size reductions are very expensive and, in general, have not produced clean, significant positive outcomes. Certainly not enough to justify the cost.

The wise use of technology can increase class size and improve academic outcomes, and students are anxious to use it. Harris Interactive conducted a survey for NACOL in 2006 (now iNACOL) and found that 47 percent of middle school and high school students wanted to take an online course.[20] The current fiscal crisis is accelerating this trend. States need to get more for their money or educational quality will suffer, as budgets have been cut almost everywhere. Online courses, technology-rich classes, public virtual schools, and online summer schools all offer states a chance to improve outcomes without spending more money.

The need—and the demand—is far outstripping the supply. Policy makers should seize the opportunity presented by a public appetite for online learning and provide the resources to satisfy it, or at least avoid subverting it. Technology-based education costs less; therefore no additional resources will be required. In fact, *less* will be required. All policy makers need to do is remove the barriers that are limiting its use.

• • •

Bringing schools into the twenty-first century will yield positive results and cost benefits. States and nations that use technology to improve education will build a significant competitive advantage as they create a better workforce, more prepared for the jobs of the next century. Schools will produce students who are more technologically savvy, and the students will have more course options than are available in schools today. With individualized education, each student will vastly improve his or her likelihood of success. These changes combined with the explosion of online education at the postsecondary level will clearly enrich human capital and therefore wealth.

11

THE NEED FOR COMPETITION
AND THE PRIVATE SECTOR

*T*he two most important ingredients in the recipe for a healthy and wealthy society are an outstanding education system and a vibrant market economy, and the premium attached to an education grows every year. In 1950, 80 percent of the jobs in the United States were unskilled labor. Today less than 20 percent of jobs are unskilled labor.[1]

There has been a shift from a world where wealth was dependent on physical and financial capital to one where knowledge is the primary source of wealth creation. This shift has magnified the need for an education to the point where an uneducated person will soon find it difficult to participate in the legal economy. The globalization of markets, combined with the shift toward a knowledge-based economy, has also resulted in increased income disparities, with well-educated countries typically much richer than countries with low levels of education. In a global, knowledge-based economy, the income gap increases as the premium for skills is made even larger, since those skills can be leveraged over the entire world. The past combination of the world's first and best education system with a market-based economy made the United States the greatest wealth- and job-creation engine the world had ever seen.

The fact that a vibrant market economy is needed for wealth creation is evident from examining market-based economies versus nonmarket economies. Comparing the United States with Cuba makes the point, though there are countless other examples. I remember visiting Eastern Europe and being stunned by the wealth differences between it and Western Europe. One only needed to compare the two Germanys to see the difference.

Competition driven by markets drives efficiency and innovation. Ayn Rand described this process in her classic work, *The Fountainhead*:

> Throughout the centuries, there were men who took first steps down new roads armed with nothing but their own vision. Their goals differed, but they all had this in common: that the step was first, the road new, the vision unborrowed, and the response they received—hatred. The great creators—the thinkers, the artists, the scientists, the inventors—stood alone against the men of their time. Every great new thought was opposed. Every great new invention was denounced. The first motor was considered foolish. The first airplane was considered impossible. The power loom was considered vicious. Anesthesia was considered sinful. But the men of unborrowed vision went ahead. They fought, they suffered, and they paid. But they won.[2]

Rand perfectly captured innovation and the entrepreneur: "the step was first, the road new, the vision unborrowed." As Barack Obama said in his first inaugural address, "It has been the risk takers, the doers, the makers of things—some celebrated, but more often men and women obscure in their labor—who have carried us up the long, rugged path toward prosperity and freedom."[3]

The entrepreneurial spirit gave us the standard of living we have today, and it also gave us a public education system with the potential to once again be the best in the world. I agree with Claudia Goldin and Lawrence Katz, authors of *The Race Between Education and Technology*, that America's drive to harness human capital in the first half of the twentieth century by creating universal public education was a significant contributor to the country's huge economic advantage in the world.[4] The GI Bill added to that advantage and was part of the development of the world's best university system, which unlike the K-12 system, has experienced significant competition. In many ways, the GI bill was a college voucher system—a competitive dynamic the K-12 system has not had. In fact, until public charter schools and public online virtual academies, there was almost no competition in the K–12 system.

As the country's educational advantage diminishes, so will its economic advantage. The free enterprise system may emerge as the tool that restores America's educational leadership.

Improving Traditional Schools

The keys to improving anything are competition and innovation, which are not uncorrelated. Just as competition creates more innovation and wealth in the commercial sector, it can—and should—create more value and efficiency in the education sector. There is already intense competition within the private school system, with good results. One of the strengths of America's university system is the competition among private and public universities for students, professors, etc. We need more competition within the public K-12 school system, but historically there has been almost no competition within public school systems. As most families could not move easily or afford private schools, they essentially had one choice for their schooling. Until public charter schools, private groups could not create public schools. Show me an institution where the customers have nowhere else to go and I will show you an institution with poor customer service and no innovation.

As President Obama and Secretary of Education Duncan have recognized, public charter schools are a big part of that competitive dynamic. The public charter school movement has grown to include over five thousand schools and over two million students in more than forty states and the District of Columbia.[5] While these numbers seem large, they represent a tiny part of the traditional public school system, where there are over ninety-four thousand public K–12 schools and over fifty-five million students.[6] Most students do not have access to a charter school, either because there isn't one near them or because the one near them is completely full and has a long waiting list.

In those locales where public charters exist—and in some cities, like Washington, DC, New Orleans, Louisiana, and Albany, New York, where they have managed to achieve impressive market share—students enjoy a choice of schools, which puts pressure on traditional schools to compete for those students. Assuming that parents prefer good schools to bad, such competition will invariably lead to schools that are academically better and that give parents and students better customer service. Parents whose children are in public charter schools are usually more satisfied with their school.

There is significant debate about whether public charter schools outperform traditional public schools on an academic basis. Selection bias makes this a difficult question to answer, as does the lack of excellent gains testing. There have been extensive studies of the Philadelphia school district, which suggest that competition lifted both public schools and charter schools but not that one outperformed the other. We will certainly see more research in the near future as charter schools continue to grow, although it is less certain that the research will ever yield a clear answer that can be applied to all charter schools. It should not be surprising that some charter schools outperform the traditional public school and that others do not. This is what we would expect.

One thing that should never be forgotten is that parents choose for their children to be in that public charter school. Students are not forced to attend the school as so many of the students in traditional public schools are, and public charter schools cannot deny students. If people are choosing to attend a school when they have other options available, the school is likely doing something right; it's literally the school's business to educate and attract students. If students are not attracted to the school, it will cease to exist. This quality mechanism does not exist for most traditional public schools. This alone makes public charter schools more likely than traditional public schools to serve the needs of their students.

While the academic performance of public charter schools is still being evaluated, one thing is clear: they outperform traditional public schools on parent/student satisfaction and on cost efficiency. They generally deliver similar performance while being funded at a much lower per-student funding level, especially when one considers all of the funds that go to noncharter public schools. It's actually quite impressive that charter schools are able to achieve similar results with significantly lower funding. If a state ever wanted to massively reduce its taxpayer budget, it could make all schools public charter schools. Outcomes would be similar or better and education spending would be reduced by 20 to 50 percent depending on the state.

However, their comparative performance is not the relevant point. Charters should be viewed as an incubator for innovation so that the traditional public school system can absorb the best practices from successful public charter schools. They should also be considered for their economic efficiency, which includes technology-based curriculum and online education. School districts that successfully adopt the best practices from the most successful schools, using the private sector appropriately, will be successful. Furthermore, the competitive dynamic created by public charter schools should make all schools better, particularly when parents have good information by which to make their decision.

The Entrepreneurial Experience in Education

Before suggesting how traditional public schools can compete with public charters, or even with private schools, let me describe the creation of K^{12}. It was created with a simple vision: that the advent of the internet would allow every child in the world to receive a world-class education regardless of their economic situation or their geographic location. For the first time in human history, education could be separated from geography. K^{12} was set up as a for-profit company because the size of the vision required an entity that would be able to scale by hiring world-class talent, innovating continually, and having access to financial capital. Additionally, it would require people working long hours in order to for the enterprise to succeed. Content creation and software development would become increasingly more costly, and it had to be done as efficiently as possible. K^{12} was designed to be a start-up no different than the start-ups that are created in Silicon Valley every year. This start-up, however, had the additional benefit of a powerful social mission, which was even more powerful than the traditional business vision that has powered most successful start-ups.

Almost every person hired the first two years worked in either curriculum or technology development. We had to ensure a quality product before expanding, because we had a higher calling than just building a business: we were here to educate children—and not just a few children but all children. We tried to follow the example set by the founder of a leading pharmaceutical firm, Merck:

We try never to forget that medicine is for the people. It is not for the profits. The profits follow, and if we have remembered that, they have never failed to appear. The better we have remembered it, the larger they have been.[7]

If you substitute *education* for *medicine* in that quote, it captures the founding culture of K[12]—and the culture that still exists today. To ensure that every possible dollar went into the product, I led nearly every business function myself for the first year. We attracted talented people like John Holdren, who was in charge of research and publications at the Core Knowledge Foundation. I remember meeting John and thinking, *He will forget more about curriculum when he goes to sleep each night than most experts ever knew.* We also attracted veteran educators and amazingly smart young people who could do just about anything.[8]

We had to create all of the systems necessary to deliver education, including the content management systems, learning management systems, and student information systems. Though we considered the idea of buying them, we couldn't afford them, and they were ill suited for our purpose anyway. Fortunately, necessity is the mother of all innovation, and we were able to rapidly build the systems we needed. We hired great software engineers, and they did what had to be done in a very short period of time. When we look back at it, we sometimes can't believe they built the systems they did so quickly.

We also had a schedule, promising our investors and prospective clients that we would open our first school in the fall of 2001. Since we didn't hire the first employees until early 2000, we didn't have much time. This is another advantage of the competitive, entrepreneurial model: it attracts dedicated staff who are not bound by union rules or a fixed schedule, so they can work as hard as it takes to get the job done. Extraordinary things are accomplished by extraordinary people exerting extraordinary effort, and that was K[12] in the six months prior to launch.

Maria Szalay, a talented MBA hired in 2001, recalled,

> Our timeline to the launch was pretty crazy. We were trying
> to figure out what exactly we were building while we were
> building it. No one took vacations that first year. During that
> summer, almost no one had a day off, including Saturdays and
> Sundays. We were sleeping on futons in the office. We were
> here seven days a week, twenty hours per day.[9]

No entity other than a start-up could have made that deadline with
the limited resources we had.[10]

Amazingly, we got it done. Our Pennsylvania Virtual Charter School,
with six hundred students (K-2 only) opened under budget and on time,
and the Colorado Virtual Academy opened up three weeks later. The
first day of school was a week before 9/11. With our headquarters being
located near the Pentagon, this had a traumatic effect on all of us. Many
of the materials we shipped were in transit and ended up being more
than a week late in several instances. Our customers were incredibly
understanding, and calling them to explain the late shipments gave me a
good insight into the need for public virtual education and how we were
helping students.

We were taking the sweat equity, the toil, and the entrepreneurship
that we've seen in the biotech, software, and semiconductor sectors and
bringing it to education. A normal entity—a nonprofit, a school district,
or a government—can rarely drive people like that for so long. Few nonprofits have ever scaled because they can't hire at the same rate nor can
they remove employees who are not working out as quickly. In addition,
nonprofits don't usually have the same access to capital.

Since that launch, K[12] has been fueled by a constant drive to improve
every year. One of my senior executives, who came from a large school
district, once told me, "You make more improvements at K[12] in a
year than we made at my previous district in a decade." In essence,

wehad brought the intelligent innovations and drive of Silicon Valley to education.

The fund-raising process for K[12] says a great deal about the outside perception of America's education system. Every education-oriented venture capitalist turned down the opportunity to invest in K[12] in its early stage because they didn't believe the public education system would adopt virtual learning in the next decade, if ever, and they didn't believe a private company would be allowed to participate in the process when it did come. The fact that this skepticism came from people who take risks for a living and understand the power of entrepreneurship speaks volumes about the perception—and reality—of innovation and speed (or lack thereof) in America's education system. Their skepticism made us drive even harder, because the skeptics were correct in one way: without private companies driving the change, the growth rate in online education in public schools would have been much slower.

The Fear of Competition and the Relentless Drive to Innovate

The frenetic pace of a start-up or fast-growing technology company is not for everyone, but finding ways to harness the energy, human capital, and incentives of free enterprise is critical to improving America's schools.

When the then Ohio governor Ted Strickland was faced with a severe economic downturn and the need for an austere budget, he used his 2009 State of the State address to encourage the citizens of the Buckeye State to "focus our energies and resources on the programs most vital to our future." And, he said, "First on that list is education."[11]

The governor devoted more than half of his hour-long speech to outlining an ambitious set of goals and plans for improving the state's education system, all based on "a very simple premise," he said—that "we should design our education system around what works."[12]

Strickland said that "simply tinkering with centuries-old education practices will not prepare Ohio's children for success in college, in the workplace, or in life." The state had to "build our education system anew."[13] The key question is how is this best accomplished.

This renovation will likely be done most efficiently and effectively by partnerships with the private sector. If an education is high quality, why would it possibly matter if the entity was for-profit or not-for-profit? I have always thought it is the end product that matters. There are no mandates that the state government buy computers or software from nonprofit entities. They don't mandate that the state buy their vehicles from nonprofit companies. Why should education be different?

For-profit companies have five advantages over nonprofit entities:

1. Scale   2. Sustainability   3. Innovation
4. Efficiency 5. Capital Access

There is no logical reason why the tax status of an entity should matter—especially when resistance to entrepreneurial innovation adversely affects the education of children. Any argument saying otherwise is indefensible and dangerous. If anything, government should be encouraging for-profit entities to be involved, as there is such strong need for effectiveness, efficiency, and innovation—not to mention the need for organizations that can scale. It amazes me that anyone would even consider excluding for-profit companies from managing schools.

Public versus Private: Where "V" is for Virtue

Many individuals have made statements that private companies should not be involved in public education, and these are almost synonymous with "we do not want change." Why does it matter who runs the charter school? We all know the inputs (the cost) and the outputs (educational gains and student/family satisfaction). Amazingly, only Arizona currently allows charter schools to be for-profit companies, and the reason has nothing to do with the education of children. The primary reason why charter schools must be nonprofit is that the opposition to educational choice knows that the movement will progress much more slowly if they forbid these schools to be for-profit companies that can scale, innovate, and drive efficiency. Nonprofit schools that rely on outside philanthropy to operate are not likely to scale and can be difficult to sustain, given the fiscal restraints. When a model is more expensive than the current system, we question that it can be scaled.

There was a movement against public virtual schools in Ohio shortly after *Businessweek* magazine and the nonprofit GreatSchools program named the Ohio Virtual Academy, a school managed by K[12], the Parent's Choice top public school in Ohio.[14] Even though the school is great for the kids and great for the parents, some opposed it.

To be fair, such inconsistency on the part of public officials comes from a long tradition of us versus them related to the public and private sectors—and from the "competition" for scarce public funds. This antagonism derives from a fundamental misunderstanding of the nature of public schools and the role of the private sector in serving and challenging them. Anyone who has worked in public education knows that competitive juices fill the classroom and the boardroom. Teachers work hard, and the pride of their work—to have their children succeed, to improve, to beat the neighboring district—is palpable.

However, the collaboration that fosters private-sector efficiency is often overlooked. It may be cutthroat on one level, but on another it depends on trust and cooperation. A food-service business contracts with a trucking company to deliver the goods; a bank has an agreement with a cleaning company to wash its floors and windows. Many hire accountants to do our books and taxes. The government doesn't build fighter jets but contracts with the private sector to design and build them instead. Without large defense contractors, military technology would not be nearly as advanced as it is.

There is much that a public service agency can do that a private company cannot do—and vice versa. What the public sector does best is provide funding, equity, and transparency in delivering services; what the private sector provides is expertise, private capital, and the ability to create good services—curriculum, research and development, building and infrastructure—in large numbers and efficiently.

Private enterprise has played a vital role in making America a prosperous, innovative nation. The private sector can attract capital and employ it far more efficiently and effectively than the public sector. Unlike private sector companies, government entities are not necessarily driven to continually improve. The best public sector organizations harness the proficiencies of the private sector to be more effective. The US military is a great example of this. Its ability to partner with for-profit technology companies has allowed it to be far more advanced than the militaries of other nations.

The right mix of collaborative and competitive relationships will put American schools on the path to higher student achievement. The Soviet economy and almost all communist economies have collapsed or languished because they lack the innovation and productivity that the private sector provides. Unfortunately, our school system suffers to some degree from the same deficiencies. These deficiencies were fine when no other nations were competing, but those days are over. Competition and private sector partnerships can only help.

Competition Lifts All Boats

When America's public school system soared—through much of the twentieth century—it had little competition from other countries. The schoolhouse doors were open to almost everyone in a wave of human capital expansion that had no peer, but it's easy to be the best when no one else is competing.

The US automobile industry is a perfect example. When the Japanese and the Koreans started producing cars for the US market, the shortcomings of the US auto industry were exposed. In the absence of foreign competition, the innovation and productivity of the American auto companies didn't matter because they all possessed many of the same weaknesses, and the oligopolistic industry structure allowed the extra costs to be passed on to the consumer. When competition from more efficient competitors came, their weaknesses were exposed and they were forced to improve.

The American education system, like our auto industry, has lost some of its advantages—not because it has declined significantly but in large part because others are doing better. This relative decline couldn't happen at a worse time, as the health of nations is now determined by human capital, not physical capital, and our students have to compete with students from all over the world. Unfortunately, most of the public schools still operate without competition.

The first place where competition in education was attempted on a large scale was Philadelphia. In 2002, for-profit companies and not-for-profit entities were given the opportunity to manage schools. When the RAND Corporation released a study suggesting that privately managed schools in Philadelphia did no better than publicly managed schools, it completely missed the point of competition.[15] Caroline Hoxby, a Harvard education economist, pointed out that all the city's schools had improved dramatically. The reason, concluded Hoxby, was competition.[16]

Competition and charter schools did exactly what they were supposed to do: spur public schools to higher achievement. Comparing the results of Philadelphia schools relative to other urban districts leaves little doubt that competition works well. With better information and more dynamic capacity, it could work even better.

Drilling down even further in Philadelphia, researchers Paul

Peterson and Matthew Chingos, writing in the research journal *Education Next*, found that for-profit school management companies in Philadelphia outperformed district-managed schools in math but not in reading, that nonprofit management organizations fell short of district schools in both reading and math instruction, and that "for-profits outperform nonprofits in both subjects."[17]

In Philadelphia, Paul Vallas saw the private companies as part of a mix of improvement strategies and was sorry to see them go. As it turns out, as Hoxby, Peterson, Chingos, and others discovered, he was right. The diverse provider model works. "They took the worst schools and they made gains comparable to the district as a whole," commented Vallas. "The bottom line is...the EMOs [education management organizations] proved to be a good whipping boy.... The rest of the school district benefited from a substantial amount of additional money the EMOs brought in."[18]

These conclusions should not be surprising. For-profit entities were designed to continually improve themselves and deliver better results for the customer. Their existence is dependent on being more efficient and more effective. In the case of schools, this means higher customer satisfaction and better academic gains. If the education system is centered on students, there will be cries for *more* for-profit companies in the system, not fewer.

Opponents of for-profit entities often suggest that the profits at these companies result in less money for the students. The evidence is suggesting otherwise. For-profit schools are on average more efficient, and they deliver more value for students.[19] If taxpayers are paying a fixed amount of dollars per pupil, they should not choose a vendor based on whether it is organized as a for-profit entity or a nonprofit entity; they should choose the vendor based on the value it delivers for students. In education, this is all that should matter, and the preference of students and families should not be ignored.

The *Wisconsin State Journal* clearly understood this when it editorialized, "Critics of virtual schools worry that for-profit companies are muscling into modern schooling, although the reason this is a problem is never really stated other than a general vilification of capitalism." It went on to say, "The business model puts customers first—and those customers, Wisconsin families, so far are very satisfied with the product."[20]

Public/Private Partnerships Work

Arkansas has been a pioneer of state-sponsored online education. Its Department of Education, in partnership with K[12], established the Arkansas Virtual School (ARVS) in 2003 as a pilot program for students in grades K-8.

We did the same in Indiana in 2007, when the Ball State University Office of Charter Schools approved the Indiana Virtual Charter School (INVCS). The INVCS joined fifteen other statewide public virtual schools that provided students with the K[12] learning program (including schools in Utah, Pennsylvania, Minnesota, and Arizona) and three public virtual schools in major cities (Washington, DC, and Chicago). By the fall of 2012, K[12] alone was serving over 125,000 students in public virtual schools and delivering over one million courses.

K[12] also partners with thousands of traditional school districts to offer public virtual school programs and courses for students who reside inside their district boundaries but cannot take classes in the school building. We have also developed an innovative science curriculum and a suite of education tools designed for classroom instruction in those public schools. As of 2011, K[12] was serving almost five hundred thousand students in some capacity. When districts actively seek technology-based solutions to help them educate their students, then we can be confident that education transformation is underway.

Such partnerships are both creative and productive. At the 250-pupil Mildred Jackson Elementary School in rural Hughes, Arkansas, for example, nine out of ten pupils qualify for free and reduced-price school lunches. The school could never afford to offer the curriculum that the teachers found in wealthier communities. However, thanks to a federal grant awarded to the Arkansas Department of Education, the school purchased the K[12] online science program, which included outfitting three classrooms at each of four grade levels (K-3) with books, workbooks, science kits, software, assessments, and training for teachers.

"They made us modern," said Principal Janice Base, who had been working in the Delta region for almost thirty years. "They gave us an opportunity. When you are in the Delta, you feel kind of like a stepchild."[21]

Scale Matters

The reason government doesn't build personal computers is the same reason it shouldn't be building school management systems: scale. The government is not likely to efficiently build a worldclass school that can be replicated across the entire country; private companies are better suited for doing that. An individual public school system doesn't have the resources nor the expertise to do the research and development necessary to bring the technological revolution to scale. Even if the public school system could do this, it is not set up to continually innovate and do it efficiently. The rate of change makes technology different than things like physical campuses.

The private sector does all of these things and does them well. One only needs to look at what has happened in telephony over the past twenty years to see the power of the private sector and the power of competition on innovation: dramatic improvements and reduced costs.

"The half-life of technology is very short, as we know," said James Konantz, a senior vice president at K[12] who was formerly the assistant superintendent for Secondary School Redesign and Charter School Development of the Los Angeles Unified School District. "You can spend a whole lot of money and get technology, but by the time education changes enough for you to use it, the half-life of the technology is gone, and suddenly, you can't do what you wanted to do. The technology is not up to the standards you need for new programs."[22]

The difficulty and expense of creating high quality online programs was recognized by Randall Greenway and Gregg Vanourek when they wrote:

Developing a high quality, virtual learning program can be costly, requiring sizable capital expenditures on computers and servers, sophisticated instructional design (the orchestration of different media—such as online, offline, images, sound—into compelling and effective instructional units), content and course-management systems (computer systems for organizing and facilitating collaboration on documents and courses), course-authoring platforms (computer frameworks that allow educators to "post" their courses onto the internet), and beta and usability testing (publishing test versions of new programs to eliminate the "bugs" and ensure ease of use). Too many programs simply load lessons developed for the traditional classroom directly onto the web without making adjustments for the new delivery methods; they are not likely to advance the "state of the art." We cannot assume that excellent teaching translates directly into excellent online lesson development.[23]

Clearly, there is a need for scale providers of online education as the technology and content become more complex. Government entities are not prepared to continually change and keep up with these improvements. Furthermore, school districts do not have the scale of capital necessary for even the first stage of investment. Even when they could succeed in creating a good product, the product is obsolete within a decade—and sometimes much faster—as the marketplace and technology continue to evolve. In order to justify the investment, it must be spread over millions of students. Private companies that serve thousands of districts are perfect to deal with the size of the investment and need for rapid change.

Ineffective Efforts of Class Size Reduction

The inability to bring good reforms to scale is one reason the reform movement has had a limited effect on school improvement. The aforementioned class size reduction, for instance, which is one of the most popular reforms of the last twenty years, is also one of the most expensive and least productive. It has been implemented in several states and the benefits are minimal with regard to academic achievement, yet the cost to taxpayers has been billions of dollars.

"If you want to raise achievement in reading of fourth graders, you have two ways to do it," said Dale Mann, managing director of Interactive, Inc., and a professor emeritus of Teachers College, Columbia University. "You can dramatically reduce class size, or you can put effective computer-mediated instruction before the children. One of them costs eight times more than the other, and it's the one that every school board loves and that all teacher unions think is terrific; which is, hire more adults."[24]

As school systems have hired more and more adults, they have faced a teacher shortage, often leading them to hire lower-quality teachers. With technology, it is possible to increase student–teacher ratios without jeopardizing student performance. This would also make it possible to raise teacher wages, since their productivity would increase, and also provide teachers with more classroom resources. Higher wages are also likely to attract more teachers and retain more teachers. The higher productivity creates many secondary benefits.

Doubling Capacity

Technology potentially solves the brick-and-mortar scale problem. The United States spends tens of billions of dollars per year building facilities—most of which are unnecessary. For example, urban high schools in cities like Los Angeles can now cost over $100 million to build.[25] A few high schools in Los Angeles have cost significantly more than this. The capacity of a school can be doubled for *much* less money. Having students take one or two classes online makes it possible for a school to offer eight periods instead of six, at more or less the same cost. This allows schools to double-shift the school day to serve twice as many students, not only eliminating the cost of constructing new schools but also reducing the cost of maintaining facilities and the costs of instruction and extracurricular activities, because the students can be amalgamated (meaning fuller classes and larger sports teams).

Creating the Best Teacher—for Everyone

Many states and districts across the country are facing teacher shortages in specific subjects and geographic areas. Math and science teachers seem to be particularly scarce in some areas. Recruiting, hiring, and training these teachers is an enormous challenge.

Technology can meet this challenge because it reduces the number of teachers schools need to hire. By using lectures from the very best teachers and creating simulations, games, and videos to help teach the concepts, each of the teachers hired will be more effective and able to serve more kids. Increased productivity allows for higher wages, thus simplifying recruiting.

Going forward, one of the keys to unlocking progress will be teaching teachers how to use technology, but this is far easier today than it was ten years ago. Young teachers, particularly, are already technology proficient; they just need to learn how to use it in the instructional process. Once teachers learn how to use technology properly, teaching becomes simpler with the vast number of tools online that can aid in instruction and classroom communication. Lessons can come alive. The very best lecturers can now reach millions of students at the click of a mouse, and *everyone* can hear the great algebra teacher explain a difficult concept. Technology standardizes the curriculum without limiting the teacher's ability to expand upon the lesson and make sure every student is engaged and mastering the lesson.

"Every one of those things increases the delivery of schooling substantially," said Dale Mann. "None of that happens without digital, because with digital, you can guarantee the fidelity of the message and you can guarantee the participation and involvement of the learner."[26]

Ramping Up Technology R&D

Sixty billion dollars of education spending has been devoted to technology over the past twenty-five years, but there have been no significant improvements in achievement.[27]

This is a significant sum of money, but given that more than $550 billion is spent on education *every year*, it is a pittance. The United States spends less than four tenths of 1 percent on computers and computer systems—barely enough to put a computer or two in a classroom and just enough to ensure that those computers will be unused.[28] Few successful companies devote less than half of one percent to their technology budget.

Teachers need devices like SMART Boards, they need to be trained on how to use them, and they need a curriculum that is seamlessly built into this network. If one of these pieces is missing, schools will not see results. In addition, SMART Boards need to have the right curriculum combined with the right teacher training or they will not improve student achievement. They might even have an adverse effect, if they become a distraction. Tablet computers will soon be in the hands of every student worldwide, and their power needs to be harnessed.

"Schools use computers as a tool and a topic," said Clayton Christensen, "not as a primary instructional mechanism that helps students learn in ways that are customized to their type of intelligence."[29]

Investing in Curriculum Development

The scale challenge is at the heart of the public school system: a rigorous curriculum and the consistent, effective delivery of that curriculum. Prior to technology-based learning, schools had to rely solely on textbooks and teacher lesson plans. With online learning, the lessons can be far more dynamic and consistent, engaging students in an interactive way that textbooks never could. According to Dale Mann:

> The American model is one in which the state departments of education have the legal mandate to provide schooling and guarantee the quality of schooling, but they do not develop curriculum. Neither do the schools. The armature, the scaffolding, the infrastructure of what goes on in the classroom is curriculum. Companies like K[12] spend more developing curriculum, and refining and improving curriculum, than any district could. They make a huge contribution, especially when they reinvent the enterprise of schooling with hybrid models that combine brick-and-mortar, conventional school delivery with digital learning.
>
> In the American model, the RD&E [research, development, and evaluation] of curriculum falls to the private sector, and it's a *huge* contribution. The federal government was once briefly in this business, in the mid-1960s, and supported a couple of curriculum development endeavors...and it caused a firestorm.
>
> If we are going to have something comparable to Singapore math...it's going to happen because companies see

a profit, a market, and an opportunity. I trust companies that combine doing well with doing good. You can make money by providing new capability to the learning enterprise.[30]

Even teacher training is lacking in the traditional schools. According to the North Central Regional Educational Laboratory (NCREL), "It is likely that less than 1 percent of all teachers nationwide are trained as online teachers. The intensity, duration, and quality of staff development for online teachers appear to vary significantly."[31] *Education Week* reports that only eleven states require at least some of their online teachers to receive training in online instruction.[32] Teachers at virtual schools need training on a variety of software applications, basic hardware maintenance, effective communication strategies (such as effective writing techniques for web-based lessons), information management skills, and instructional intervention.

School systems have not had the resources to buy the kind of high quality education software that will raise student achievement. Part of the problem has been the absence of an industry to create those tools. That changed with the advent of K[12], which provided management services to the schools, making it possible to justify the investment of dollars to build great content online. As online learning grows, the investment in courses will continue to increase. K[12] also invests significant capital training online teachers.

Gaining Productivity

Computer technology reduces dependence on school buildings, since students can be taught outside of a school's four walls. According to the National Clearinghouse for Educational Facilities, the capital outlay for public school systems in 2005–2006 was almost $60 billion; another $30 billion was spent on maintenance. Even without skyrocketing fuel prices, which cost America's massive school transportation system $20 billion a year, the brick-and-mortar school system is expensive.[33] Thus, just the cost of infrastructure and of bringing the students to it costs more than $110 billion per year—an expense that is bound to keep growing unless something changes.

In a 2009 preinauguration radio address, President-elect Obama promised

the most sweeping effort to modernize and upgrade school buildings that this country has ever seen. We will repair broken schools, make them energy efficient, and put new computers in our classrooms. In order to help our children compete in a twenty-first-century economy, we need to send them to twenty-first-century schools.[34]

We should question whether upgrading buildings is going to allow children to compete globally in the twenty-first century, but the message about sending students to twenty-first-century schools is exactly right. There are many great schools with poor buildings and vice versa. Rather, consideration should be given to investment in scalable technology and software, which can have a far bigger effect on student learning. With today's online learning platforms, we can provide education to the public without having to build hundreds of buildings in which to school them. This technology will also aid developing nations to leapfrog the brick-and-mortar phase of education, making time—and action—of the essence for American children.

Using the right technology, class size can increase from twenty-five to thirty and translate into an enormous increase in productivity. That frees up a lot of money for more technology, more innovation, and increased teacher salaries. Computers provide a much more efficient and cost-effective way of creating what Clayton Christensen called "student-centric technology." He explained, "Like all disruptions, student-centric technology will make it affordable, convenient, and simple for many more students to learn in ways that are customized for them."[35] By using technology, we can reverse the productivity decline we have witnessed the past fifty years. Once we begin the process, the savings yielded by the productivity improvement will permit more investment in technology and even further productivity improvements. It should produce a cycle that keeps going and going.

The Goal Is to Serve Public Education

The K[12] vision is not to compete with public education but to serve public education. Private companies should be a service vendor to public education, creating the technology, curriculum, tools, and services that support America's public education system in being the best in the world. K[12] will help it deliver more customized, interactive, efficient, and engaging education to students.

The speed at which society is changing is so fast, we cannot expect our public schools to keep up. My grandfather died in 2003 at the age of ninety-three, and as I drove back to his funeral in Bethlehem, Pennsylvania, I realized that he had seen more changes in his lifetime than anyone had seen in the prior two millennia—from phones, electricity, aviation, and indoor plumbing to cell phones, fax machines, televisions, and radios. One example: Bethlehem Steel was founded shortly before he was born, and it grew to be the second largest producer of steel and one of the largest companies in the United States by the 1950s. By 2000 it was bankrupt. This amount of change is indeed stunning, yet our kids will see far more changes than he saw, as the pace of change accelerates.[36]

The young people of today—and the future—must be prepared to learn continuously and to regularly update their skill sets. Learning how to learn online is critical, because it opens up a (literal) world of learning. Classroom learning will not be able to keep up with the pace of change, nor will it be practical to do so. This type of learning must be available anywhere, anytime, any place. Course offerings, already diverse, will rapidly expand for academic courses and vocational courses in the years ahead. MOOCs (Massive Open Online Courses) will make new, sophisticated subjects widely available.

The dynamism of the modern economy is not something to fear; it should be embraced as an opportunity, albeit one that requires constant learning. Innovation, entrepreneurship, and competition have made the United States a great nation, and they are traits that need to be nurtured as our public education system develops in the coming decade.

The public and private sectors need not view each other as rivals or competitors; they should instead focus on partnerships that will make them both more efficient and more effective as they strive to raise student achievement. Perhaps the greatest positive change in education will occur when states, school boards, and school districts begin to think of themselves as purchasers of educational services for the students who reside in their district rather than exclusive providers of these services. Once this happens, change will come quickly, and education will be individualized and student-centric.

12

WHERE TECHNOLOGY AND EDUCATION MEET: THE FUTURE

*T*hose in the middle of a revolution are not always the best judges of where it will end up. What's clear today, however, is that a new system of educating children is unfolding, and the journey is far from complete. Although we don't know the journey's final destination, it's nonetheless worthwhile to look a little further down the road.

Classrooms with More Students

I agree with Clayton Christensen that online education is no longer just a futurist's dream; it is here. I believed that in early 1999, when I wrote the original business plan for K[12]. The current economic crisis might even accelerate the pace of change as policy makers realize how much more efficient it will be to augment schooling with technology and the internet.

The technology exists to greatly improve classroom results while reducing capital expenditures and costs in the system, thus creating opportunities for higher teacher pay and more technology spending. The efficiencies emanating from this process can contribute to the reversal of the productivity losses of the last fifty years, but school districts have many models for using educational technology. One of the keys is for policy makers to enact laws that will use this technology in the best ways. States, districts, schools, principals, teachers, parents, and most important, students will benefit from using technology-based education. Once this realization is widely understood, the pace of adoption is going to accelerate dramatically.

When I think of an online school, I see a teacher in a room with twenty-five or even fifty students, all of them with computers. The teacher isn't lecturing every minute of the day; the teacher is addressing specific questions from the students, most of whom are interacting with their computer, working at their own pace. If it is an elementary school, there are specialty teachers to help the teacher with specific subjects or learning needs. In all instances, the teaching model is a teacher-on-demand model, delivering the instruction that is needed exactly when it is needed to whom it is needed. There's no reason why classrooms in today's world need to exist in a physical building; they can exist all over the world! Indeed, this is the essence of online learning.

In a classroom, teachers should be teaching with a complete set of tools to engage the students. This includes interactive whiteboards, games, simulations, animations, videos, sample problems, and lesson plans that meet the state or Common Core State Standards. The assessments should be built-in, allowing a teacher to know exactly what each student has mastered on a daily basis, and preselected websites should come wired in to the lessons to allow students and teachers to explore beyond the lesson. Parents should also have access to the same lessons and get daily emails when their child is having difficulty. The classroom and home should be integrated. Afterschool programs and tutors should also have this information.

Fortunately, *all* of this exists today and has been shown to deliver good results. As evidence continues to accumulate, this model will become more widely accepted.

A Multitude of Choice

Chicago is a model of education innovation, and the city's leadership team has facilitated the creation of a variety of schools. Among them is a hybrid program the city opened with K^{12}, so parents now have a hybrid choice along with a multitude of brick-and-mortar options (though the school is full and has a large waiting list). City leaders have also facilitated the creation of a hybrid school for dropouts and a variety of charter schools with different methodologies. Large districts are capable of providing Core Knowledge schools, KIPP (Knowledge Is Power Program) academies, foreign language immersion schools, vocational schools, science and math magnets, performing arts schools, and every other type of school that students desire. The public school system should seek to offer these options as long as the schools succeed and have a constituency among the customers (parents). A full-time virtual school will hopefully be available as well.

Adaptive Learning and Artificial Intelligence

Educational software and content is still in its infancy. With hybrid and virtual schools and today's content and learning systems, a strong foundation has been built. Technologists are already designing systems that incorporate more social networking, peer-to-peer learning, and adaptive learning software. The current generation of systems creates individualized pathways for each student, and these pathways will only get more engaging, interactive, and customized.

Individualized remediation allows students to move faster and more easily through curriculum, and lessons in the future will address even more individual learning needs than they do today. Eventually, the systems will be able to figure out how each student learns most effectively and deliver content accordingly. As cognitive science learns more about how the brain works, online learning can take advantage of it. Imagine a world in which students are as drawn to learning and solving problems as they are to video games. I believe this world is not far away.

With online textbooks and tablets, textbook adoption no longer makes sense. The power of digital content is that it can rapidly change and improve, which is the opposite of adoption processes that freeze content for multiple years.

Good-bye, Grade-based Education

I envision the disappearance of a grade-based school system and a return, in a twenty-first-century way, to the one-room schoolhouse. Children of all ages will be in the classroom of the future with the new technology assessing their proficiency level at any given moment. Arbitrary grade levels might disappear as education comes to be thought of as a continuous stream of knowledge and skill acquisition, eliminating the need to break it into the discrete chunks that we call grade levels today. In addition, rather than having grade-level state tests, these tests should be condensed into a single, computer-based, adaptive test. Students would take it at various time intervals, and learning gains could be measured accordingly.

Such grade merging will result in the blurring of high school and college, in the three-year university (maybe two years spent learning on campus and one off), and in a halt to the spiraling costs of a college education. High school may also move to three years, which becomes possible if students take summer school online. By reducing the number of years for both high school and college, the cost of education drops significantly for taxpayers, students, and parents. Colleges could actually go to two years if students finished the first two years of college-level courses during high school. In addition, with the lower cost of college, the capacity problem at the nation's selective colleges—a situation that has seen minimal increases in the last forty years despite a massive increase in the number of qualified candidates—would be simultaneously solved.

More Kids to College and a Return to Vocational Schools

More students will be attending college as the number of dropouts declines. With school available anywhere—from Boys & Girls Clubs to juvenile detention centers—children can be educated anywhere, anytime. Neither the gifted nor those struggling will be held back. Parents will no longer face the prospect of discovering that their bright and bubbly sixth grader is two years behind, with no clear remedy. (The best remediation is not falling behind to begin with, as the mathematics of remediation shows.) Vocational education will also return in a major way, as technology will allow education to become more specialized and students will have more customized paths to the career they seek.

Vocational education declined in schools because the system pushed every student toward college—a noble goal but one that left students who did not go to college without a clear career pathway. This may have inadvertently increased the dropout rate, as these students saw less value in completing high school. Without doubt, it did result in a shortage of prepared students for skilled trades in many geographic areas—but online schools can change this. Online courses can help students find their pathway and follow it. States with vacant jobs and a shortage of skilled employees should do everything possible to drive these changes in their schools.

A School for Every Student

The school of the future will be customized. Instead of one Miss Dilbert for thirty kids, there can be one Miss Dilbert for each child. Adaptive software will allow individualized education, leveraging teachers to address individual student's specific needs. Paradoxically, it will simultaneously allow teachers to get more granular while reaching thousands—and in some cases *millions*—of students.

Future class sizes may be larger, but student–teacher ratios will remain unchanged in the short term. This will occur because schools will have specialty teachers who do small-group interventions. I had classes at Berkeley with eight hundred students but section sizes of perhaps twenty—a big difference when it comes to comparing class size and student–teacher ratios.

The traditional brick-and-mortar school can't customize education the way online school can, which is why grades and desks are still lined up in rows. The modern school has attempted to deliver customized schooling without having the means to do so, contributing to the spiraling costs of education and the nearly flat achievement scores in the process. Meanwhile, flex academies are already offering customized learning in a cost-efficient way, providing teachers who specialize in focused, small-group instruction, not lectures in a brick-and-mortar building.

By giving up the order of the old system—rigid curriculum and rigid discipline—the modern school may have made matters worse. Instead of customizing the delivery of a set of standards (which it couldn't do), the system created the "child-centered" classroom. Unfortunately, rigor was weakened in the process, and the technology didn't exist for individualized learning.

Delivering a customized education to all students under the current system would require not just twice the number of teachers but probably ten times. America can't afford that; no country can or will be able to. The country can, however, afford online schools, courses, and technology in the classroom. This technology—combined with the right content, software, and teacher training—allows individualized education to be a reality now and is more cost effective than the traditional model. And it is only going to get better. In some ways, technology-based education is just a means to achieve individualized education, which is the promised land.

One Goal, Many Options

The ultimate objective is a world-class education for every child. That may sound like a pie-in-the-sky wish, but so were the proposals at the beginning of the last century to offer every American a high school education.

Hunter in Philadelphia showed what is possible. Teachers can use technology to enhance their lessons, to ensure curricular consistency, and to engage with students. Individualized education refers not just to individualization within the course but to the student's program itself. High schools should move to offering electives online, expanding student choices from tens to thousands while saving them money. As in the case of Hunter, students, schools, and taxpayers would all win.

Brick-and-mortar schools will still exist, and the overwhelming majority of children will attend them, but the schools will be centers of individualized learning, with engaging interactive content rather than a series of chalk-and-textbook, grade-delineated classrooms. At high school and potentially middle school, each child will have a computer to work at his or her own pace in customized programs; technology will deliver it to them in ways best suited to their individual needs and strengths. In addition, as adaptive content capabilities increase, those computers will be able to figure out each student's knowledge level—across a range of subjects—and tailor the content delivery to that level.

Tailoring content-delivery strategies is very different than changing the content; the former ensures mastery of the curriculum through a deep understanding of a child's ability, and the latter ensures mastery by changing the curriculum—often by dumbing it down. Throughout this tailoring process, master teachers, who function as individualized instructors, can provide extra help to students.

There will be special environments like orphanages, youth clubs, youth correction centers, prisons, and homes for young mothers that are able to facilitate the use of the online school. There's no reason there can't be tens of thousands of these learning annexes across the country—across the world.

Educating the incarcerated is a particularly powerful application of online education. Attaining a high school or college degree can do wonders to reduce recidivism. Obtaining employment without a high school diploma is difficult; obtaining employment with a criminal record is difficult; trying to get a job when dealing with both is extraordinarily difficult. It is little wonder recidivism rates are so high. If prisoners could get an education while incarcerated, employment opportunities would increase when they are released. As mentioned previously, states might even want to consider reduced sentences for nonviolent criminals who obtain a degree.

Similar logic applies to students who do not have a high school diploma. If they have the motivation, why not let them complete their education? With online high schools, the problem of much older students being in the classroom almost disappears. There is no reason to cut off funding at twenty or twenty-one years old

Often, the light leading someone to the value of education doesn't turn on until they get into the real world and realize why they need it. This is especially true for at-risk students. Once they are out of school, however, they feel too old or embarrassed to go back. Fortunately, online education removes this stigma. States should embrace these students and fund degree completion, regardless of age.

The virtual school itself will be a school that is open anytime, anywhere. Virtual schools, hybrid schools, and flex schools will proliferate across the country, with significant increases in student achievement. Students will be empowered by getting the education necessary to fulfill their dreams.

The results from online learning have been coming in, and they are encouraging. According to a 2004 NCREL meta-analysis of fourteen web-delivered K-12 distance-education programs, between 1999 and 2004, "In almost every comparison, students in distance education programs performed as well as students in classroom-based programs."[1] A 2005 NCREL report also found "new evidence supporting the apparent effectiveness of online programs and schools, and generally demonstrating the potential of online learning as a promising instructional intervention that can, when implemented judiciously and with attention to 'evidence-based' practices, apparently improve student academic performance."[2]

The variety and number (hundreds of thousands) of students being served by online schools is impressive. Though full-time virtual schooling may not be right for every student, it is right for many—particularly those who fully engage with the school. Even if it's less than 5 percent of students who do this, they deserve the option.

Individualized online courses and technology-based curriculum in the classroom are invaluable resources that can benefit every student, and the technology is available *now* to school districts that are ready to put America's education—and human capital—back on the global map.

CONCLUSION

The future of education will be marked by the extensive use of technology-based learning so that there can be individualized education for all students. Technology will be integrated in the classroom, and there will be full-time online schools, online classes, hybrid schools, and online tutoring. Unlike television, motion pictures, or personal computers, the internet and its ability to provide two-way interaction will finally be the technology that improves education. It is already doing so.

As the market expands, so will the vendors and offerings. At everyone's fingertips, because of the internet, parents and students will be able to buy whatever course they want. The new era in education will be defined by parent/student choice, individualized education, and improved, consistent technology. The system will also see extensive productivity gains.

The role of the public school system will remain the same: to guarantee equal access to the best education possible. In the future, however, this will mean a more intensive effort setting learning standards, developing more frequent and sophisticated adaptive student assessments, and maintaining an ongoing evaluation of vendors' abilities to meet these standards.

The new education world is unlikely to include a voucher system. If schools embrace technology, and states embrace public charter schools, there's no reason why vouchers would be needed. The key is for the public school system to allow choice. If parents want their child to take Chinese or Arabic, that choice should be available through the public education system. There is no reason why high school students can't take vector calculus. Students should not be limited by lack of on-site subject matter expertise. Online learning can bring expertise to any student.

Technology will also become more sophisticated. Gaming engines will be designed for learning and learning management systems that support far more advanced media, adaptive learning software, and artificial intelligence. Content and online learning will become increasingly autodidactic, which will allow teachers to give more individualized instruction. Great teachers will be able to reach millions of students, not tens.

With unlimited resources, I'd engage a top movie director, game designer, classroom teacher, cognitive neuroscientist, and instructional designer and sit them all down with a top historian to create a US history course. The end result would likely be something of high quality that is part dramatic film, part sophisticated game for reinforcing the content, and part wonderful narrative from a great writer. Learning would be engaging and exciting.

Implementing this vision is expensive—or will be until the productivity gains of a fully integrated online education system are realized. When a course can be used by fifty to one hundred million students, however, it becomes affordable. That's why scale is so necessary.

Technology has changed almost every aspect of American life—except our schools. Online learning, in its many forms, has become the most important trend in American education and will eventually be able to deliver an individualized, world-class education to anyone, anywhere on the globe. This is already beginning to happen in the developing world.

Yes, technology will completely revolutionize education. The question is whether it will do it the right way or the wrong way. Will technology be used to increase teaching and learning productivity? To increase time on task? To individualize education? Will policy makers increase statewide access to online learning, release budget money to create and buy the right software, let parents log on to school curriculum and instruction? Will they encourage competition and innovation?

If these questions are answered quickly and correctly, there is no doubt that America will once again have a public school system that is the envy of the world—a vision K^{12} had over a decade ago and has watched become increasingly possible every day as we expand our service to states, districts, and students.

EPILOGUE

The Next Twenty Years

*E*ducation is about to undergo remarkable change over the next twenty years. This is true not only for K-12 but for postsecondary education as well. Technology is the key to all these changes.

It's always fun to try to predict the future, so I'll end this book with twenty predictions for the next twenty years. Some of these are obvious and already beginning while others are yet to come.

1. A large number of students will go to school completely online. This will likely be 5 to 10 percent of students in the United States. Hybrid schools will also expand dramatically. The availability of online schooling will improve the quality of education for athletes, artists, musicians, and anyone with an intense passion for something, as they will have more time to pursue their passion.

2. Every high school student will be taking at least one to two courses online every year. They will be able to take all electives online in the not too distant future.

3. Online course libraries with qualified teachers will be expanded significantly, giving high school students the ability to choose from thousands of courses. The course library available to high school students will be larger than the course library available at most universities today.

4. The lines between high school and college will get blurry as most high school students will be taking college courses for credit.

5. Teaching in classrooms will be done via electronic whiteboards with highly interactive engaging lessons. Students will work on an individualized basis, with teachers helping students on an as-needed basis. Remediation will be surgical and individualized based on assessments. Much of it will be autodidactic, enabled by sophisticated learning technologies. These changes will significantly increase student achievement.

6. Summer school will explode as online learning makes this cost effective. In this way schooling will become year-round and finally leave the archaic agrarian calendar. This will help eliminate the summer regression that afflicts so many children and increases instructional time.

7. Online learning will greatly increase the high school graduation rate because the flexibility and interactivity will keep more kids in the system. Online and hybrid programs will bring many dropouts back into the system and allow them to complete their degrees. Online learning will also increase college graduation rates. Education will become a large export industry for the United States.

8. States and municipalities will save tens of billions of dollars on school construction. Middle schools and high schools will dou-

ble and triple their capacity as students take a significant number of courses online.

9. Teachers will earn more because they will be able to leverage their skills over a larger number of students, and the predicted teacher shortage will be averted.

10. Highly sophisticated learning games will be developed to teach critical courses, such as algebra, that are as engaging as the video games that children currently play.

11. Courses will become adaptive so that the pathways students take will be dependent on their knowledge and skills as determined by assessments. All courses will be designed to handle various learning styles and scaffolded remediation will be built into the courses.

12. Colleges and high schools will likely move to three-year programs as the need for four years is questionable and less cost efficient. At a minimum, almost all colleges will require students to devote one year of their four-year college experience to online education. This will expand the capacity of almost every university and significantly lower the cost.

13. There will be an explosion in vocational education and a large part of this will be done online. Students will be able to choose from a variety of public schools as opposed to the singular choice most students currently have.

14. Online high school completion and associate's degree programs will become prevalent for incarcerated youths, which will lower the recidivism rate. Some states will offer reduced sentences for nonviolent criminals who complete degrees.

15. Foreign language will begin in elementary schools, when the brain is best prepared to learn foreign languages. Courses will be available in multiple languages and foreign language proficiency will increase.

16. The content of education will change to reflect the skills needed for the twenty-first century. Students will have to be technology proficient and work on collaborative projects even if they never physically interact.

17. Online learning will make lifelong learning a reality. As the speed of societal and technological change continues to accelerate and life expectancy increases, people will need to update their skill sets multiple times in their careers. With online learning, this will be achievable and affordable. MOOCs will lower the cost of higher education and enable greater access to higher quality learning for everyone.

18. School communities will be global, and we will see the emergence of global K-12 schools.

19. Courses will be delivered on mobile devices that are highly engaging. This will be cradle-to-grave education, which will become a necessity in the rapidly changing society today's students will experience. Textbooks and adoption processes will disappear within a decade.

20. Privately managed public schools will expand significantly through charter schools, giving the students a large variety of choices and delivering large savings for taxpayers. Students will be able to choose among different types of schools such as Core Knowledge, language immersion, etc. The competition among these schools will greatly increase the quality of all schools.

ACKNOWLEDGMENTS

I started out with a simple idea fourteen years ago that K-12 schools could go completely online. At that time, I had been involved in education for less than two years, and most of that was in early childhood education. I had no idea of the remarkable journey that I was about to embark on. The whole process—writing a business plan, raising capital at the height of the internet bubble, hiring the initial team, raising capital and hiring people after the bubble burst, and waging a crusade for educational liberty for all students across the fifty states—is itself a book. Over the course of that journey, I have been fortunate to meet and get to know some of the most innovative and interesting people, including political leaders, school leaders, investors, professors, board members, union leaders, employees, teachers, celebrities, concerned parents, and some phenomenally dedicated students. Of all the hours I spend working, my favorite are the ones I get to spend with the students who are benefitting from technology-based education.

When we started K^{12}, we never imagined the variety of children that it would serve. In some ways, the *Field of Dreams* approach was taken: "build it and they will come." We had no idea who would come, but they did, and they came in droves. These included children from rural areas, children who had been bullied, highly gifted children like athletes and actors, children seeking a more rigorous curriculum, and children with a large variety of special needs for whom online learning works the best. I owe many thanks to all the families who have come to K^{12} and a special thanks to the families who agreed to be profiled in this book. Also, a special thank you to all parents who have helped bring innovation and educational liberty to their states.

This book has taken longer to write than I originally anticipated, as every time I go to edit a new draft, more innovation has occurred in the time between. Since this could be an endless cycle, I put out the book now so that the amazing story of the technology-based transformation in the world of education can be told.

The first thanks must go out to my oldest daughter, who was in many ways my inspiration as I sought out—to no avail—an online math course. From this fruitless search emanated the idea for K^{12}. I owe her and the rest of my family much thanks, as they have been guinea pigs for many of the products K^{12} has developed. They have been full-time students, taken individual courses, supplemented their brick-and-mortar courses, and enrolled in camps. I am happy to report that they are all surviving the ordeal and, in fact, thriving.

I also owe immeasurable thanks to Michael and Lowell Milken. In addition to recruiting me into education a long time ago, they made K^{12} possible because of their unwavering support. They were willing to invest in the vision—and continue to invest in this vision—when nobody else would. Their advice and counsel have proved invaluable over the years.

A special thanks to Mike for teaching me that no idea is too big and Lowell for teaching me about K-12 education.

Without William Bennett K^{12} would have not been possible. He is someone I have admired for a long time. As US Secretary of Education, he brought attention to the need for changes in the education system, and his book *The Educated Child* was instrumental in the early blueprint for K^{12}. Without Bill's leadership as the chairman of K^{12} in its early years, I am not sure we would have made it over the hump that has destroyed so many educational start-ups.

I also send thanks to Elanna Yalow, who helped me think through the original business plan and, more important, started me down the road of constantly studying educational research. I must also thank former Governor of Pennsylvania Tom Ridge, former US Deputy Secretary of Education Eugene Hickok, and former Secretary of Education for Pennsylvania Charles Zogby, who were all pioneers in allowing the creation of online schooling, along with former Florida Governor Jeb Bush.

I also owe thanks to the many employees of K^{12} who helped with this book and who have taught me so much about online education and education in general. These include John Holdren, who is the most knowledgeable curriculum expert I have known, and Bror Saxberg, who taught me about cognitive neuroscience, as well as the many employees who helped me with this book, including Jim Konantz, Mary Gifford, Allison Cleveland, Bruce Davis, Chip Hughes, Karen Ghidotti, Jennifer Sims, Jeff Kwitowski, Bryan Flood, Eric Waller, Celia Stokes, Julie Linn, and Margie Jorgensen. A special thanks to two employees who have been with me almost since the beginning: Peter Stewart and Maria Szalay. Peter has taught me so much about schools, and his creative spirit has pushed educational technology into new channels. Maria advocated adaptive learning before it was trendy and helped me in many ways with this book. To avoid listing thousands, I owe a general thanks to all K^{12}

employees and teachers, as they have moved technology-based education forward faster than I could have dreamed. I have no doubt they will continue to do so.

I also must thank my previous board chairman, Andrew Tisch, who allowed me to spend some time writing this book and whose leadership and investment in K^{12} helped move online learning forward. Similar thanks must go out to past and current investors of K^{12}, who provided and continue to provide the capital that will allow children from around the world to benefit from this education transformation.

On the production of this book, I owe thanks to Katie Connelly, who put in many hours on this project and who can actually read my handwriting, and Sabrina Ortiz, who found the final sources needed to complete this book. I also want to thank my editor, Jen Weaver-Neist, and publisher, Richard Cohn, who made this book possible.

Lastly, I thank the states, school districts, nonprofit schools, administrators, teachers, parents, and students who are customers of K^{12}. You are the users of technology-based learning; without you, it would not exist.

NOTES

Introduction

1. William J. Bennett, Chester E. Finn, and John T. E. Cribb, *The Educated Child: A Parent's Guide from Preschool through Eighth Grade* (New York: The Free Press, 1999), 619.

2. David Gelernter, *Machine Beauty: Elegance and the Heart of Technology* (New York: Basic Books, 1998), 129. See also Gelernter's *Drawing Life: Surviving the Unabomber*, as antitechnology terrorist Ted Kaczynski selected Gelernter as his first target, sending Gelernter a package bomb that blew off part of the Yale professor's hand.

3. Paul E. Peterson, "Ticket to Nowhere," *Education Next* 3, no. 2 (Spring 2003).

4. Frederick M. Hess, ed., *The Future of Educational Entrepreneurship: Possibilities for School Reform* (Cambridge, MA: Harvard Education Press, 2008), 2.

5. National Center for Education Statistics, Institute of Education Sciences, "Pupil/teacher ratio: 1960–61 through 2007–08," Digest of Education Statistics, US Department of Education (2009), fig. 6.2: http://nces.ed.gov/programs/digest/d09/figures/fig_06.asp.

6. Barack Obama, "Inaugural Address," transcript, *New York Times* (January 20, 2009): http://www.nytimes.com/2009/01/20/us/politics/20text-obama.html.

7. Christopher B. Swanson, "Cities in Crisis: A Special Analytic Report on High School Graduation," Editorial Projects in Education Research Center (April 2008).

8. Bureau of Labor Statistics, "College Enrollment and Work Activity of 2010 High School Graduates," news release, US Department of Labor (April 2011): http://www.bls.gov/news.release/hsgec.nr0.htm; Tamar Lewin, "College Graduation Rates Are Stagnant Even as Enrollment Rises, a Study Finds," *New York Times* (September 27, 2011): http://www.nytimes.com/2011/09/27/education/27remediation.html; Complete College of America, "The Completion Shortfall": http://www.completecollege.org/completion_shortfall/; National Center for Higher Education, "Six-Year Graduation Rates of Bachelor's Students, 2009," NCHEMS Information Center for Higher Education Policymaking and Analysis: http://www.higheredinfo.org/dbrowser/?level=nation&mode=map&state=0&submeasure=27; National Center for Higher Education, "Three-Year Graduation Rates of Bachelor's Students, 2009," NCHEMS Information Center for Higher Education Policymaking and Analysis: http://www.higheredinfo.org/dbrowser/index

.php?measure=19. See also Henry M. Levin and Cecilia E. Rouse, "The True Cost of High School Dropouts," *New York Times* (January 25, 2012): http://www.nytimes.com/2012/01/26/opinion/the-true-cost-of-high-school-dropouts .html?_r=2&nl=todaysheadlines&emc=thab1.

9. Thomas L. Friedman, *The World Is Flat: A Brief History of the Twenty-First Century* (New York: Farrar, Straus and Giroux, 2006).

10. Susan Sclafani, "New Expectations for a New Century: The Education Imperative," Office of Vocational and Adult Education, United States Department of Education (July 20, 2008), slide 2: http://www2.ed.gov/about/offices/list /ovae/resource/newexpectations.ppt.

11. Anna Habash, "Counting on Graduation: Most States Are Setting Low Expectations for the Improvement of High School Graduation Rates," press release, The Education Trust (October 23, 2008): http://www.edtrust.org/dc/press -room/press-release/counting-on-graduation"-most-states-are-setting-low-expectations-for-the. See also National Center for Higher Education, "American Education Survey, Educational Attainment by Degree-Level and Age-Group: Percent of Adults 35 to 44 with an Associate's Degree or Higher, 2009," NCHEMS Information Center for Higher Education Policymaking and Analysis: http://www.higheredinfo.org/dbrowser/?level=nation&mode=data&state=0 &submeasure=240.

12. Randall Greenway and Gregg Vanourek, "The Virtual Revolution: Understanding Online Schools," *Education Next* 6, no. 2 (Spring 2006), 35.

13. US Department of Education, "Toward a New Golden Age in American Education: How the Internet, the Law and Today's Students are Revolutionizing Expectations," National Education Technology Plan (2004), 7–8.

14. Brown v. Board of Education, 347 U.S. 483 (1954): http://www.nationalcenter.org/brown.html and http://www.nps .gov/brvb/index.htm.

15. Larry Cuban, *Teachers and Machines: The Classroom Use of Technology since 1920* (New York and London: Teachers College Press, 1986), 9.

Chapter 1

1. The National Commission on Excellence in Education, "A Nation at Risk: The Imperative for Educational Reform, A Report to the Nation and the Secretary of Education," US Department of Education (April 9, 1983): http://reagan .procon.org/sourcefiles/a-nation-at-risk-reagan-april-1983.pdf.

2. Ibid.

3. Ibid.

4. Paul E. Peterson, "Ticket to Nowhere," *Education Next* 3, no. 2 (Spring 2003): http://educationnext.org /tickettonowhere.

5. Ibid., fig. 1.

6. National Center for Education Statistics, Institute of Education Sciences, "NAEP 2008 trends of academic progress: Reading 1971–2008 / Mathematics 1973–2008," executive summary, US Department of Education: http://nces.ed.gov /nationsreportcard/pdf/main2008/2009479.pdf.

7. Jay Greene, "A Comprehensive Problem," *Education Next* 6, no. 1 (Winter 2006): http://educationnext.org /a-comprehensive-problem/.

8. National Center for Education Statistics, Institute of Education Sciences, "Trends in International Mathematics and Science Study (TIMSS): Average mathematics scores of fourth- and eighth-grade students, by country," US Department of Education, (2007), table 1: http://nces.ed.gov/timss/table07_1.asp.

9. National Center for Education Sciences, Institute of Education Sciences, "Highlights from PISA 2009: Performance of US 15-Year-Old Students in Reading, Mathematics, and Science Literacy in an International Context," US Department of Education (2010): http://nces.ed.gov/pubs2011/2011004.pdf.

10. Christopher B. Swanson, *Cities in Crisis 2009: Closing the Graduation Gap*, Editorial Projects in Education, Inc. (Bethesda, MD: April 2009), 14: http://www.americaspromise.org/~/media/Files/Resources/CiC09.ashx.

11. Tim Rutten, "By All Account, a Failure: State Figures on LAUSD Student Dropout Rates Are Stunning and Shameful," *Los Angeles Times* (July 19, 2008): http://articles.latimes.com/2008/jul/19/opinion/oe-rutten19.

12. Ibid.

13. Sam Dillon, "Schools Slow in Closing Gaps Between Races," *New York Times*, US Education, (November 20, 2006): http://www.nytimes.com/2006/11/20/education/20gap.html.

14. Arne Duncan, "The Digital Transformation in Education," transcript of US Secretary of Education Duncan's remarks at the State Educational Technology Directors Association Education Forum, US Department of Education (November 9, 2010): http://www.ed.gov/news/speeches/%E2%80%9C-digital-transformation-education%E2%80%9D -us-secretary-education-arne-duncan.

15. Alliance for Excellent Education, "Public Education Policy and Progress," Straight A's 7, no. 5 (March 5, 2007): http:// www.all4ed.org/publication_material/straight_as/7/5.

Chapter 2

1. K¹² internal data and resources. For further information, please visit www.k12.com or call 866-YOUR-K12.
2. National Center for Education Statistics, "Total US Expenditures for Elementary and Secondary Education," Common Core of Data, US Department of Education (2006), table 2: http://www2.ed.gov/about/overview/fed/10facts /edlite-chart.html#1.
3. US Census Bureau, "Profile America: Facts for Features," press release (June 27, 2011), CB11-FF.15: http:// www.census.gov/newsroom/releases/archives/facts_for_features_special_editions/cb11-ff15.html.
4. Jay Mathews, "The Philadelphia Experiment: The Story behind Philadelphia's Edison Contract," *Education Next* 3, no. 1 (Winter 2003): http://educationnext.org/thephiladelphiaexperiment.
5. Ibid.
6. Paul E. Peterson, *Saving Schools: From Horace Mann to Virtual Learning* (Cambridge, MA: Harvard University Press / Belknap Press, 2010), 21–36; Patricia Graham, *Community and Class in American Education, 1865–1918* (New York: Wiley, 1974).
7. National Center for Education Statistics, Institute of Education Sciences, "Enrollment of the 20 largest degree-granting college and university campuses: Fall 2010," *Digest of Education Statistics*, US Department of Education (2011), table 1: http://nces.ed.gov/fastfacts/display.asp?id=74.
8. National Center for Education Statistics, Institute of Education Sciences, "Teacher Attrition and Mobility: Results from the 2008–2009 Teacher Follow-Up Survey," US Department of Education (August 2010): http://nces.ed.gov /pubs2010/2010353.pdf.
9. International Society for the Study of Behavioural Development, "TIMSS—Mathematics and Science Achievement in International Comparison: Goals, Design, and Research Questions," no. 1 (1998), 8: http://www.issbd.org/resources /files/newsletter_198.pdf. For more information on the TIMSS, see the TIMSS & PIRLS International Study Center of the International Association for the Evaluation of Educational Achievement at the Lynch School of Education, Boston College: http://timssandpirls.bc.edu/isc/publications.html.
10. K¹² internal data and resources (see chap. 2, n.1).
11. Milken Institute: http://www.milkeninstitute.org/publications/searchpubs.taf.
12. Nick Anderson, "International Test Score Data Show US Firmly Mid-Pack: Shanghai Tops International Test Scores," *Washington Post* (December 7, 2010), fig. 1: http://www.washingtonpost.com/wp-dyn/content/graphic/2010/12/06 /GR2010120607984.html.
13. "Shanghai Test Scores Have Everyone Asking: How Did Students Do It?" *Christian Science Monitor*, accessed January 25, 2012: http://www.csmonitor.com/World/Asia-Pacific/2010/1209/Shanghai-test-scores-have-everyone-asking -How-did-students-do-it/(page)/2.
14. The Organisation for Economic Co-operation and Development (OECD), *Strong Performers and Successful Reformers in Education: Lessons from PISA for the United States* (OECD Publishing, 2011), 92: doi:10.1787 /9789264096660-en.
15. Paul E. Peterson, "From the Editors: What Is Good for General Motors," *Education Next* 9, no. 2 (Spring 2009): http:// educationnext.org/what-is-good-for-general-motors.
16. Ibid.
17. Ibid.
18. Elizabeth Green, "City's Grading of Schools Defies Popular Notions," *The Sun* (November 5, 2007): http:// www.nysun.com/new-york/citys-grading-of-schools-defies-popular-notions/65891.

Chapter 3

1. Todd Oppenheimer, *The Flickering Mind: Saving Education from the False Promise of Technology* (New York: Random House, 2003), 3.
2. Newton N. Minow, "Television and the Public Interest," a speech before the National Association of Broadcasters (May 9, 1961), 398: http://www.law.indiana.edu/fclj/pubs/v55/no3/Speech.pdf.
3. Terry Moe, Larry Cuban, and John Chubb, "Virtual Schools: Will Education Technology Change the Role of the Teacher and the Nature of Learning?" *Education Next* 9, no. 1 (Winter 2009): http://educationnext.org/virtual-schools.
4. Oppenheimer, *The Flickering Mind*, xiii.
5. Larry Cuban, *Oversold and Underused: Computes in the Classroom* (Cambridge, MA: Harvard University Press, 2001).
6. Frederick Hess, "Technically Foolish: Why Technology Has Made Our Public Schools Less Efficient," *The Weekly Standard* (March 29, 2006): http://www.weeklystandard.com/Content/Public/Articles/000/000/012/006upcia .asp?pg=1.
7. Oppenheimer, *The Flickering Mind*, xiv.
8. Minow, "Television and the Public Interest," 1961.
9. David Nagel, "Q&A: iNACOL's Susan Patrick on Trends in eLearning," *The Journal* (October 29, 2009): http:// www.thejournal.com/articles/2009/10/29/q-a-inacols-susan-patrick-on-trends-in-elearning.aspx.

10. National Center for Education Statistics, Institute of Education Sciences "Number and enrollment of public elementary and secondary schools, by school type, level, and charter and magnet status: Selected years, 1990–91 through 2008–09," *Digest of Education Statistics*, US Department of Education (2010), table 100: http://nces.ed.gov /programs/digest/d10/tables/dt10_100.asp.

11. National Center for Education Statistics, Institute of Education Sciences, "Enrollment in public elementary and secondary schools, by state or jurisdiction: Selected years, fall 1990 through fall 2010," Digest of Education Statistics, US Department of Education (2010), table 36: http://nces.ed.gov/programs/digest/d10/tables/dt10_036.asp.

12. Randall Greenway and Gregg Vanourek, "The Virtual Revolution: Understanding Online Schools," *Education Next* 6, no. 2 (Spring 2006), 34–41: http://media.hoover.org/sites/default/files/documents/ednext20062_34.pdf. See also National Center for Education Statistics, Institute of Education Sciences, "Distance education courses for public elementary and secondary school students: 2002–03," *Digest of Education Statistics*, US Department of Education (March 2005), 7: http://nces.ed.gov/surveys/frss/publications/2005010/index.asp.

13. David K. Randall, "Virtual Schools, Real Businesses; K12's Ron Packard Is Winning the Fight against the School Establishment," *Forbes* (August 11, 2008).

14. Clayton Christensen, with Michael Horn and Curtis Johnson, *Disrupting Class: How Disruptive Innovation Will Change the Way the World Learns* (New York: McGraw-Hill, 2008), 12–11.

15. Ibid., 91.

16. Alan J. Borsuk, "Wisconsin Has Another Entrant in Bid for Virtual Charter School," *Milwaukee Journal Sentinel* (February 13, 2002).

17. David Gelernter and William J. Bennett, "Commentary: Improving Education with Technology," *Education Week* (March 14, 2001).

Chapter 4

1. Jones family, interview by Peter Meyer, October 3, 2008.

2. Ibid.

3. Home School Legal Defense Association, "Over Two Million Children Are Homeschooled," press release (January 4, 2011): http://www.hslda.org/docs/media/2011/201101140.asp.

4. K[12] internal data and resources (see chap. 2, n.1).

5. The Center for Education Reform, "Charter School Law," accessed October 11, 2012: http://www.edreform.com /issues/choice-charter-schools/laws-legislation/.

6. Cf. Richard Buddin, "The Impact of Charter Schools on Public and Private School Enrollment," Cato Institute Policy Analysis, no. 707 (August 28, 2012).

7. Ann Alonzo, "Letter to the Editor: Support WIVA for Future Students," *Fond du Lac Reporter* (March 9, 2008).

8. Wisconsin Virtual Academy, "Who We Are," accessed January 25, 2012: http://www.k12.com/wiva/who-we-are.

9. Alonzo, "Letter to the Editor," *Fond du Lac Reporter.*

10. Reza Shadmehr and Henry Holcomb, "Neural Correlates of Motor Memory Consolidation," *Science* 277, no. 5327 (July 1997), 821–825, doi: 10.1126/science.277.5327.821. See also Shadmehr's website for a copy of the study: http:// www.shadmehrlab.org/Reprints/science.pdf.

11. Gwendolyn Bounds, "How Handwriting Trains the Brain: Forming Letters Is Key to Learning, Memory, Ideas," *Wall Street Journal* (October 5, 2010).

12. Ibid.

13. Jones family, interview by Peter Meyer, October 3, 2008.

14. Alan J. Borsuk, "Wisconsin Has Another Entrant in Bid for Virtual Charter School," *Milwaukee Journal Sentinel* (February 13, 2002).

15. K[12] internal data and resources (see chap. 2, n.1).

16. "Lake Mills, William J. Bennett Introduce the 'Wisconsin Virtual Academy,'" US Newswire (February 18, 2002); James W. Hopson, pub., Tim Kelly, ed.,"Virtues Abound in Virtual Schools: The Business Model Puts Customers First—And Those Customers, Wisconsin Families, So Far Are Very Satisfied with the Product," *Wisconsin State Journal* (August 4, 2003), A8: http://newspaperarchive.com/wisconsin-state-journal/2003-08-04.

17. K[12] internal data and resources (see chap. 2, n.1).

18. Hopson and Kelly, "Virtues Abound," *Wisconsin State Journal.*

19. Sharon Hayes, interview by Peter Meyer, December 2, 2008.

20. Sam Dillon, "Online Schooling Grows, Setting Off a Debate," *New York Times* (February 1, 2008).

21. "Lake Mills, William J. Bennett Introduce the 'Wisconsin Virtual Academy,'" US Newswire (February 18, 2002).

22. Hopson and Kelly, "Virtues Abound," *Wisconsin State Journal.*

23. Dillon, "Online Schooling Grows," *New York Times.*

24. Ibid.

Chapter 5

1. Facts and figures used in "The Philadelphia Story—Online" were extrapolated from a K¹² PowerPoint presentation, K¹² "Hunter Research Brief" (March 2008), and personal communication and interviews with K¹² personnel who worked at William H. Hunter Elementary School.

2. Katherine Jones, "Poverty's Effect on Childhood Academic Achievement," Associated Content Society (September 6, 2007): http://www.associatedcontent.com/article/365487/povertys_effect_on_childhood_academic .html?singlepage=true&cat=4.

3. K¹² internal data and resources (see chap. 2, n.1).

4. Lezlie B. McCoy, "Hunter Elementary Goes Extra Mile," *Philadelphia Tribune* (April 3, 2001).

5. K¹² internal data and resources (see chap. 2, n.1).

6. Jay Matthews, "The Philadelphia Experiment," *Education Next* 3, no. 1 (Winter 2003): http://educationnext.org /thephiladelphiaexperiment.

7. Jacques Steinberg, "In Largest Schools Takeover, State Will Run Philadelphia's Schools," *New York Times* (December 22, 2001): http://www.nytimes.com/2001/12/22/us/in-largest-schools-takeover-state-will-run-philadelphia-s.html.

8. Alexander Russo, "Political Educator," *Education Next* 3, no. 1 (Winter 2003): http://educationnext.org /politicaleducator. As Russo pointed out, Vallas was one of a growing number of "nontraditional" superintendents who were changing the face of American education, especially in large cities. San Diego chose Alan Bersin, a former federal prosecutor, to run its schools in 1998, and New York City tapped a former US assistant attorney general, Joel Klein, to run its schools in 2002. Wrote Kenneth Wong, author of *Rethinking School Reform in Chicago* and professor of political science at Vanderbilt, "The mayoral takeover [of the public school system] in Chicago in 1995 heralded a return to a strong central administration. Daley's choice as schools CEO, Paul Vallas, the mayor's former budget director, saw a need to apply accountability standards to all schools and students system-wide. While decentralization may lead to successful reform in some schools, system-wide improvement is not likely to occur unless district leadership has the political will and the capacity to implement performance-based accountability.... As the first non-educator to take the helm of a large urban district, Vallas inspired a trend in urban school reform across the nation. His leadership in the revitalization of the Chicago school system gave credibility to the idea that one need not have progressed through the school bureaucracy in order to be an effective superintendent. As a result, in recent years cities like New York, Los Angeles, Seattle, and Washington, DC, have all turned to so-called nontraditional superintendents—lawyers, businessmen, former military officers, politicians—to lead their school systems." Kenneth Wong, "The Big Stick," *Education Next* 3, no. 1 (Winter 2003): http://educationnext.org/thebigstick.

9. Ibid.

10. See Herbert R. Kohl, reply by E. D. Hirsh Jr., "'The Primal Scene of Education': An Exchange," *The New York Review of Books* (April 13, 1989): http://www.nybooks.com/articles/archives/1989/apr/13/the-primal-scene-of-education-an -exchange.

11. Jay Matthews, "The Philadelphia Experiment," *Education Next* 3, no. 1 (Winter 2003): http://educationnext.org /thephiladelphiaexperiment.

12. Mensah M. Dean, "Tainted Program a Hit at Hunter School," *Philadelphia Daily News* (December 6, 2005).

13. Interview by author with Peter Stewart, October 8, 2008.

14. Interview by author with Sue Furick, October 6, 2008.

15. Interview by author with Barbara Foster-Dolt, October 9, 2008.

16. Ibid.

17. Interview by author with Sue Furick, October 6, 2008.

18. Ibid.

19. Mensah M. Dean, "Tainted Program a Hit at Hunter School," *Philadelphia Daily News*, 4Star edition, December 6, 2005.

20. Ibid.

21. Foster-Dolt interview, 2008.

22. This is not to say we had 100 percent buy-in. There were about twenty-five grade-level teachers in our program. By the end of the first year, about 95 percent were on board and excited.

23. Foster-Dolt interview, 2008.

24. Pennsylvania Department of Education, "Pennsylvania System of School Assessment," resource materials (2005–05 through 2011–12): http://www.portal.state.pa.us/portal/server.pt/community/pennsylvania_system_of_school_ assessment_(pssa)/8757/resource_materials/507610.

25. Peter Whoriskey, "Rural Mississippi Elementary School Falls Behind," *Washington Post* (November 11, 2007).

Chapter 6

1. National Center for Education Statistics, Institute of Education Sciences, "Selected statistics on enrollment, teachers, dropouts, and graduates in public school districts enrolling more than 15,000 students, by state: 1990, 2000, and 2006," *Digest of Education Statistics*, US Department of Education (March 18, 2009), 129–139: http://nces.ed.gov/pubs2009/2009020.pdf.
2. Brian Jacob, "High Stakes in Chicago," *Education Next* 3, no. 1 (Winter 2003): http://educationnext.org/highstakesinchicago/.
3. "Who We Are: Renaissance," Chicago Public Schools website, accessed October 11, 2012: http://cps.edu/NewSchools/Pages/WhoWeAre.aspx.
4. Julie Peterson and Jordan Meranus, "The Third Try," *Education Next* 8, no. 3 (Summer 2008).
5. Ibid.
6. Rosalind Rossi, "Renaissance 2010 Draws 57 Applications in Second Round: Ideas for Several Single-Sex Schools Included in Proposals," *Chicago Sun-Times* (August 23, 2005).
7. Sharon Hayes, interview by Peter Meyer, December 2, 2008. Hayes had once tried her hand running a suburban school, twenty-five miles south of the city, but came back to the city after just two years. "I'm an urban educator," she said matter-of-factly.
8. Ibid.
9. Ibid.
10. Ibid.
11. Ibid.
12. Ibid.
13. K12 internal data and resources (see chap. 2, n.1).
14. Susan Patrick, interview by Peter Meyer, November 5, 2008.
15. Yun Xiang, Michael Dahlin, John Cronin, Robert Theaker and Sarah Durant, *Do High Flyers Maintain Their Altitude?: Performance Trends of Top Students*, The Thomas B. Fordham Institute (Washington, DC: September 2011): http://edexcellencemedia.net/publications/2011/20110920_HighFlyers/Do_High_Flyers_Maintain_Their_Altitude_FINAL.pdf.
16. K12 internal data and resources (see chap. 2, n. 1).
17. Ibid.

Chapter 7

1. Sam Dillon, "Online Schooling Grows, Setting off a Debate," *New York Times* (February 1, 2008).
2. James W. Hopson, pub., Tim Kelly, ed., "Virtues Abound in Virtual Schools: The Business Model Puts Customers First—And Those Customers, Wisconsin Families, So Far Are Very Satisfied with the Product," *Wisconsin State Journal* (August 4, 2003), A8, url ch. 4 no. 16.
3. Kinnic Phan, "Legislative Brief 08-6," Legislative Reference Bureau (May 2008): Virtual Charter Schools: legis.wisconsin.gov/lrb/pubs/lb/08lb6.pdf. See also 2007 Wisconsin Act 222, S. 2007–2008, § 5. 118.19 (1): https://docs.legis.wisconsin.gov/2007/related/acts/222.
4. Dillon, "Online Schooling Grows," *New York Times*.
5. Charlie Sykes, "The Fight for Virtual Schools: Updated,": accessed January 2013. http://www.620wtmj.com/blogs/charliesykes/45183707.html?corder=reverse.
6. Ibid.
7. Ibid
8. Ibid.
9. Ann Alonzo, "Letter to the Editor: Support WIVA for Future Students," *Fond du Lac Reporter* (March 9, 2008).
10. Editorial, "Doyle, WEAC Wrong to Try to Scuttle Virtual Schools Compromise," *Sheboygan Press* (February 26, 2008), A5; Editorial, "Study but Don't Cap Online Schools," *Wisconsin State Journal* (February 26, 2008); Editorial, "Virtual Schools, a Failed Compromise: The State Senate Scuttled a Compromise That Would Have Kept Wisconsin's Online Schools Alive and Instead Imposed an Unnecessary Cap," *Milwaukee Journal Sentinel* (February 22, 2008), 16.
11. For more information about the International Association for K–12 Online Learning in the press, see https://www.inacol.org/press/press_releases.php.
12. Phan, "Legislative Brief," 2008.
13. Sharon Hayes, interview by Peter Meyer, December 2, 2008.
14. Mensah M. Dean, "Bennett Aside, K12 Program Praised," *Philadelphia Daily News* (October 25, 2005).
15. Ibid.

Chapter 8

1. Southern Regional Education Board, "Five Academic Reasons: Why State Virtual Schools Are Important to Your State" (October 2007), 1.

2. Another major testimonial to the liberating power of computer technology is Martha Mason, who lived most of her life in an iron lung and was able to write her memoirs, at age sixty-five, thanks to a voice-activated computer.

3. Portable, Practical, Education, Preparation, Inc.: http://www.ppep.org/main.html.

4. Teen pregnancy is a huge drag on our nation's education progress. According to Family First Aid, the United States has the highest rates of teen pregnancy and births in the Western industrialized world. Teen pregnancy costs the United States at least $7 billion annually. Thirty-four percent of young women become pregnant at least once before they reach the age of twenty—about 820,000 a year. Eight in ten of these teen pregnancies are unintended and 79 percent are to unmarried teens. Family First Aid, "Teen Pregnancy Stats: Facts and Prevention," accessed October 9, 2012: http://www.familyfirstaid.org/teen-pregnancy.html.

5. Rob Reynolds, "Breaking and Entering into a New Era of Correctional Education," *Xplanazine* (blog), June 7, 2004.

6. National Agricultural Center, "Agriculture: Demographics," US Environmental Protection Agency (June 27, 2012): http://www.epa.gov/oecaagct/ag101/demographics.html.

7. Harris Cooper, "Summer Learning Loss: The Problem and Some Solutions," ERIC Digest (May 2005): http://www.eric.ed.gov/ERICWebPortal/search/detailmini.jsp?_nfpb=true&_&ERICExtSearch_SearchValue_0=ED475391&ERICExtSearch_SearchType_0=no&accno=ED475391.

8. Mike Streich, "Reducing Instructional Days & Increasing Classes: Time in the Classroom Reduced to Balance State Budgets," *Suite101* (June 10, 2009): http://suite101.com/article/reducing-instructional-days-increasing-classes-a124211#ixzz2162ZxWFA.

9. State of Michigan, "Extending the School Day and Year for the Education Achievement Authority of Michigan," http://www.michigan.gov/documents/eas/Extended_School_Day_and_Year_Final_v11_final_379078_7.pdf.

10. Hank Pellissier, "High Test Scores, Higher Expectations, and Presidential Hype: Should South Korean Schools Point the Way for American Reform?," Great Schools, Inc., http://www.greatschools.org/students/academic-skills/2427-South-Korean-schools.gs?page=all.

11. Ibid.

12. Office of Justice Programs, "Juveniles as Offenders: Time of Day," *OJJDP Statistical Briefing Book*, US Department of Justice (December 21, 2010): http://ojjdp.gov/ojstatbb/offenders/qa03301.asp.

13. See David A. Cook, Thomas J. Beckman, Kris G. Tomas, and Warren G. Thompson, "Adapting Web-Based Instruction to Residents' Knowledge Improves Learning Efficiency: A Randomized Controlled Trial," *Journal of General Internal Medicine* 23, no. 7 (July 2008), 985–990: doi: 10.1007/s11606-008-0541-0.

14. Ruth Cloven Clark and Richard E. Mayer, *e-Learning and the Science of Instruction: Proven Guidelines for Consumers and Designers of Multimedia Learning* (San Francisco: John Wiley and Sons, Inc., 2008). There is pertinent information in chapter 9, "Applying the Segmenting and Pre-training Principles: Managing Complexity by Breaking a Lesson into Parts," 183–198.

15. Erik Kain, "High Teacher Turnover Rates Are a Big Problem for America's Public Schools," *Forbes* (March 8, 2011): http://www.forbes.com/sites/erikkain/2011/03/08/high-teacher-turnover-rates-are-a-big-problem-for-americas-public-schools.

16. Sam Dillon, "Schools Slow in Closing Gaps Between Races," *New York Times* (November 20, 2006): http://www.nytimes.com/2006/11/20/education/20gap.html.

17. Robert Rothman, "Closing the Achievement Gap: How Schools Are Making It Happen," *The Journal of the Annenberg Challenge* 5, no.2 (Winter 2001/2): http://annenberginstitute.org/challenge/pubs/cj/gap_cj.htm.

18. K¹² internal data and resources (see chap. 2, n.1).

19. Peter Meyer, "Learning Separately: The Case for Single-Sex Schools," *Education Next* 8, no. 1 (Winter 2008): http://educationnext.org/learning-separately.

20. David Von Drehle, "The Myth about Boys," *Time* (July 26, 2007): http://www.time.com/time/magazine/article/0,9171,1647452,00.html.

21. Michelle L. Brandt, "Video Games Activate Reward Regions of Brain in Men More than Women, Stanford Study Finds," news release, Stanford School of Medicine (February 4, 2008): http://med.stanford.edu/news_releases/2008/february/videobrain.html.

22. Ibid.

23. Fumiko Hoeft et al., "Gender Differences in the Mesocorticolimbic System during Computer Game Play," *Journal of Psychiatric Research* 42, no. 4 (2008): 253–8.

24. K¹² internal data and resources (see chap. 2, n.1).

25. Christopher B. Swanson, "Cities in Crisis 2009: Closing the Educational Gap, Educational and Economic Conditions in America's Largest Cities," Editorial Projects in Education Research Center (April 2009), 13–14.

26. K¹² internal data and resources (see chap. 2, n.1).

27. National Center for Education Statistics, Institute of Education Sciences, "Current expenditures per pupil in fall enrollment in public elementary and secondary schools: Selected years, 1961–62 through 2007–08" *Digest of Education Statistics*, US Department of Education (2010), table 188 and chapter 2: http://nces.ed.gov/fastfacts/display.asp?id=66.

28. Adam Schaeffer, "They Spend WHAT? The Real Cost of Public Schools," *Cato Institute Policy Analysis*, no. 662 (March 10, 2010): http://www.cato.org/pubs/pas/pa662.pdf.

29. Amy Anderson, John Augenblick, Dale DeCescre, and Jill Conrad, "20/20 Costs and Funding of Virtual Schools: An examination of the Costs to Start, Operate, and Grow Virtual Schools and a Discussion of Funding Options for States Interested in Supporting Virtual School Programs," Augenblick, Palaich & Associates on behalf of the BellSouth Foundation (October 2, 2006), 13: http://www.inacol.org/research/docs/Costs&Funding.pdf.

30. National Center for Education Statistics, Institute of Education Sciences, "Public elementary and secondary revenues and expenditures, by type of locale: 2008-09," *Digest of Education Statistics*, US Department of Education (2011), table 190: http://nces.ed.gov/programs/digest/d11/tables/dt11_190.asp.

31. National Center for Education Statistics, Institute of Education Sciences, "Contents of Elementary and Secondary Education: Indicator 36: Public School Expenditures," *The Condition of Education* (2011), section 4: http://nces.ed.gov/pubs2011/2011033_5.pdf.

32. Paul Abramson, "15th Annual School Construction Report, School Planning & Management," special supplement (February 2010).

33. Alliance for Excellence in Education, "Education and the Economy: Boosting the Nation's Economy by Improving High School Graduation Rates," (March 2011), 2: http://www.all4ed.org/files/NationalStates_seb.pdf.

Chapter 9

1. "Lake Mills, William J. Bennett Introduce the 'Wisconsin Virtual Academy,'" US Newswire (February 18, 2002).

2. For more information on E. D. Hirsch, see "E. D. Hirsch, Jr.," Core Knowledge: http://www.coreknowledge.org/ed-hirsch-jr.

Chapter 10

1. Annie E. Casey Foundation, "EARLY WARNING! Why Reading by the End of Third Grade Matters," KIDS COUNT executive summary (2010): http://www.aecf.org/~/media/Pubs/Initiatives/KIDS%20COUNT/123/2010KCSpecReport/Special%20Report%20Executive%20Summary.pdf.

2. K12 internal data and resources (see chap. 2, n.1).

3. Ibid.

4. Susan Patrick, interview by Peter Meyer, November 5, 2008.

5. Jay P. Greene, "A 'Comprehensive' Problem: The Disconnect Between Fantasy and Reality," *Education Next* 6, no. 1 (Winter 2006): http://educationnext.org/a-comprehensive-problem.

6. National Center for Education Statistics, Institute of Education Sciences, "Pupil/Teacher Ratios and Expenditures per Student," *Digest of Education Statistics*, US Department of Education (1995), 74, table 30: http://nces.ed.gov/pubs98/yi/yi30.pdf.

7. Peter Meyer, "New York City's Education Battles," *Education Next* 8, no. 2 (Spring 2008): http://educationnext.org/new-york-citys-education-battles. See also Sol Stern, *Breaking Free: Public School Lessons and the Imperative of School Choice* (New York: Manhattan Institute, 2003).

8. Greene, "A 'Comprehensive' Problem," 2006.

9. Paul E. Peterson and Matthew M. Chingos, "For-Profit and Nonprofit Management in Philadelphia Schools," *Education Next* 9, no. 2 (Spring 2009): http://educationnext.org/for-profit-and-nonprofit-management-in-philadelphia-schools. The researchers found that public schools managed by for-profit companies outperformed district-managed schools in math and outperformed nonprofit-managed schools in both math and reading.

10. Jay Greene, "Joanne Jacobs on Bullies," (blog), April 25, 2008: http://jaypgreene.com/2008/04/25/joanne-jacobs-on-bullies.

11. Clayton Christensen, with Michael Horn and Curtis Johnson, *Disrupting Class: How Disruptive Innovation Will Change the Way the World Learns* (New York: McGraw-Hill, 2008).

12. *Education Week*, "Highest to Lowest Graduation Rates in the Nation's 50 Largest School Districts, Class of 2007," Editorial Projects in Education Research Center (2010): http://www.edweek.org/media/34arrow-c1.pdf.

13. Max Roosevelt, "Student Expectations Seen as Causing Grade Disputes," *New York Times* (February 18, 2009): http://www.nytimes.com/2009/02/18/education/18college.html.

14. Ibid.

15. K12 internal data and resources (see chap. 2, n.1).

16. Daniel Golden, "Bill Gates' School Crusade," *Bloomberg Businessweek* (July 15, 2010): http://www.businessweek.com/magazine/content/10_30/b4188058281758.htm.

17. Frederick M. Hess, *When Research Matters: How Scholarship Influences Education Policy* (Cambridge, Massachusetts: Harvard Education Press, 2008).

18. Ibid.

19. Frederick M. Hess, "When Education Research Matters," *Education Outlook* (February 2008): http://www.frederickhess.org/5122/when-education-research-matters.

20. Allison Powell, C. Bonk, et al, eds., *K¹² Online Learning: A Global Perspective, Proceedings of World Conference on E-Learning in Corporate, Government, Healthcare, and Higher Education* (Chesapeake, VA: Association for the Advancement of Computing in Education, 2008), 2353–2380.

Chapter 11

1. Susan Sclafani, "New Expectations for a New Century: The Education Imperative," Office of Vocational and Adult Education, United States Department of Education (July 20, 2008), slide 2: http://www2.ed.gov/about/offices/list/ovae/resource/newexpectations.ppt.

2. Ayn Rand, *The Fountainhead*, (New York: The Bobbs-Merrill Company, 1943), 679.

3. Barack Obama, "Inaugural Address," transcript, *New York Times* (January 20, 2009): http://www.nytimes.com/2009/01/20/us/politics/20text-obama.html?pagewanted=all.

4. Claudia Goldin and Lawrence F. Katz, *The Race between Education and Technology* (Cambridge, MA: Belknap Press, 2008).

5. Nick Pandolfo, "Charter-School Enrollment: Two Million Students and Counting," HechingerEd (blog), The Hechinger Report: http://hechingered.org/content/charter-school-enrollment-two-million-students-and-counting_4641/.

6. Ibid.

7. George Merck, "Address to the Medical College of Virginia," (Richmond: December 1, 1950). Quoted in James C. Collins and Jerry I. Porras, *Built to Last* (New York: Harperbusiness, 1997), 48.

8. I often tell the story of Tom Boysen, who I hired to be my first head of schools. He had a distinguished career that included being state superintendent of Kentucky schools. When I first met Tom, I was a senior in high school and he was superintendent of my school district.

9. K¹² internal data and resources (see chap. 2, n.1).

10. Maria has remained at K¹² and does an outstanding job of continuing to improve the quality of K¹² content and the efficiency of the creative process. Despite the long hours, a high percentage of people who were at K¹² in 2000 are still here today. Our social mission is a big result of this.

11. Ted Strickland, "State of the State Address," transcript, *Business First* (January 28, 2009): http://www.bizjournals.com/columbus/stories/2009/01/26/daily32.html?page=all.

12. Ibid.

13. Ibid.

14. Prashant Gopal, "America's Best High Schools: A State-by-State Look at the Best-Performing High Schools in the US. Does Your Child Already Go to One?" *Bloomberg Businessweek* (January 15, 2009): http://www.businessweek.com/lifestyle/content/jan2009/bw20090114_146291.htm; http://images.businessweek.com/ss/09/01/0115_best_schools/37.htm.

15. Ron Zimmer, Suzanne Blanc, Jolley Christman, and Brian Gill, "Evaluating the Performance of Philadelphia's Charter Schools," RAND Corporation (WR-550 EDU, 2008): http://www.rand.org/pubs/working_papers/WR550.html.

16. Interview with Caroline Hoxby, November 8, 2011.

17. Paul E. Peterson and Matthew M. Chingos, "For-Profit and Nonprofit Management in Philadelphia Schools," *Education Next* 9, no. 2 (Spring 2009): http://educationnext.org/for-profit-and-nonprofit-management-in-philadelphia-schools.

18. Dale Mezzacappa, "The Vallas Effect," *Education Next* 8, no. 2 (Spring 2008): http://educationnext.org/the-vallas-effect.

19. K¹² internal data and resources (see chap. 2, n.1).

20. James W. Hopson, pub., Tim Kelly, ed., "Virtues Abound in Virtual Schools: The Business Model Puts Customers First—And Those Customers, Wisconsin Families, So Far Are Very Satisfied with the Product," *Wisconsin State Journal* (August 4, 2003), A8: http://newspaperarchive.com/wisconsin-state-journal/2003-08-04.

21. K12 internal data and resources (see chap. 2, n.1).

22. Ibid.

23. Randall Greenway and Gregg Vanourek, "The Virtual Revolution: Understanding Online Schools," *Education Next* 6, no. 2 (Spring 2006), 40.

24. Dale Mann, interview by Peter Meyer, December 16, 2008.

25. Christina Hoag, "LA Unveils $578 Million School, Costliest in the Nation," AP/*Huffington Post*, Los Angeles (August 22, 2010).

26. Mann, interview, 2008.

27. Clayton Christensen, with Michael Horn and Curtis Johnson, *Disrupting Class: How Disruptive Innovation Will Change the Way the World Learns* (New York: McGraw-Hill, 2008), 81.

28. Michelle R. Davis and Kathleen Kennedy Manzo, "Spending Law Offers Educators Several Options for New Aid," *Education Week* (February 25, 2009). Even though the Obama-inspired stimulus package of new federal funds for education included an extra $650 million for educational technology programs, that amount was spread over two years and still represented only three-tenths of 1 percent of total new federal education spending.

29. Christensen, *Disrupting Class*, 81.

30. Mann, interview, 2008.

31. Randall Greenway and Gregg Vanourek, "The Virtual Revolution: Understanding Online Schools," *Education Next* 6, no. 2 (Spring 2006), 40.

32. Ibid.

33. National Clearinghouse for Education Facilities, "Data & Statistics," National Institute of Building Sciences: http://www.edfacilities.org/ds/statistics.cfm. According to the National Center for Education Statistics, in 1998 the average public school building in the United States was forty-two years old. The mean age ranged from forty-six years in the Northeast and Central states to thirty-seven years in the Southeast. About one-fourth (28 percent) of all public schools were built before 1950, and 45 percent of all public schools were built between 1950 and 1969. About 17 percent of public schools were built between 1970 and 1984, and 10 percent were built after 1985. The increase in the construction of schools between 1950 and 1969 corresponds to the years during which the Baby Boom generation was going to school. For the 2005–2006 school year, there were 97,382 public elementary and secondary schools (92,816 the year before); 87,585 were regular elementary and secondary schools; 2,128 were special education schools; 1,221 were vocational/technical schools; and 6,448 were other/alternative schools. Laurie Lewis, Kyle Snow, and Elizabeth Farris, "Condition of America's Public School Facilities: 1999," National Center for Education Statistics (June 2000), 37: http://nces.ed.gov/pubs2000/2000032.pdf; Cassandra Rowand, "How Old Are America's Public Schools?" National Center for Education Statistics (1999): http://nces.ed.gov/pubs99/1999048.pdf.

34. Barack Obama, "Remarks of President-elect, Radio Address on the Economy" (December 6, 2008).

35. Christensen, *Disrupting Class*, 29.

36. Donna M. Ragucci and Robert D. Gulbro, "Bethlehem Steel: Downfall of a Giant," Proceedings of the International Academy for Case Studies 11, no. 1 (New Orleans: Allied Academies International Conference, 2004), 86: http://www.sbaer.uca.edu/research/allied/2004/caseStudy/pdf/26.pdf.

Chapter 12

1. Randall Greenway and Gregg Vanourek, "The Virtual Revolution: Understanding Online Schools," *Education Next* 6, no. 2 (Spring 2006), 40; iNACOL, "Effectiveness of K-12 Online Learning," Research Committee Report (2007): http://www.inacol.org/research/docs/VSresearch-summary.pdf.

2. Ibid.